Hearing Haneke

The Oxford Music / Media Series
Daniel Goldmark, Series Editor

Hearing Haneke

THE SOUND TRACKS OF A RADICAL AUTEUR

Elsie Walker

OXFORD

UNIVERSITY PRESS

Oxford University Press is a department of the University of Oxford. It furthers
the University's objective of excellence in research, scholarship, and education
by publishing worldwide. Oxford is a registered trade mark of Oxford University
Press in the UK and certain other countries.

Published in the United States of America by Oxford University Press
198 Madison Avenue, New York, NY 10016, United States of America.

Publication of this book was supported by the Lloyd Hibberd Endowment of the American
Musicological Society, funded in part by the National Endowment for the Humanities and
the Andrew W. Mellon Foundation.

Library of Congress Cataloging-in-Publication Data
Names: Walker, Elsie M., 1975– author.
Title: Hearing Haneke : the sound tracks of a radical auteur / Elsie Walker.
Description: New York : Oxford University Press, 2017. |
Series: The Oxford music/media series | Includes bibliographical references and index.
Identifiers: LCCN 2017021656 (print) | LCCN 2017038673 (ebook) |
ISBN 9780190495923 (updf) | ISBN 9780190495930 (epub) |
ISBN 9780190495909 (cloth : alk. paper) | ISBN 9780190495916 (pbk. : alk. paper)
Subjects: LCSH: Haneke, Michael, 1942—Criticism and interpretation. |
Motion pictures—Sound effects.
Classification: LCC PN1998.3.H36 (ebook) | LCC PN1998.3.H36 W34 3017 (print) |
DDC 791.4302/33092—dc23
LC record available at https://lccn.loc.gov/2017021656

9 8 7 6 5 4 3 2 1

Paperback printed by WebCom, Inc., Canada
Hardback printed by Bridgeport National Bindery, Inc., United States of America

For my daughters,
Charlotte Hope and Dorothy Jane.
Thank you for making me hear everything better.

And in memory of my mother,
Varvara Richards.
Thank you for giving me a voice.

CONTENTS

ACKNOWLEDGMENTS

I must begin by mentioning that extracts from the chapters on *Funny Games* and *Caché* originally appeared in *Music and the Moving Image* 3, no. 3 (Fall 2010):15–30. I thank the editors of this journal, Ron Sadoff and Gillian Anderson, not only for their permission to reprint these extracts, but also for their kindness. The *Music and the Moving Image* conference that they host has become an essential part of my life, both for the camaraderie and for the inspiration I find there. I know that many ideas within this book are a direct result of my having met so many extraordinary scholars at this annual event. Thanks, too, to the original anonymous readers for my book submission who gave me invaluable feedback, and to Senior Editor Norm Hirschy for his patience, largesse, and clarity. I am grateful to Daniel Goldmark, Series Editor, for his permissive and precise guidance, and to the entire production team at Oxford University Press.

Writing this book has led me to reflect more on all the sounds I make, and on how to hear the people around me better. My most personal thanks go to Jim Burton, the best listener I know I'll ever know. He is the one who introduced Haneke's films to me in the first place, and I was pregnant with our first child when I watched most of them for the first time. It was a harrowing experience, as well as being one of the most significant for me. Jim helped me through the emotional highs and lows of my coming to terms with what the films had to say, and his love and faith in me is in every line of this book.

I want to give special thanks to some friends who have movingly shared their stories with me, along with helping me find a stronger female voice of my own: Cristina Cammarano, Céline Carayon, Louise Detwiler, Lana Foley, Tara Gladden, Claudia Gorbman, Diane Illig, Loren Marquez, Susan McCarty, Heather McGee, Vicky Pass, Michelle Schlehofer, Katherine Spring, Robynn Stilwell, Erin Stutelberg, Leslie Yarmo, and Diana Wagner. Thank you to Catherine Grant and Liz Greene for showing me what it means to be truly generous scholars. I am especially grateful for a kindred spirit through the entire experience of writing this book: Danijela Kulezic-Wilson.

I am thankful for the freedom that my job at Salisbury University allows me to pursue my professional dreams. The campus is a rare place of congenial intellectualism, and there are many colleagues who make my working life wonderful. Here, I particularly thank Jerry Tabor for the musical knowledge he shares with Fulton Faculty, along with introducing me to the documentary *Touch the*

Sound. Thanks to Sarah Surak for helping me understand more about how the original German of *The White Ribbon* is translated into English. Thanks to the Dean of the Fulton School of Liberal Arts at Salisbury University, Maarten Pereboom, and SU President Janet Dudley-Eshbach for their unwavering support. I give special thanks for the multiple conference travel grants and the Fulton School Faculty grant that I received to help me complete this book. Thank you to my students at SU for joining me in thoughtful, spirited, and compassionate discussions. And thanks again to my greatest mentor, Michael Hattaway, who continues to help me more than he can possibly imagine, even when I cannot hear him.

This book pays tribute to my father, Marshall Walker, because *Amour* is the last film we discussed before he died. He was brave enough to watch the film when he was dying, and he wanted to talk about it with me. This book is for my mother, Varvara Richards, because she taught me to speak up for other people and she was the first person who really listened to me. She died while this book was in production, but I heard her voice urging me on all the same. I will keep hearing her voice and saying the words she gave me for the rest of my life. This book is also for my daughters, who fill my days with noise and laughter, and who give me the strength I need to keep imagining the future and speaking out for progressive change. Charlotte Hope and Dorothy Jane—you make the sweetest sounds I'll ever hear.

Prelude

WHY DOES HEARING HANEKE'S FILMS MATTER?

Michael Haneke's films are designed to make us hear anew. They subject us to many hostile noises of life, along with sonically stressing the preciousness of humanity that we must perceive in order to save it. We can easily take our senses, *especially* our sense of sound, for granted. Millions of people around the world are engaging with this idea by watching a new genre of YouTube videos: footage of people hearing or seeing for the first time. These videos capture the extraordinary in the ordinary, celebrating the power of those abilities that most of us have stopped consciously appreciating. In a recent article for *The New Yorker*, Joshua Redman examines the exhilarating sense of newness that we can thus experience by proxy. Drawing on the work of the philosopher L. A. Paul, he suggests that the videos allow us to witness "transformative experiences" on a par with other rites of passage (Redman 2015). Paul herself defines the "transformative experience" as one that can "change your point of view [. . .] and perhaps even change the kind of person you are or at least take yourself to be" (Paul 2014, 16).

One YouTube video shows a woman named Sarah Churman testing a new hearing aid for the first time (Churman 2011). As soon as she hears her own voice, she is both delighted and shocked. She struggles to speak over her own laughing and crying. Offscreen, her husband gently laughs with her, and we realize that she is probably hearing him for the first time too. This video has been played more than twenty-six million times, suggesting a widespread recognition that the experience of witnessing another human being's delight in hearing has a special, and enduring, level of potency.

The return to hearing for the first time is elusive, which goes some way to explaining the power and popularity of Churman's video. As the sound designer and editor Walter Murch writes, our hearing develops before we are even born, just four and a half months from conception:

> From then on, we develop in a continuous and luxurious bath of sounds: the song of our mother's voice, the swash of her breathing, the trumpeting of

her intestines, the timpani of her heart. Throughout the second four-and-a-half months, Sound rules as solitary Queen of our senses: the close and liquid world of uterine darkness makes Sight and Smell impossible, Taste monochromatic, and Touch a dim and generalized hint of what is to come. (Murch 1994, vii)

Murch's poetic phrasing suggests a desire to recapture the very first things we hear with full appreciation. Yet we obviously lack the faculties to describe the beauty of what we hear when we first experience that sense: as unborn infants, we will not perceive or conceptualize our mother's heart as a "timpani," for instance, and such a word evokes musical possibility while also reminding us that the return to our first hearing is impossible. Moreover, as Murch also observes, once the baby is born she or he is bombarded with other senses, and Sight becomes "King" (viii).

The idea that we live in a visually saturated culture is commonplace, much as film was usually written about as a "visual medium" until comparatively recently. Sight has surely been "King" of film analysis, at least up until the last two decades when we have seen a surge of new attention to sound tracks. This scholarship is not only an important corrective to the visually biased work that came before it, but also reminds us that film can *aurally* represent reality, which in turn prompts us to perceive the world in new ways. Though we cannot necessarily have transformative experiences precisely like those of Churman, we are only beginning to collectively understand what films can do to reawaken our capacity to hear. And even if we can never return to the initial glory of aural stimulus as Murch imagines it, this reawakening has lasting, multilayered implications.

On a more medium-specific level, Haneke's cinema demands that we hear new sonic possibilities of representation. His sound tracks make us listen to every move of his main characters, as well as every single thing they could choose to hear in the world around them. Further, his films make us hear what is right and wrong about the characters' social contexts in ways that resonate far beyond the films themselves, and often shockingly so. Haneke himself has repeatedly observed the waning power of images that have lost the capacity to shock, especially in the current multimedia context through which we are bombarded with visual information on a daily basis. Within his own work, sound becomes a kind of salvation, prompting us to engage with others' perspectives and to perceive the value of human life despite the violent or dispassionate noises of the world. Because there is obvious intentionality behind every single sound in a Haneke film, and we are never invited to become lost in a wash of homogenously mixed noises or familiarly constructed music, we have to hear everything at moment-to-moment levels of intensity. This is a huge part of what makes his films especially demanding and discomfiting. But to return more positively to the work of Paul and Redman, listening to Haneke's work can transform us by making us more conscious perceivers of *all* sonic stimulus.

This book is about what's at stake in our fully hearing Haneke's films, which extends beyond cinema to the world at large. Every chapter of this book begins from a place of curiosity, by asking questions about how each film fosters our greater aural alertness in broadly applicable terms. Whether we are hearing the sounds of numerous objects that foreground overwhelming consumerism in *The Seventh Continent*, or the silences that call attention to a shameful postcolonial legacy in *Caché*, Haneke's sound tracks are designed to amplify our social conscience. Listening attentively to *Code Unknown* means acknowledging disparate voices within a multicultural context and understanding the violence of *not listening* to those same voices. Listening to *Funny Games* means having to hear a level of suffering that many other thrillers do not require that we perceive, and especially the excruciating pain of a family being victimized. The sound track of *The Piano Teacher* subjects us to an intensely intertextual experience of female subjectivity, adapting many sources to communicate numerous cultural limits on a woman's expressivity. Every aural detail of *The White Ribbon* gives us a psychoanalytically terrifying context for the outbreak of World War One. And our taking in the sound track of *Amour* means honoring the life-defining importance of lasting love, even when death quickly approaches.

As Redman writes, "we settle into life, and it becomes commonplace and knowable, until something comes along to remind us how vivid and moving it can be." In being designed to reignite our sense of hearing, Haneke's films are gifts to us in this way. As painful as the narratives of his films are, they offer us the transformative possibilities of new sonic awareness. His sound tracks redefine cinema in ways that can help us rehear everything—including our own voices, and everything around us—better.

1

Introduction

HEARING HANEKE THROUGH THE CRITICAL RUCKUS

> It seems to me that the ear is fundamentally more sensitive than the
> eye. To put it another way, the ear provides a more direct path to
> the imagination and to the heart of human beings.
> —Michael Haneke (2000, 174)[1]

Listening to Haneke's cinema hurts. His films subject us to experiences of disturbance, desperation, grief, betrayal, and many forms of violence. They are unsoftened by music, punctuated by accosting noises, shaped by painful silences, and charged with aggressive dialogue. The director has become a controversial subject of scholarly debate, as well as one of the most celebrated living filmmakers. His films have been labeled "difficult, didactic, rarefied, abstruse, and excessively dark" (Grundmann, 2010a, 6). Haneke himself is often accused of being coldly dispassionate about the traumas he shows us: the director and the nastiest actions within his work are thus frequently, problematically aligned. So, the above quotation, in which he expresses his interest in our *hearts* as well as our imaginations, is surprising. The primary purpose of this book is to delve deeply into how and why Haneke's work fosters our greater aural alertness. Along the way, we will understand the director's moral compass, political progressiveness, and compassion for humanity better.[2]

Over the last several years, Michael Haneke's films have prompted an explosion of scholarly work, including several book-length studies and hundreds of articles. The strong patterns among his films make them ripe for auteurist analysis. His having won the Palme d'Or twice at the Cannes Film

---

[1] Haneke gives this argument for the comparative sensitivity of the ear (in relation to the eye) while discussing television reports on atrocities, such as the war in Yugoslavia. He argues that such visual reports were once shocking but have now ceased to shock: "[today] most of the people regard this coverage as unwelcome irritation" (Haneke, 2000, 174).

[2] Any straightforward correlation between an artist and his or her work is, of course, speculative and potentially misleading. That said, where other critics assume Haneke's misanthropy, our counterreading of the humane themes in his films leads us to assume his compassion.

Festival—for *The White Ribbon* (2009) and *Amour* (2012)—secures his status as a leading European auteur. He has received much recent mainstream acclaim too. In 2013 he won the Academy Award for Best Foreign Language Film for *Amour*, in addition to the film receiving Academy Award nominations for Best Actress, Best Picture, Best Original Screenplay, and Best Director—a rare feat for a non-Anglo-American production. Despite the surge of widespread critical attention to Haneke's work, there is still much more to say about his use of sound tracks: the aural components of his films are often mentioned (with emphasis on the lack of music), but usually in passing and in subsidiary relation to visual patterns.[3] Moreover, Haneke's use of silence, and the *absence* of sound when we expect it, is seldom studied. We will redress the balance by analyzing the sound tracks of Haneke's films over and above their visual elements. We will thus echo the films themselves, for their sound tracks often demand greater attention, or communicate more immediate meaning, than their visuals.[4] As the top quotation indicates, Haneke focuses on sound to sensitize and engage an audience. He writes sounds "in capital letters" throughout his screenplays to distinguish them from everything else "in lowercase letters" (Cieutat 2010, 144). He thus textually indicates how much he consciously foregrounds sound, even in preproduction.

Given that Haneke makes sonically driven films to reach his audiences' hearts and imaginations, it is strange that many critics assume he is dispassionate about representing painful experiences. Philippe Met, for instance, refers to Haneke as "the Iceman" whose "frigid chunks of cinematic truth" constitute a "global *warning*" (2012, 175, original emphasis). Catherine Wheatley stresses Haneke's notorious claim that he wants to "rape the [audience] into autonomy" (2009, 78). J. Hoberman accuses Haneke of having a fascist mindset that allows him to "despise the mass audience's vicarious pleasure in make-believe mayhem" (as cited by Wheatley 2007). Thomas Elsaesser calls Haneke

---

[3] There are some noteworthy exceptions, such as Michel Chion's article on the sound track of *Caché*, and several articles by Lisa Coulthard that focus on aural patterns across Haneke's films, but this book is the first extended study of its kind.

[4] Haneke's emphasis on playing with fundamental elements of film form is frequently connected with that of numerous other auteurs—including representatives of German New Wave cinema, such as Rainer Werner Fassbinder, Wim Wenders, and Werner Herzog (Speck 2010, 168); other filmmakers who have profited from cinephile-driven funding opportunities in France, such as Theo Angelopoulos, Abbas Kiarostami, and Krzysztof Kieślowski (Saxton 2008, 85); other directors who create subversive cinema using "strategies of irritation," such as David Lynch and Lars von Trier (Loren and Metelmann 2013, 197); and other European modernist filmmakers like Andrei Tarkovsky and Michelangelo Antonioni, as well as Robert Bresson (Trifonova 2007, 68). All these other internationally recognized filmmakers push the boundaries of conventional aural techniques, but it is beyond the scope of this book to thoroughly consider how Haneke's sound tracks intertextually draw from other films without risking too many tokenistic, fleeting allusions. We dwell only on those comparative examples that we have space to consider at length. This book is not about establishing Haneke as a lone pioneer: it is, rather, about finding some new ways to perceive his aural radicalism.

a hypocritical "control freak," adding "violence is bad for you, says the director who inflicts violence on me" (2010, 56).[5] Alex Gerbaz even aligns Haneke with the killers of *Funny Games* by saying he uses one of them (Paul) as "his mouthpiece to converse with the audience" (2011, 167). Similarly, Jonathan Romney views *Caché* as "a terrorist attack on the audience" (Kumar and Swiatek 2012, 312). In response to the often torturous content of his films, Speck redirects the criticism against Haneke toward his audience by assuming they must have "a masochistic streak" (2010, 161).

Yves Montmayeur's recent documentary *Michael H.—Profession: Director* (2013) attempts to balance out Haneke's notoriety by foregrounding his humanism. Ironically, Montmayeur includes the most shockingly violent scenes from Haneke's films without much narrative context. These scenes include the brutal murder of a teenage girl in *Benny's Video* (1992), the onscreen suicide of a desperate man in *Caché* (2005), the mass shooting at the end of *71 Fragments of a Chronology of Chance* (1994), the protagonist stabbing her own breast in the last moments of *The Piano Teacher* (2001), and the husband euthanizing his wife in *Amour. Michael H.—Profession: Director* begins with the murder from *Benny's Video*, including the appalling, closely miked cries of the teenage girl dying offscreen after the main character shoots her. Then the documentary cuts to a close-up on Haneke's unblinking eyes as he watches this scene before coolly saying "in all my films, I have made an attempt to approach the truth" (see Figure 1.1). Anyone seeing this who might be unfamiliar with the director's work could reasonably assume a level of pathology in Haneke's willingness to show such horrendous action, let alone watch it himself, without giving us time to recover and consider its meaning. The result is a ghoulish and sensationalistic distortion of the time his films allow for us to absorb what happens and why it matters, and the special quiet after every culminating moment of violence. The documentary thus reinforces the critical myopia about Haneke, the preexisting misunderstandings that have led to judgments about him and his films being indefensibly cruel.

We can adopt a more nuanced approach to Haneke's cinema. The films themselves deserve and reward a stronger comprehension of their ethical logic, contrary to those reactions that assume Haneke's unconscionable misanthropy. When it comes to deepening our understanding of Haneke's approach, the work of Bertolt Brecht is an important influence.[6] Brecht was profoundly committed

---

[5] For Elsaesser, the sadistic elements of Haneke's films are redeemed by the director's "autocritique" on some occasions—for example, Elsaesser cites the disturbing film-within-a-film scene in *Code Unknown* (2000) during which an offscreen director (voiced by Haneke) torments his lead actress (the lead of the film proper, played by Juliet Binoche) in the filming of a violent scene (2010, 55).

[6] Along with Brecht, the Frankfurt School's critique of culture industries, as exemplified by Theodor Adorno, is another important influence on Haneke (Trifonova 2007, 77–78). Adorno argues that mainstream media does not demand the audience's effort because "the message is invariably that of

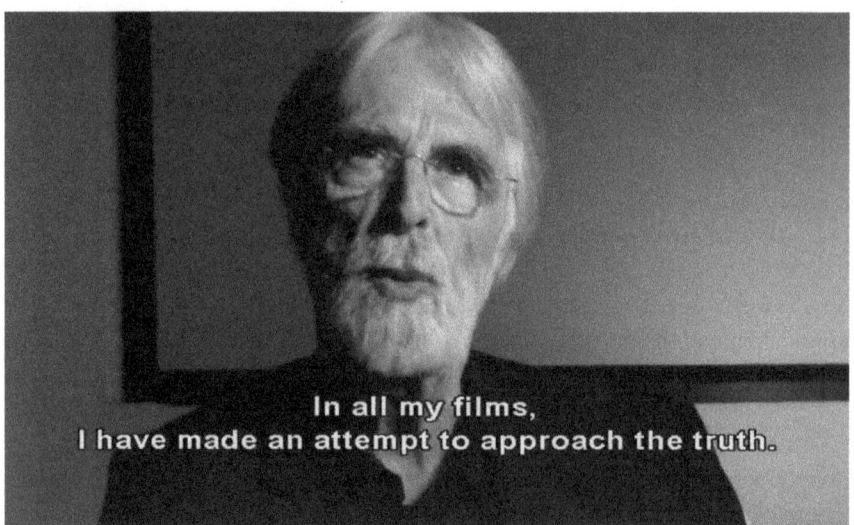

FIGURE 1.1 Haneke coolly pronounces his commitment to the truth after watching the murder scene from *Benny's Video*: this moment from Montmayeur's documentary does not reflect the director's compassionate morality.

to inspiring his audiences' socially conscious engagement with his theater and, by extension, with the world around them. Rather than allowing audiences to "get lost" within all-consuming entertainment, the Brechtian text requires that audiences be consistently active participants in the creation of meaning. Moreover, the Brechtian text is one that explores social truths in a multidimensional and self-consciously constructed manner, one that encourages audiences to reflect upon their own processes of understanding that should extend into their own lives. As David Sterritt argues, by demanding that moviegoers "decipher and interpret their meanings" rather than being allowed to passively consume them, Haneke's films are very much "in the tradition of Bertolt Brecht" (2010, 254).[7] Brecht is so often mentioned in relation to Haneke's cinema that the connection has become something of a cliché.[8] That said, critics frequently

---

identification with the status quo" and the viewer can swallow "premasticated" media products whole (Forrest 2012, 556). His emphasis on the possibilities within art to challenge dominant ideology run parallel to the objectives of Brecht's epic theater, and Haneke's cinema in turn.

[7] Similarly, Roy Grundmann connects Haneke's strategies with Brecht in light of his "roots in Brechtian-influenced theater culture, which was still flourishing during the 1960s and 70s, when he first worked as a script advisor and editor at a German television station and then as a stage director at German and Austrian theaters" (2008, B14). Jörg Metelmann has also written about Haneke as "a successor to Bertolt Brecht's approach to theater," applying the concept of *Verfremdung* to explain how his work opposes Hollywood's manipulative strategies of covert manipulation: he says Haneke's films "tear the realities shown on the screen from the shadow of their 'being-so' into the light of their 'having-been-*made*-so'" (2010, 168).

[8] For just a few other representative examples, see Brunette (2010, 57, 79), Grundmann (2010a, 35, 46), and Wheatley (2009, 26–27).

associate Brecht with Haneke's perceived coldness and detachment without balanced attention to the emotional content of his films.[9] Similarly, Brecht's epic theater is often mistakenly referred to in terms of coldness and critical detachment without full consideration of its affective strategies.

Brecht himself considers reasoned responses most important, but *not entirely at the expense* of his audiences' deep-seated feelings. In the context of arguing for the "radical transformation of the theatre" which, for him, must correspond with "the whole radical transformation of the mentality of our time,"[10] Brecht writes:

> The essential point of the epic theatre is perhaps that it appeals less to the feelings than to the spectator's reason. Instead of sharing the experience the spectator must come to grips with things. At the same time it would be quite wrong to try and deny emotion to this kind of theatre. It would be much the same thing as trying to deny emotion to modern science. (1964, 23)

Here, Brecht admits the subjectivity of even the most ostensibly objective (or scientific) enquiry. Therefore, to assume his failure to acknowledge the inevitability of emotional reactions is to underestimate the complexity of his dramaturgical approach. Throughout the well-known collection of his essays titled *Brecht on Theatre: The Development of an Aesthetic*, it is only the particular emotion of empathy that Brecht explicitly and consistently warns against. For Brecht, the kind of theatre that prompts audiences to align themselves wholeheartedly with its protagonists may disable those same audiences from being able to step back enough to assess the social meaning of what they see. To cite a representative example, Brecht critiques a production of *Oedipus* in which the pitiful delivery of the line "Jocasta has died" by her servant left the audience "[p]lunged in self-identification with the protagonist's feelings" so that "virtually the whole audience failed to take part in the moral decisions of which the plot is made up" (1964, 28).

Haneke certainly dissuades us from empathizing with his characters, not least because many of his protagonists bear the same names (variations on George and Anne), thereby encouraging us to view them as representative beings rather than as sharply individuated characters with whom we can identify.

---

[9] For some reviews that connect Haneke's work with both Brecht and "coldness," see Bleasdale (2011), Kunzru (2009), and Peterson (2006).

[10] Brecht argued that theatre, along with art and literature, should create a complete reconfiguration of the entire "ideological superstructure" of his time: he thus borrowed a phrase from Marx's *Das Kapital* that, as John Willett explains in his editorial notes to the translation of *Brecht on Theatre*, stands "for the whole body of art, ideas, morality, etc., of any given society, which Marx saw as resting on certain basic economic relationships" (1964, 23). Haneke's *The Seventh Continent* lends itself most readily to a Marxist reading, particularly as its sound track places extreme emphasis on the objects that define a society of commodity fetishism.

However, even a cursory summary of a few Hanekean storylines highlights his immediately affective, rather than solely detached or alienating, subjects: a family commit suicide together (*The Seventh Continent*); a family is terrorized by murderers within their own home (*Funny Games*); and a man nurses his wife in her last, painful stages of life before euthanizing her (*Amour*). At the same time, Haneke gives us these narratives with such a Brechtian emphasis on stylistic unconventionality that we must comprehend their form and socially loaded significance, even while we are deeply disturbed by their content.

Haneke's extremely sparing and sometimes startling use of music is eminently Brechtian in disallowing our surrender to pure affect. In the context of discussing his own unconventional use of music in *The Threepenny Opera*, Brecht explicitly warns against using music to aestheticize drama (1964, 84). In particular, he resists the use of so-called serious music that "still clings to lyricism, and cultivates expression for its own sake" (87). He provides a vivid critical description of the concert hall audience: "entire rows of human beings transported into a peculiar doped state, wholly passive, sunk without trace, seemingly in the grip of a severe poisoning attack. Their tense, congealed gaze shows that these people are the helpless and involuntary victims of the unchecked lurchings of their emotions" (89). This exact description ironically anticipates the post-credit opening of *Amour*, which begins with audiences taking their seats for a classical concert. The film maintains focus on how the audience hears the music rather than cutting to show the performer, and because we watch the audience settling into the familiarly ritualistic experience of a classical concert, we are ourselves invited to react on a different, metadiegetic level—we are, in short, made self-conscious in ways that the onscreen audience is not. Through such a scene, and like Brecht before him, Haneke avoids the "narcotic attraction" of musical expressiveness so that his audiences are always encouraged to be more alert than any onscreen audience (Brecht 1964, 85). Even when Haneke does use the inherently affective power of music, it never straightforwardly lightens or brings elegance to the action. He never softens his traumatic stories with any aesthetically pleasing or emotionally coercive sound, the impact of which might encourage us to suspend our critical faculties. Haneke protects us from becoming so engulfed by artistic style that we lose sight of what *any* action means.

The Gestus

Since Brecht's playwriting revolves around the "Gestus," defining this concept is crucial for an even fuller understanding of how much his work resonates with Haneke's cinema. The Gestus is a moment on stage through which a whole social situation can be read. This moment combines a physical gesture with a gist or attitude that is memorably revealing. The most famous example of the

Gestus is from Brecht's play *Mother Courage*. Brecht wrote the play during the Second World War but it is set during the Thirty Years War of the seventeenth century, thus using historical reference points to comment on the sociopolitical desperation of the present. The central character of the play is Anna Fierling, a mother of three who runs a canteen and makes profit from the war by trailing the army and trading with soldiers.[11] At the end of Scene 3, she is so busy with trying to save her business that she fails to prevent one of her sons from being dragged off the stage for execution. In a 1949 production of the play under Brecht's direction, the actress playing Mother Courage (Helene Weigel) gave the character a defining moment: a silent scream. After hearing the gunfire of her son's execution offstage, she bent her head back and opened her mouth wide, but made no sound.

The Gestus is what Roland Barthes calls "a pregnant moment," an artificial instant, "a hieroglyph in which can be read at a single glance . . . the present, the past and the future," a "crucial instant, totally concrete and totally abstract" (1977, 73). In this moment from *Mother Courage* we understand the impact of the past (how Mother Courage has failed her son) and the impact of the present (the shock and grief she cannot release), along with anticipating the sadness of her future. The Gestus sums up an entire personal *and* social situation. In this case, Mother Courage's loss stands for the general cost of war. She must not scream for her own safety, highlighting her social context. In addition, her silent scream is a point at which image and sound do not match, requiring an audience's imaginative investment in "hearing" the sound she does not make. It is, in short, a moment that demands our self-consciously active, cognitive involvement, while *also* being deeply affective.

The Gestus is part of Brecht's overall emphasis on *Verfremdung*, a term frequently and mistakenly simplified through translation as "alienation." Brecht defines *Verfremdung* as follows:

> What is involved here is, briefly, a technique of taking the human social incidents to be portrayed and labeling them as something striking, something that calls for explanation, is not to be taken for granted, not just natural. The object of this "effect" is to allow the spectator to criticize constructively from a social point-of-view. (1964, 125)

In relation to the creative suggestiveness of Brecht's definition, Ulrike Garde points out that "alienation" is an inadequate translation of *Verfremdung* due to its negative connotations. Although Brecht was wary of allowing audiences much empathetic involvement in characters' experiences, his own definition of using *Verfremdung* does not mean to necessarily "antagonize" or "detach" the audience entirely but, rather, to create a sense of "surprise" or "astonishment" at

---

[11] Perhaps Haneke's recurrent use of the name "Anna" knowingly echoes the main character of Mother Courage—she is sometimes referred to as "Canteen Anna."

the everyday or normalized experience.[12] In connection with Mother Courage's silent scream, Paul Allain and Jen Harvie remind us that many scholars mistakenly assume that Brecht encouraged so much detachment that he "did not want his audience to feel any emotion." By contrast, they argue that Brecht wanted his audiences to be able to "rationalize their emotional responses [. . .] in order to be able to ascertain the social foundation of characters' motivations and their own reactions to these" (2006, 37).

Brecht's use of the Gestus is a model for understanding the aural significance of Haneke's cinema. With each chapter of this book, we zero in on many sonic moments that are charged on multiple levels of meaning, and likely to create surprise and astonishment in terms of breaking with cinematic norms. In Brecht's theatre, the Gestus is an especially loaded moment as it represents social reality. For the purposes of analyzing Haneke's cinema, we interpret "social" to mean any culturally loaded, contemporary contexts beyond the characters' immediate diegetic worlds. For instance, we will analyze how and why Haneke challenges genre-related conventions in *Funny Games,* defying many sonic norms of family-in-peril thrillers so that we may hear the cost of violence anew. Equally, we will historically contextualize how and why the sound track of *Caché* amplifies the lasting legacies of colonial oppression. Though Haneke is not always driven by overtly Marxist imperatives, as Brecht was, his films parallel Brecht's work by demanding that we experience the radically reawakening possibilities of artistic construction.[13] The goal here is not to redefine the well-known concept of the Gestus, but to use the term in explaining what makes Haneke's sound tracks singularly impactful.

Let us consider how Mother Courage's silent scream resonates with Haneke's cinema in more precise terms. First, consider that her *silence* is crucial: it is the shock of not hearing her that makes the moment so memorable. This is akin to Haneke's use of silence as well as his frequently separating visual from aural messages. Haneke argues that the visuals and sounds of films should be handled differently, or work distinctly from each other, so that the filmmaker can make "not only twice as much, but rather ten times as much, because one has a counterpoint. Nothing needs to run parallel."[14] Moreover, consider that Mother Courage's scream embodies and encapsulates an entire personal and social situation with

---

[12] Indeed, Garde points out that this mistranslation of the term *Verfremdung* is indicative of "a whole range of misreadings of Brecht" (2006, 58), a point that parallels how many critics have associated Haneke's so-called Brechtian techniques with negative objectives.

[13] Grundmann explains that Haneke does not tend to focus on Marxist themes of "class struggle, imperialism of third world countries" so much as "more traditional humanist issues" and "metaphysical themes" (2010a, 3). However, the sound track of *The Seventh Continent* still lends itself strongly to a Marxist reading, as we shall see.

[14] These are Haneke's own words, as cited by Seeßlen (2010, 332). When he uses the term "counterpoint" here, he refers to visual and aural elements that do not work straightforwardly together but, instead, create tension through running "counter" to each other. This is a common usage of the term in sound track studies, as opposed to the strictly musical definition of the term as meaning polyphony or interweaving melodic strands (for example, in a fugue texture).

extreme economy, and involves the audience in decoding its meaning, a description that applies to numerous aural cues in Haneke's films. To take one brief example, there is the "repetitive, cacophonous" sound of the three-minute ping-pong machine sequence in *71 Fragments of a Chronology of Chance*, a sound that indicates the isolated and automated life of the killer-to-be, revealing that he is socially alienated (playing with a machine rather than a partner), along with heightening the audience's perception of their own "corporeal, perceiving presence" (Peucker 2000, 186). In addition, Mother Courage's silent scream is a strong example of Brecht's *Verfremdungseffekt* (sometimes known as the "V-effect"), the use of a stylistic device to prompt the audience's active response in relation to social comprehension. In this case, something familiar (a scream) is presented in a strange way, prompting the audience to experience a level of distance from the action, enough to consider how Mother Courage's actions led to her own grief. Similarly, Haneke repeatedly shows everyday surroundings along with sounds of familiar things that are amplified beyond the norm, prompting us to critically consider the worlds that his characters move within, as well as the characters themselves. In *The Seventh Continent*, for instance, sounds of numerous familiar objects—from a car wash to a television—repeatedly amplify the empty consumerism of its characters' lives. Consider, also, that the moment of Mother Courage's scream is deeply affecting, even as it provokes its audience to be self-conscious in their perception (noticing the absent sound) and participants in the action (imagining the sound). Similarly, Haneke's films require this level of self-conscious participation along with being grueling. As we shall explore, the opening three minutes of near-silence for *Caché* are most compelling in this regard. Like Brecht's epic theatre, and Mother Courage's silent scream in particular, Haneke's films provoke responses hovering between detachment and engagement, intellectual comprehension combined with emotional reaction. Again, their power is more complex than the clear-cut sadism that is habitually attached to Haneke's name. Finally, we cannot help but perceive that Mother Courage's silent scream is a moment of rule-breaking: we "should" hear what we do not, and the moment forces our awareness of what we have been denied, which is representative of Brecht's anti-illusionist approach to truth-telling. Haneke is a rule-breaker too, especially when it comes to sound.

Though any list of cinematic sonic "rules" would be inevitably reductive, there are certain norms that are worth emphasis here: the dominance of dialogue within a clear-cut hierarchy of film sound, with sound effects and music being subsidiary; the prevalence of sounds that are used for continuity, to "hide" or suture cuts and provide a sense of coherent seamlessness;[15] the sparing use

---

[15] Sonically sutured cuts are those that feature aural continuity, which have the effect of subtly masking the construction of the film itself. Conversely, non-sutured cuts are those where the sound changes *on* the cut in a way that calls attention to itself, highlighting the editing of the film and its overall construction by implication.

of silence that leaves space for unanswerable questions; the incorporation of music as a guiding presence to prompt identifiable emotional reactions and/or for its inherently pleasing or easily digestible qualities; and, above all, a close correspondence between what we see and hear, or an ultimate impression of audiovisual complementarity. All these conventions are so common in contemporary, mainstream, Western-world cinema that they almost go without saying, but Haneke's sound tracks frequently defy all of them.

Haneke's "Epic Cinema"

Like Brecht's epic theatre, Haneke's cinema challenges dominant ideology by calling attention to its own unconventional construction: for the director, this is about being "more honest."[16] Haneke describes his intentions in ways that (indirectly) chime with Brecht's resistance to norms of representing theatricalized "reality," as exemplified by his having musicians play on stage rather than hiding them in an orchestra pit. Haneke says, "my approach provides an alternative to the hermetically sealed-off illusion which in effect pretends at an intact reality and thereby deprives the spectator of the possibility of critical participation. In the mainstream scenario spectators are right off herded into mere consumerism" (Haneke 2000, 172). Though Haneke is not specific about the examples of mainstream cinema that he means to challenge,[17] he stresses how to gauge the relative worth of a given film: "a film's essential feature, its criterion of quality, should be its ability to become the productive center of an interactive process" (Haneke 2000, 171).[18] Surprisingly, Grundmann argues that Haneke communicates no faith in "viewers' critical faculties and their willingness to perform intellectual synthesis" (Grundmann 2007, 12). Conversely, we will find that Haneke's films inherently *depend upon* our making necessary leaps of intellectual comprehension. The director himself speaks of strategies by which he aims to ensure that his audiences adopt active positions of interpretation: "I'm always attempting in my works to shake up the confidence the viewer has in what he's [*sic*] seeing. . . . The

---

[16] This is part of Haneke's "Director's Statement" for the *Code Unknown* DVD release by Artificial Eye.

[17] Haneke makes some more particular, and admittedly problematic, generalizations about what American cinema does: "my films are polemical statements against the American 'taking-by-surprise-before-one-can-think' cinema and its disempowerment of the spectator. It is an appeal for a cinema of insistent questioning in place of false because too quick answers, for clarifying distance in place of violating nearness. I want the spectator to think" (as cited by Vogel 1996, 73).

[18] Haneke's own comments about influence do not emphasize his obvious artistic affinities with European cinematic predecessors (such as Jean-Luc Godard, Antonioni, or Bresson) but, rather, the generalized power of mainstream American cinema to which he is fundamentally opposed (and to which *Caché* and both versions of *Funny Games* most directly "respond").

more you shake it up, the more you disturb that sense of trust and confidence . . . the less capable the viewer will be of being manipulated by the images he or she is seeing" (Mottram 2006). This quotation makes Haneke's desire to undo the manipulative power of images quite explicit. Through his radically unconventional emphasis on sound, he is committed to nothing less than a re-evaluation of what cinema can do.

Each subsequent chapter of this book is focused on one of Haneke's films from a particular theoretical perspective. Chapter 2 is an auteurist analysis of *The Seventh Continent*, establishing the dominant aural patterns of Haneke's sonic world.[19] Chapter 3 focuses on the impact of the thriller *Funny Games* within a genre studies context, emphasizing how and why its sound track breaks with cinematic norms for representing violence. Chapter 4 is a post-colonial approach to *Code Unknown* as it aurally stresses both diversity and possible unity within a narrative about contemporary French cultural politics. Chapter 5 studies the rippling effects of *The Piano Teacher*'s sound track as a disturbingly ironic, feminist adaptation of multiple literary, cinematic, and musical works. Chapter 6 is a second postcolonial analysis, thematically centered on the lasting, insidious, and all-too-often "hidden" legacy of colonialism that is signified by the sonic subtleties of *Caché*. Chapter 7 delves into the subtextual aural logic of *The White Ribbon* from a psychoanalytic perspective, using Lacanian concepts of the Symbolic and the Real to explain its historical weight and nightmarish resonance. The final chapter on *Amour*'s sound track is a return to more auteur-centered analysis, partly because the film provides rich sonic surprises in the full context of Haneke's other work. *Amour* is the director's most moving appeal to our imaginations and hearts, and we explore it as the culmination of his rule-breaking, sonically driven cinema to date. None of these approaches to the films is meant to place restrictions on how they might be perceived but, instead, to show how much they reward close analysis through particular ways of hearing. After all, despite his overtly stated intentions, Haneke is not didactic about what precise meanings we should take from his films. He says "a hundred people in front of a screen in a cinema see not one film, they see a hundred different films" (Haneke 2000, 171). Equally, he gives the meaning of his films over to his audiences: "A film cannot stop at the screen. Cinema is a dialogue" (as cited by Conrad 2012).

---

[19] For a range of other auteurist studies of directors' distinctive sonic styles, see James Wierzbicki's edited collection *Music, Sound, and Filmmakers*. Wierzbicki's introduction provides a useful summary of how to define sonic style in relation to the history of auteur theory, and he argues that "relatively few" filmmakers "*have* a sonic style" (5). That said, he foregrounds the important example of Alfred Hitchcock's directorial interest in and control over all aural elements of his films (Wierzbicki 8). Much like Haneke's well-known practice of writing sound into his screenplays—and see the screenplay for *The White Ribbon* for an instructively detailed example—Hitchcock routinely dictated a "sound script" that indicated "all the places where sounds should be heard" (Wierzbicki 8).

This book engages with all the contentious ruckus around Haneke's work in order to begin a new dialogue: for whatever terrors his films subject us to, and whatever theories we use to understand them, his relentless emphasis on aural detail is always more about compassion than cruelty, and more about social conscience than misanthropy. Haneke's cinema makes us listen to awful things, but it also teaches us about the cost of our not hearing, and the moral significance of our being aurally alert.

2

The Seventh Continent

THE NOISES OF CONSUMERISM, THE MUSIC OF SOMETHING MORE

How can a sound track convey the vulnerability of human lives and the power of consumer culture? Is it possible for sound effects to amplify the horror of a family choosing to die without reveling in their tragedy? By what logic can a film demand that we listen to a child's life ending, and experience that horror in excruciating detail, without our being disabled from the critical capacity to engage with the needlessness of her death? What sonic patterns can establish a director as an aural auteur? Can a sound track make us newly alert to what threatens humanity in the real world? These are the big questions behind this auteurist analysis of Haneke's first feature film, *The Seventh Continent* (1989).[1] The story revolves around a bourgeois family of three who commit suicide after destroying almost everything they own. Despite its shocking content, *The Seventh Continent* establishes Haneke's compassionate emphasis on making us hear the emptiness and loss of some ordinary human lives. While the family provides no clear-cut reason for choosing death, the sound track stresses a hostile, capitalist social context that makes their decision understandable: the noises of transactional and mechanical processes dominate the aural hierarchy more than any meaningful, interpersonal conversation.

Aural Patterns of the Auteur

This chapter establishes the fundamentals of Haneke's sonic style. Like Mother Courage's silent scream, the sound track is constructed to unsettle us, raise

---

[1] The original German film title is *Der siebente Kontinent*. Throughout this book, we use the film titles most commonly used in the English-language scholarship on Haneke to date: where the English title is favored for this film, for example, most critics refer to *Caché* with its original French title. For more on the linguistic inconsistency of scholars' references to Haneke's films, see Wheatley (2009, xiii).

FIGURE 2.1 The grainy billboard advertisement for Australia that we first see in the opening sequence of *The Seventh Continent*. At several other pivotal moments of the film the same image is shown without the text, and newly animated by moving waves along with sounds: the sound track thus gives the image greater weight, and a new otherworldly status as the implied, ghostly, and impossible-to-reach "Seventh Continent."

questions, challenge conventions of representation, and demand our emotional and intellectual reactions to it as such. At the fundamental level of form, it offers us a self-consciously atypical experience: the aural patterns of *The Seventh Continent* are strident enough that they *demand* to be perceived. The film draws us into what Haneke calls "an interactive process," relying upon our willingness to make meaning from its strangeness, a strong parallel to Brecht's application of the term *Verfremdung*. For example, Haneke uses sound to noticeably change the implications of images: a beach image is first shown in Part One as a billboard alongside quiet traffic [3:50–3:57], and then shown at the end of Part One as a real landscape with moving waves and sound effects [33:43–34:04] (see Figure 2.1). The sounds of gathering waves along with light birdsong invest the added motion with ominous implications, transforming the image's initial touristic and idyllic aspect to an anticipation of small life being drowned out by massive threat. This is a representative example of the director's emphasis on the power of sound to determine meaning, often over and above the visual message.

   The Seventh Continent features sonic patterns that dominate Haneke's cinema, and which thus establish him as an aural auteur. First, it focuses on a family of three with first names that are repeated in different forms through Haneke's *oeuvre*: the father Georg, the mother Anna, and their daughter Evi. The repetition of these names suggests Haneke's "knowingness with regard to auteurist critical agendas" (Saxton 2008, 85). In other words, the echoing names across his films invite us to read his cinema as a coherent body of work. Our hearing the same names across Haneke's films also encourages us to read his characters as representative figures rather than as sharply distinguished individuals. This, in turn, relates to his emphasis on making social, and often transnational, statements over and above stories of uniquely defined people.

Other sonic patterns are equally, stridently Hanekean. We are forced to perceive the aural impact of every action because the texture is usually comparatively thin, and most noises are closely miked. The film thus amplifies the tangibility of the diegetic space as well as denying us the possibility of becoming engulfed in a wash of homogenized sound effects. The relentless emphasis on aural detail makes the sound track of *The Seventh Continent* an intensely physical experience, one that invests numerous banal objects with life. The sound track frequently changes *on* the cut, emphasizing the film's unconventional, non-sutured form. This has the result of keeping us consistently alert and on guard, even when we witness everyday scenes. The distinction between musical and non-musical sound breaks down, most obviously when background Muzak is used without calling attention to itself as anything more than another noise. Because the music infrequently demands attention to itself, those occasions when it comes to the fore are all the more commanding. Along with the sparing use of music, the film features many silences and near-silences. The most obvious moments of quiet come with the blackouts that punctuate many sequences. Haneke himself explains that the blackouts get longer when there is more to contemplate (Brunette 2010, 13): thus the absence of aural and visual stimulus is far from straightforward negation in that it allows for the positive possibilities of interpretation. The blackouts with silence prompt us to ask questions, or approach answers, without ever providing a sense of closure in themselves. Throughout *The Seventh Continent*, silences are also used in the contexts of abbreviated or fragmented conversations. Silences suggest subtext, unspeakable reaction, avoidance, denial, confrontation, and sometimes, more positively and rarely, peace and acceptance. Like Mother Courage's silent scream, all these moments of no sound demand our imaginative engagement.

The audiovisual rhythm of *The Seventh Continent* is noticeably irregular, further enforcing our alertness, and making the traumatic representations of suicide all the more disturbing. In an interview with Serge Toubiana, Haneke himself emphasizes the importance of rhythmic unpredictability:

> Whatever story you tell, there's already been one like it. So how do you have a deeper impact on the viewer? One of the possibilities is the rhythm, which is what film is actually all about. It's much closer to music than to literature. (Brunette 2010, 20)[2]

---

[2] Haneke may be influenced by Sergei Eisenstein's musical descriptions of filmic possibilities. He echoes Eisenstein in that his figurative emphasis on sonic concepts parallels his literal emphasis

The rhythmic unpredictability of *The Seventh Continent* helps ensure that the film does not fit recognizably within "any standard film genre" (Sterritt 2010, 250). Were we to summarize the impact of film in further musical terms, we would say that its timbre is consistently abrasive. We might compare its repeated details (such as the image of Australia or the blackouts) to serial music in that each repetition is more like the manipulation of a tone row than the return of a familiar melody or identifiable leitmotif.[3] The "music" that is *The Seventh Continent* is far from aesthetically pleasing in a familiar sense. When two lines of sound create a thickening texture, the result is not harmony, but discordance that goes unresolved: for example, when the father and mother murmur "morning" to each other over the sound of a radio newscaster reporting on relentless conflict between Iran and Iraq [4:22–4:48]. This is a representative moment combining banality (the everyday word) with terror (the news of bombings). Such discordance subtly critiques the family's choice to carry on with "business as usual" as an act of irresponsible obliviousness. Their routine greeting underlines their separation from the world at large, long before their death.

We apply musical concepts (such as "discordance") to non-musical elements (such as speech) because Haneke encourages us to understand the entirety of his films in musical terms. Not only does he write sounds as well as speech into his screenplays, thus "scoring" every aural element most precisely, he also describes his directorial role with actors as being like that of a "conductor" who must keep his orchestra "dynamic" (Grundmann 2010b, 601). Further, he says:

> I believe that every art form works with structures, and structures are produced by repetitions. Without exception the repetitions and variations in my films have their basis in music. (Riemer 2000, 161–162)[4]

---

on sound tracks. Eisenstein privileged music to the extent of extensive collaborations with Prokofiev (*Alexander Nevksy* [1938] and *Ivan the Terrible, Part 1* [1945] and *Ivan the Terrible, Part 2* [1958] being the key examples). He fitted his montages to Prokofiev's music through listening until he said he could "imagine a series of images which could correspond with the music, or a section of the music which could correspond with an imagined film sequence" (Robertson 2009, 146). Although Haneke usually privileges sound effects over music, the fact of his writing sonic details into his screenplays parallels this kind of process whereby aural cues are treated as much more than mere accompaniment to visual action. It is beyond the scope of this book to fully explore the parallels between Haneke and Eisenstein, but for more on Eisenstein's approach to parallel aural and visual artistic stimuli, see his article "Synchronization of the Senses" (from *The Film Sense* [1942] 1947 , 69–109). For more on his understanding of cinema as a total art form, and as "audiovisual counterpoint" see Kulezic-Wilson (21, 36, 40, 82–85). And for more on Eisenstein's conceptualizations of visual media (both painting and cinema) as musical, see Robertson (2009, 13–46).

[3] The repetitive sonic structure of *The Seventh Continent* can be usefully contrasted with that of a much more recent film, *The Tree of Life* (2011). The latter film deals with some disturbing themes of death and domestic violence, but it is sonically structured around calming repetitions of voiceover phrases, musical cues, and sound effects that evoke a cumulative sense of macrocosmic cycles as powerful as the waves on shore that we see in its climactically unifying final sequence.

[4] Other critics have already commented on the "musical" forms of Haneke's films. Brinkema, for instance, calls *Funny Games* "Haneke's most Cagean piece, marked by interruptions, digressions, and

The Seventh Continent is representative of Haneke's exacting approach to scoring and conducting all sounds and silences. We will therefore continue to apply musical concepts to his cinema where appropriate. Although each aural pattern is uniquely handled by each of Haneke's films—the silence at the end of *The Seventh Continent*, for instance, means something very different from the silence at the end of *Amour*—one overarching point applies to them all: understanding Haneke's films entails perceiving the deliberation with which he uses every sound (or lack thereof). Our analysis of *The Seventh Continent* paves the way for perceiving the logic of Haneke's entire sonic universe as it makes demands of our imaginations and hearts. We include the timings of crucial sound effects and dialogue, as well as for music cues, to stress that *all* aural elements demand our interpretative attention.[5]

The Aural Patterns of *The Seventh Continent*

From the outset, the sounds of *The Seventh Continent* are unconventionally abrasive: the film begins with the *forte* sounds of an automatic car wash [0:07–3:47], and a seemingly innocuous procedure is thus invested with sinister life. We see the family inside the car, but cannot hear them. And even before we see them inside, the car is shown in several parts from the outside, along with the sounds of spraying, hosing, brushing, drying, and the car's movement through the conveyor tunnel. There is no conversation in competition with this automatic process, one that requires that the family sit passively in waiting. Towards the end of the washing, as the car is moving slowly forward, signs in front of the car come into prominent view. They read, in German and English, "Do not brake" (see Figure 2.2).

The opening throws us *in medias res*, disallowing us the freedom to feel any measure of control over the sounds that happen to us along with its characters. Even when the family subsequently seems to control the sounds of the film, or when the sounds do not come solely from an automated machine like the car wash, the sound track is accosting. This applies to the sequence following the first car wash, where we witness the family's morning routines: waking to

---

even a dared invitation to abandon the diegesis altogether—and, also, yes, a playfulness that shocks." He then argues that *Benny's Video* is Haneke's "Morton Feldman work" in the way it repeats details to introduce subtle differences in a minimalist manner, a pattern that equally applies to *Caché* (2010, 361). Seeßlen uses more general musical terminology to define how Haneke's films take "breaks from conventional rhythm" and feature "dissonant editing technique[s]" that make cuts visible (2010, 334). Similarly, Stoehr refers to shots or scenes that are not closely tied to Haneke's main plots, but which nevertheless "create room for interpretation and speculation" as "grace notes" (2010, 481).

[5] Every effort has been made to pinpoint timings for the particular aural effects discussed in this book, all of which come from specific editions of the films referenced in the works cited. However, the reader should be aware that every timing is variable depending on the specific DVD or Blu-ray edition being used.

FIGURE 2.2 The car moves us closer to the signs ("Nicht bremsen!/Do not brake!") along with the appearance of Haneke's name during the opening sequence: the director knowingly braces us for something beyond our control.

an alarm clock and then the first radio news broadcast, dressing, feeding fish, making and eating breakfast (see Figure 2.3). The sounds are more threatening than ordinary because we do not see the family's faces: indeed a full nine minutes pass before we get a full facial close-up.[6] Thus, the family's voices are not fully de-acousmatized for much of the exposition.[7] Instead of seeing faces, we see parts of bodies in action: mother's hands using the coffee maker, father's hands tying his shoelaces, daughter's hands spreading butter on her toast. Because each sound consistently amplifies the action and agency that we cannot immediately attach to a face, sound itself has a disturbing presence, one that suggests equivalency between the car wash (a faceless automation) and the members of the family.

[6] Haneke's emphasis on showing the fragment to represent the whole—such as images of hands without faces, along with characters' voices detached from their physical movements—echoes the cinema of Robert Bresson (Peucker 2010, 17). That said, we should be careful about assuming that the emotive impact of this tendency is the same in both directors' works—for example, in *Pickpocket* (1959), Bresson repeatedly shows the hands of the protagonist as he learns deft tricks for stealing while he speaks dispassionately about what he did through a voiceover. There is a consistently obvious tension between his increasingly assured, slick hand movements and the worn-out, self-critical sound of his voice as he remembers the details of his criminal life. In *The Seventh Continent*, the emphasis on hands detached from bodies relates to a thematic emphasis on human bodies working like objects, which is usually reinforced by (rather than shown in tension with) the characters' detached voices.

[7] As Michel Chion most influentially explains, the acousmatic voice is one that is separated from its bodily source, a classic example being the Wizard of Oz as depicted in the 1939 film (1994, 129–130). The acousmatic voice creates an expectation of de-acousmatization: that is, the moment at which the voice and bodily source are audiovisually united. In their disembodied and uncanny power, acousmatized voices are often associated with horror, as Fenimore (2010) discusses with regard to the strange

FIGURE 2.3 The first shot of the three family members together focuses on their hands at the breakfast table.

In the repeated close-ups of the family's hands completing activities and the repeated absence of their faces, the family is audiovisually represented as mechanized beings. Their lines of dialogue are seldom *forte*, and are combined with the sounds of machines and numerous *things* related to domestic duties or public activities. Consequently, it seems that "objects have triumphed over people" (Brunette 2010, 14). The sound track most noticeably amplifies all the family's transactions at a grocery store, a gas station, a hardware store, and a doctor's office. This pattern prompts us to repeatedly perceive the family as representatively objectified consumers instead of individuals with independent agency. Their very existence is inseparable from the things they purchase. Though we might therefore feel a high degree of detachment from the family and the entire film, *The Seventh Continent* requires a high level of emotional engagement. We must perceive the poignant perishability and fragility of humanity as we experience the film's many inhumane and disembodied sounds. The voices that are often separated from faces, along with the frequent speech coming from offscreen, make us long for the phantasmatic cinematic union of face and body or the implied restoration of humanity.[8] *The Seventh Continent* so obviously withholds an illusionist

---

power of Mrs. Bates's voice in *Psycho* (1960). Though *The Seventh Continent* is not a genre film as such, Benjamin Noys argues that we could read the film as a "horror" where capitalism "never materializes itself into a simple "monstrous" form" (2011, 148). Certainly acousmatic voices work here, as in horror, like "cracks in the world of synchronized sound," "tearing the parts of cinema, revealing the incision between body and voice" (Fenimore 2010, 80, 82).

[8] Mary Ann Doane calls the illusion of audiovisually coherent human presences on screen "phantasmatic" because they are "reconstituted by the technology and practice of cinema" (1980, 33–34). If

way of representing people as coherently intact and audibly in control of their world that we cannot help feeling what it denies us. The ending of the film provides no restorative comfort either: a written statement explains that the family were discovered and an inconclusive investigation was conducted. The allusion to an actual police investigation relates to the fact that Haneke decided to create the film after reading of a similar family that actually committed suicide (Wheatley 2009, 56). By extension, the film communicates Haneke's desire to help us hear the threat of capitalism in our own (Western) world.

The Seventh Continent repeatedly reminds us how easily humanity can get lost in a context of endless consumerism and empty speech. Even on those occasions when the lead characters' voices are close-miked, the film denies us a sense of intimacy with them: instead, there is a sonic emphasis on the denial of human connection that implies a threat to us along with dividing the characters themselves. The family's speech allows us precious little certainty about their internal lives. Their conversations are reserved, and the personal letters read in voiceover are relatively unrevealing. Two letters are from Anna to her parents-in-law, politely updating them on family news, and one is from Georg to his parents in preparation for suicide. The letters are focused on superficial appearances of being in control: for example, Anna mentions the awfulness of her brother's depression after her mother's death, but dwells more on the inconvenience of her having to manage business and household affairs during his sickness than the significance of his hospitalization.[9] The letters are read by the actors (Birgit Doll and Dieter Berner) in flat monotones that suggest lifelessness rather than genuine attempts to communicate. The content of Georg's letter anticipating his family's suicide *could* be deeply touching but his unchanging tone flattens his emotive phrases like "I look forward to my death," Evi is "not afraid of dying," and "please do not be sad." He communicates a level of insensibility to his own words that amounts to a death-in-life. Therefore, the voiceovers ironically deny us the sense of closeness often afforded by the same technique in other films.[10] Nonverbal sounds often tell us more about the family than they reveal of themselves through dialogue *or* voiceover.

---

we consider that sounds are often recorded separately from images, and that films typically incorporate visual and sonic editing, we can begin to appreciate how much construction is involved in creating the seemingly straightforward illusion of coherent beings on screen.

[9] In a later scene, when Anna's brother begins sobbing over their mother's death, "it seems to take forever for Anna to move closer to solace him" (Brunette 2010, 16). He makes the most unguarded emotional noise in the film, but she is still guarded in responding.

[10] For a representative example, consider the voiceover in *Never Let Me Go* (2010) that provides a crucial sense of intimacy with one of the clone characters with whom we are subversively encouraged to align ourselves. Conversely, the film of Haneke's that uses most voiceover, *The White Ribbon* (2009), does not bind us to the narrator. He speaks from a strangely unrevealing, retrospective position, and ironically underlines the film's unsettling diegetic content in that his narration is relatively dispassionate. We explore the atypical use of voiceover in *The White Ribbon* much further in the chapter about that film.

FIGURE 2.4 "And hop, and hop, and hop," Evi's teacher shouts (her face offscreen). Each child becomes indistinct in the lineup of regimented jumps.

The closest we can get to the main characters is by hearing as they do. We hear every sound the family makes as if we were within their space: almost all their actions are amplified, enforcing an impression of physical alignment, if not intimacy, with them. The sounds of *The Seventh Continent* are seldom overtly subjective, so we are not straightforwardly connected to the family, but we are forced to hear a world against them as they *might*. For example, in one brief scene we see one young girl after another from Evi's school jumping over a vaulting horse in their gymnasium. The teacher stands offscreen, shouting "and hop, and hop, and hop" ("und hüpfen, und hüpfen, und hüpfen") as each girl leaps over the vaulting horse [41:50–42:19]. The action is quick enough to make the girls' faces indistinguishable from each other: the camera is positioned to capture only the moments of movement, during which each girl is a flurry of color rather than an individual form (see Figure 2.4). Evi may be one of the girls that jumps, but we cannot tell which one: the point is not to separate her from the others, but to demonstrate that she is but one of many girls who will be routinely commanded this way. The impact of this is thoroughly Brechtian in prompting a cognitive *and* emotionally charged, push-me-pull-you response. The ordinary action of the girls is made strange through the absence of their faces and the emphasis on the sounds of their patterned movement on command. The scene thus defamiliarizes ordinary action, encouraging our distance from it, but also draws us in enough to notice Evi being lost in the visual flurry. It is shocking to see children being audiovisually represented as such regimented objects, and we cannot help noticing that Evi is unidentifiable in the flurry. We must understand that Evi and her classmates embody the damage of a ruthless culture devoid of meaningful human interaction—they move on command and in uniformity, not freely and play-fully as happy children do.

The relentless and near-perfect rhythm of the numerous girls jumping onscreen creates a sense of cold and futile repetition. Perhaps Evi herself wishes to break from this pattern by claiming her own difference: in an early scene, she feigns blindness at school. Her pretense suggests her desire to perceive things differently, and perhaps through hearing more than seeing.[11] The scene begins with the film's first sound advance: a child saying "she's in there" over a black screen [11:21], followed by a cut to Evi's school. (In earlier scenes the film establishes a pattern of sounds ending or entering *with* the cut to an image.) The voice belongs to one of Evi's schoolmates alerting a teacher to Evi's distress. The voice being attached to a black screen suggests that Evi is in darkness, both literally and symbolically. The teacher exposes Evi's lie by threatening to leave her entirely alone and then tricking her into looking at her waving hand, thus focusing on the symptom rather than the cause. After receiving a call from the teacher, Evi's mother questions her about what happened, starting with the question, "Are you crazy?" in an accusatory rather than compassionate tone. When Evi refuses to admit her deception immediately, Anna soon lowers her tone, more calmly insisting she simply wants "to hear the truth" and promising she "won't harm [her] in any way." After a long pause, Evi reluctantly says "yes" to having feigned blindness. Anna responds by giving Evi a hard slap on the face, a shocking action immediately followed by the film cutting (or "slapping") into blackness [24:39]. The slap is amplified while everything else in the scene is comparatively quiet. The sudden cut to black silence emphasizes a symbolic return to where Evi was before, even as the film has now prompted a change in us: we cannot help perceiving the child's desperation even if she withholds any explicit explanation. Indeed, her relative quiet, and her minimal speech, disallows us closeness with her *and* poignantly underlines her aloneness. The film invites us "to hear the truth" more than Anna can bear or either one of them can say. This is the truth of a child living as a controlled object.

The World's Harsh Noise, and Choosing to Leave It

The overall impact of listening to *The Seventh Continent* is emotionally over-whelming, and always in excess of what is ever spoken. The sounds cumulatively convey a hostile atmosphere in which we always know we might be surprised

---

[11] Brunette calls attention to visual details that suggest Evi's rationale for pretending blindness: the camera allows us to glimpse a newspaper article with the headline "Blind—but Never Again Alone" and the explanatory subheading "After a Horrible Accident, Anita Can Count on the Affection of Her Parents More Than Before" (2010, 17).

by an assaulting sonic burst. Experiencing the film means being subjected to sound after sound that connotes pain, injury, shock, effort, or tediousness, even in everyday scenes. Its sounds rarely mean kindness, communicating a world of unending callousness. Indeed, sound is a form of violence in *The Seventh Continent*. This is clearest in the sequence leading up to the family's suicide. The destruction begins with a piercing screech of the kitchen tap when Anna turns it on to make coffee (a sound repeated from the opening breakfast scene) [1:11:17]. The ordinary object "speaks" to, or anticipates, the agony to follow, especially in the absence of the family's faces (another reminder of the opening). The film has an ABA structure, in that the destruction sequence repeats many such details from the exposition. However, as Anna is preparing breakfast, she hears a new sound of banging in the next (living) room. She enters that space to find Georg has knocked down shelves, with Evi standing by. He flatly states, "I think the only way we'll make it is if we go about it systematically." Anna says nothing, but her eyes dart around the room, suggesting alarm or at least stimulation. Though we now see her face clearly, her reaction is strangely difficult to read in the absence of speech (see Figure 2.5). The moment is thus oddly alienating, although the buildup to the traumatic climax has already begun; it is another example of the film's Brechtian, push-me-pull-you impact.

Next, we see the family enjoy an extravagant breakfast including champagne, expensive cheese, and deli meats, though they remark on none of it with pleasure. Here, their faces are withheld from us as they were in the film's opening (see Figure 2.6). Georg gently tells Evi (addressing her as "princess") that she had better put on shoes so that she does not hurt her feet. His surprisingly tender vocalization of care for her body is painfully marked in the absence of

FIGURE 2.5 Anna's look communicates several possibilities: shock, fear, exhilaration, anxiety, oppression, willingness: it is impossible to be sure of her emotional state.

FIGURE 2.6 Another shot that withholds the main characters' faces from us, like the first one of the family together (Figure 2.3). Here, they eat their last extravagant meal before destroying everything they own. This visual reminder of how we first saw them together (as hands at the table) suggests their unchanging selves, and that their desire to die was present from the beginning.

their faces: he speaks of her as a person he cherishes while the visual action still treats them both as objects. The relative quiet of this breakfast scene, along with the flat dialogue delivery without faces, has the ironic impact of building tension: the disjunctive combination of what we see (the family as objects), what we hear (the family's resignation to their own suicide), and what we now anticipate witnessing (the trauma of their deaths) creates a profoundly rupturing experience.

Following six seconds of blackness and silence [1:13:21–1:13:28], there is an extended sequence of the family deliberately destroying almost all of their possessions, signifying "the emotional void of consumer accumulation."[12] We hear and see the parents taking down pictures, removing clothes and hangers from a wardrobe, ripping shirts, cutting various clothes, tearing drapes and cutting them. Evi's small gloved hands cut through her clothes, rip and cut up her own drawings, and tear books apart. Her parents break records, empty desks, tear the sofa, rip up photo albums, axe and saw through furniture and bathroom fixtures, mirrors and glass. Every act of destruction is amplified along with close-ups or medium close-ups. The emphasis on things in the demolition sequence conveys Haneke's message that people have replaced "truly *living* with reflexively *doing things,*" and that their lives have become "a wan, enfeebled shadow of how they'd feel if they were richly, *genuinely* alive" (Sterritt 2010, 250).

---

[12] This is Meghan Sutherland's phrase, as cited by Kumar and Swiatek (2012, 314).

Suddenly, Anna shouts "no!" on a close-up of Georg's hand with the axe, right before he smashes the fish tank [1:21:59]. Having not seen their faces during every destructive act (except when they destroyed family photographs), we now see Georg and Anna's faces attached to their bodies as the water streams out. The full sight of them, along with the rush of water, brings a sense of release. But this release also entails killing. Evi enters the scene and screams "No, let me go! Leave me!" as her mother restrains her. Anna scolds Evi to "Calm down!" The child eventually relinquishes control, falling into her mother's arms. We hear her crying over a montage of close-ups on fish as they wriggle into death [1:23:47–1:24:25] (see Figure 2.7).

Throughout this sequence, the timbre of each sound effect is amplified with the sort of calculated cumulative affect that is traditionally associated with musical scoring. The notable absence of dialogue until Anna's involuntary shout and Evi's protest emphasizes the counterintuitive calculatedness of the family's approach to suicide, as well as the vulnerability of their voices in relation to the brutal accumulation of noises. In addition, there is no music to soften the impact: instead, the film consistently requires our aural alertness to human loss and destruction. The sound of death (the fish) is comparatively weak, quiet, and pathetic, devastatingly anticipating the family's own quiet end. The sound track stresses that the world of things has won insofar as there is so much to destroy, and the result is a mess of pieces rather than any one thing being fully annihilated. Because everything stays in the apartment, everything is contained implosively within it—there is no centrifugal release for the family to parallel the rush of water from the fish tank.

By the end of this sequence, the sense of aural erosion has reached a peak. This has been building throughout the film because everything we hear

FIGURE 2.7 One example from the montage of dead fish: a strange spectacle of death.

is abrasive on some level: the quiet sounds of Georg and Anna having sex are empty of passion (grunts and sighs without eroticism); and quiet sounds can be most painful (the dying fish), just as loud sounds accost us in surprising ways (the water tap screeching on). Sounds of everyday life, such as Georg's shower (the water, soaping his face, spitting out water, moving the nozzle) are severe [21:18–21:44].[13] Even the home telephone sounds like an alarm [22:24–22:33]. During the scene at Anna's optometrist practice, there is the more dimly irritating sound of drilling on the street. The sound becomes prominent on the cut to a shot directly outside her shopfront, though the drilling begins earlier, while an old female patient tells Anna a nasty tale from her childhood: when her classmates teased a little girl for being ugly with eyeglasses, she took revenge by cursing them all into losing their perfect sight.[14] Our becoming aware of the drilling, *and* the fact of its having begun before we were perhaps conscious of it, may lead to our perceiving the aural erosion that is present *throughout* the film, even when it is less obvious. This is a subtle way of making us more conscious of everyday noises that we can easily miss: we perceive the literal impact of noise pollution, and the symbolic, cumulative impact of persistent sonic presences that are inhuman and/or inhumane.

Although we might not register such subtle details as the drill, we cannot help noticing the strange sonic violence of many everyday actions in *The Seventh Continent*. Even an ordinary trip to the supermarket is a memorably affronting aural experience. When Anna and Georg pick out groceries (bread sticks in plastic wrapping, clinking wine bottles, meat chopped at the deli), the sound track is dominated by each *thing*, and we again lose sight of their faces. When they go through the checkout, one packet after another beeps as its barcode is scanned by the cashier, and her rapid-fire typing into the cash register sounds aggressive against the quiet Muzak in the background. There is no conversation between husband and wife: the transactional process dominates [16:38–18:55].

André Bazin famously argued that one great advantage of cinema, in contrast with theatre, is being able to invest all *things* with anthropomorphic life:

> The human being is all-important in the theatre. The drama on the screen can exist without actors. A banging door, a leaf in the wind, waves beating on the shore can heighten the dramatic effect. Some film masterpieces use

---

[13] Similarly, *71 Fragments of a Chronology of Chance* features numerous everyday noises (from putting on socks to an alarm clock) that are "too loud," consistently suggestive of a relentlessly hostile world.

[14] It is difficult to pinpoint exactly when the drilling sound begins because it enters the mix so subtly, but it is certainly present by 15:24 minutes, as the woman's story reaches the climactic point of the girl making her curse. The drilling continues subtly until a cut to black [16:05]. When the films cut back to a daylight image just outside Anna's office [16:10], as Georg is collecting her from work, the drilling is suddenly prominent for the duration of the take (that is, until 16:24, after a hard cut to show Anna applying lipstick inside the car).

man only as an accessory, like an extra, or in counterpoint to nature, which is the true leading character. (2005, 102)

This quotation should be understood in the context of Bazin's focus on the positive possibilities of cinema to represent realism. Among other things, Bazin championed widescreen and minimal editing to allow the audience the depth of field and freedom to survey images as they might in their own natural world, at their own pace. Since he resisted the too-obvious intervention of the director, it is unlikely Bazin would have embraced Haneke's overtly manipulative style in *The Seventh Continent*. That said, the degree to which the film invests objects with expressive life resonates with Bazin's notion of people as mere "accessories:" the aurally strident objects are a strong contrast with the family's often dulled and monotonous voices. None of the actors uses the full expressive ranges of their voices: the timbre of their speech is thin, and the pitch and dynamics limited, so much so that Evi's passionate shout of protest against her father's killing the fish is a lasting shock.

Despite the narrative revolving around the family, the sound track is *never* dominated by their speech. Instead, it is broken up by a choppy structure of unpredictably featured objects with extremely different tonal properties, pitches, dynamics, and rhythms. Speech is comparatively sparse or abruptly cut short, most notably with the radio news broadcasts that are routinely switched off. Even though the subject matter of these broadcasts is potentially distressing, the flattened monotone of the newscaster's delivery cancels out affective interest—this motif is even more pronounced in the two other films of Haneke's so-called Glaciation trilogy[15] (*Benny's Video* and *71 Fragments of a Chronology of Chance*), both of which feature dispassionate newscasters reporting over images of socially charged violence.[16] The choppy sound track of *The Seventh Continent* parallels the film's visual motif of broken-up bodies. Much as the camera repeatedly shows hands separated from faces, the sound track breaks up the "body" of the film. The diegetic music cues are mostly registered as yet more "noises" that

---

[15] Haneke himself coined the term "Vergletscherungs-Triologie" ("Glaciation Trilogy") (Sterritt 2010, 253). Themes of the trilogy include dehumanized everyday life, guilt, and denial passed across generations, "historical amnesia," and the erosion of European state power in the face of "commercial consumption" (Grundmann 2010a, 18). Each of the three films culminates in a seemingly irrational act of violence that forces us to confront the many harms of contemporary societies (Sterritt 253).

[16] *71 Fragments of a Chronology of Chance* most memorably features televisual news stories narrated with familiar monotony. For example, a female newscaster speaks of many deaths related to guerrilla war attacks waged by the Kurdish Workers' party PKK. The television story cuts to show raw footage where the "bloodbath" occurred, and a male reporter's voiceover intones "screams of pain, full of impotent rage, this man is trying to retrieve his dead brother's shoe from the bloodstained floor of the village café." The footage then shows a heartbreaking image of a woman grieving, along with the reporter's next, incomplete voiceover line ("This woman has lost her husband in a struggle which he, like the other victims . . .") before the film suddenly cuts to black. This moment of disruption is an implicit, blunt rebuke of the newscaster's and journalist's failures to represent the whole story, on both literal and emotional levels [32:24–34:20].

break up the sound track (Muzak on the radio, in the car, at the supermarket, and on television). So, even music does not provide us with suturing consolation, and it seems unrelated to the family's life except for being a plausible component of their sonic environment. Where film music in general is far more often used to relate to, reinforce, or reflect on onscreen action, the music of *The Seventh Continent* is curiously dissociated from the family's life—it is just another part of the film's broken body. This is a crucial facet of Haneke's disallowing our complacency by breaking with conventional aural form, the impact of which is both disturbing and cognitively demanding. Again, being subjected to his sound track means being constantly on the alert, and never having the impression of seamless or familiar understandability. The repeated, unconventional sonic ruptures relay the wrongfulness and "unnaturalness" of the film's capitalist reality that makes human lives dispensable. The use of anempathetic diegetic music makes us feel social dispassion in another deceptively simple, devastatingly plausible way.

Music to Hear

Having established the strange pattern whereby music becomes but one of many unfeeling "noises," there *are* two sequences of *The Seventh Continent* where emotive music comes to the fore. First, there is the scene featuring an extract from Alban Berg's Violin Concerto "To the Memory of an Angel," originally dedicated to Alma Mahler's daughter and then Berg's own when she died (Seeßlen 2010, 32).[17] Within the context of *The Seventh Continent*, the music encourages us to perceive Evi as representative of threatened youth, rather than as a uniquely victimized child. This parallels the school gymnasium scene that "loses" her within a group of girls, even though she is visually isolated here. The music enters the dockside scene where Evi waits while her father negotiates the sale of his car [1:02:59–1:04:04]. As the music plays, the only other sound is Evi's footsteps. It is the first music that is not dismissible as background noise and/or as banal pop music or Muzak in *The Seventh Continent*. It also has the most musical status as Berg's best-known instrumental work. For Charles Warren, the music comes together with the "beauty and orderliness" of the film's structure and the final actions of the family, all of which transport the audience "to a new place," washing over us "like those waves that come to life in the poster image of an Australian shore" (2010, 497). In this context, Warren argues that there is there is some goodness in the family's act of self-annihilation, preceded as it is by the destruction of worldly things. Similarly, Robin Wood argues that Haneke's use of Berg's music signifies "the director's

---

[17] As Haneke points out to Willy Riemer (2000, 169), *The Seventh Continent* received an award at a film festival in Ghent for "the most effective use of music in a film, even though it only used a few bars from a violin concerto by Alban Berg."

wish to find a larger perspective, we might say a sublime and liberated alternative, to the condition of the world."[18] Because the modernist violin concerto quotes Johann Sebastian Bach's setting of a chorale "Es ist genug!" ("is it enough, Lord, take my soul . . ."), which is in turn derived from older sources, Wood says the music makes the family's suicide echo "through the centuries" (2007, 48). Both Warren and Wood thus stress the music's benign and uplifting possibilities.

Such readings of Berg's music make sense only if the fragment we hear in *The Seventh Continent* is taken at face value, and is decontextualized from its original placement in the concerto. The fragment that we hear is from the most sonorous, and classically pleasing section of the entire work, whereas the entire concerto features a tension between sections built out of a twelve-tone row and sections that are freer and more harmoniously accessible. Such tensions are representative of Berg's work, and the resultant unpredictability is a musical parallel to how Haneke uses recognizable elements of film form along with frustrating our expectations. Much as the hands we see in isolated close-ups within *The Seventh Continent* invite us to imagine entire bodies offscreen, the musical fragment from Berg's concerto potentially prompts us to recall or refer to the entire concerto. And the concerto itself is a deeply contradictory, ambiguous experience, one that evades simplistic assertions of transcendence or beauty.

When Manon Gropius (daughter of Gustav Mahler's widow, Alma Mahler, and Walter Gropius) died from polio at age eighteen, Berg devoted himself to completing the concerto in her memory.[19] It premiered in 1936, a year after Berg's death as the result of an infected insect bite (Pine). So, the work is now inevitably connected with a waste of life, and the cruel irony of a composer's never hearing what he wrote. The concerto is divided into four movements that chart the girl's journey from pre-birth to death. The first, Andante movement begins with sounds of a violin "tuning up," perhaps alluding to the beginning of a life: the moments that precede clear melody or harmony are suggestive of pre-personhood. The Allegretto movement then features an extended quotation from Carinthian folk tune, suggestive of the girl's life.[20] The third, Allegro movement begins with a startling "shriek" that conjures up "the horror of the death struggle" (Anderson 1995). The fourth movement, the Adagio, begins with an allusion to the Lutheran chorale "Es ist genug!" ("It Is Enough!") by Bach, Cantata BWV 60. A violinist plays Bach's original

---

[18] This is Warren's summary of Wood's claims (2010, 496). Similarly, Alexandra Lloyd argues that the music suggests that Evi "is already in some way connected to another world" (2016, 193). She even argues that the "beauty of the music also suggests that this portent of death does not need only to be read negatively" (194).

[19] The music also references the girl with whom Berg had a child when he was seventeen (Pine)— so, the music is about private grief that cannot be acknowledged, or that is disallowed within a social context.

[20] For more on this musical allusion, including the specific Carinthian song ("Ein Vogel auf'm Zwetschgenbaum"), see Brown (2015).

arrangement, alternating with four woodwinds before introducing a newly moving "Song of Woe." Here, Berg uses "quasi-dramatic elements" by instructing the soloist to visually and aurally take a role of leadership over the other instrumentalists. The other instruments join the violinist gradually, but then break away (Anderson 1995). Toward the end of the piece, the Carinthian folk tune from the Allegretto movement returns, alluding to the girl as she lived. We thus have a work of extremely opposing ideas: it evokes life and death, communal strength and disturbing divisiveness, togetherness and isolation, optimism and anxiety.

Haneke says that the musical quotation from Berg's concerto "has a lot to do with the film action," a comment that suggests we should dwell on its non-transcendent meaning within the specific narrative context. He adds that for those who know the musical allusion to a Bach chorale, "it has the potential of discovery," yet he is uncharacteristically withholding of just what the discovery might be (Riemer 2000, 169). The lyrics of "Es ist genug!" are as follows:

> It is enough!
> Lord, when it pleases Thee,
> Relieve me of my yoke!
>
> My Jesus comes:
> So goodnight now, O world!
> I'm going to my Heavenly home.
>
> I'll surely journey there in peace,
> My great distress will stay below.
>
> It is enough.
> It is enough.

Such lyrics obviously resonate with Evi's final decision to die with her parents. However, the faith of these same lyrics is destabilized in the context of Berg's concerto. The entire musical work is sometimes achingly lovely, and sometimes frighteningly turbulent. These contrary impressions are in the structural tensions of the music itself, playing as it does upon slippery distinctions between tonality and atonality, predictability and unpredictability. Though the fragment that we hear in *The Seventh Continent* is from the Adagio, one of the loveliest sections of the entire work, we must remain conscious of what it means in the context of that same work about the premature death of more than one child. The overall concerto takes us through a multidimensional experience of grief. It literally ends on an ambiguous chord. To imply, as both Warren and Wood do, that the music gives a comforting contour to the reality of Evi and her family's death is to strip the cue of all its complex built-in associations. Moreover, their arguments undermine how that same cue is contextualized within Haneke's film.

Warren and Wood ignore the danger of romanticizing the music's significance in the film, but a closer reading of *The Seventh Continent* discourages
this. If we consider that Evi is watching a boat pass as the music plays, it takes
on another dimension within the diegesis. The aural motif of a boat horn subtly punctuates several scenes of *The Seventh Continent*, and it recurs moments
after this particular music cue is abruptly cut off. The sound of the boat horn
connotes a journey, and it is repeatedly associated with the family's choice for
death. We hear the distant sounds of a boat horn before Anna picks up the
sleeping pills from her doctor for the family's suicide [58:26–58:38]. The sound
of boat horns recurs right before she tucks Evi into bed on the eve of their
suicide [1:10:50–1:10:53], and again while Anna holds Evi as she cries for the
dying fish [1:23:38–1:23:44]. Since Haneke uses sound and music almost always
diegetically, this aural motif associated with death is all the more commanding through its being non-diegetic until the scene featuring Berg's music. The
harsh sound of the boat horn *after* Berg's music is cut off signifies a separation
between the family's imminent death and the music's aesthetic appeal—the two
sounds clearly "clash" with each other in the one scene.[21]

The boat slowly passing by Evi may be an oblique reference to the famous
motif of boats passing in *Tokyo Story* (1953), in which it signifies a Zen willingness to accept the cycles of life and death. However, in *The Seventh Continent*,
when Berg's music is abruptly cut off, we cannot help feeling the shock of the
moment. As Chion points out, the music initially seems to come from "the air"
without being immediately attached to a diegetic source, but then "we realize
only retroactively that the music was diegetic, ending suddenly and brutally
when a car owner starts his car" (2010, 164). The music being suddenly brought
back to earth (that is, to the diegesis) in this abrupt manner undercuts romantic readings of its uplifting implications.[22] Building upon this, as the music first
enters this scene it is attached to the image of Evi walking along the dock past
a line of piled up car wrecks: the contrast between the elevating musical form
and the disfigured cars behind Evi is marked, complicating the concerto's evocation of possible salvation (see Figure 2.8). So, to assume Berg's music is there
to aesthetically soften or give meaning to the suicides would be reading against
the grain of *The Seventh Continent*. After all, in the sequence of destruction
alone, the sound track emphasizes the family's suicidal process as an *appallingly*
systematic act. Haneke offers us the musical "breather" but, crucially, he cuts

---

[21] In connection with this, consider that Haneke's other films present a complicated view on
revered music—this is foregrounded in *The Piano Teacher* (2001) as it attaches canonized music to the
sadomasochistic lead character, which we explore further in due course.

[22] Perhaps the Berg cue *does* serve to remind us of the world of *both* beauty and complication from
which Evi will be forever separated. As Oliver C. Speck writes, Haneke repeatedly emphasizes the tragedy of a child being denied the chance to grow up. Unlike the girl who is beaten to death offscreen in
Code Unknown, Evi is at least given a few moments of music, and the "haunting" power of Berg's music
strongly amplifies her tragedy (Speck 2010, 174).

FIGURE 2.8 The cue from Berg's Violin Concerto plays while Evi walks in front of piled-up car wrecks. The music and image "clash," much as the image of Evi's youthful pretty face seems out of place within the *mise-en-scène*.

it off. This is important for representing loss with a moral compass, disallowing our uncompromised comfort as a child anticipates her own death at her parents' hands.

When music comes to the fore again in the film, it is both deeply connected to the trauma of the family's suicides *and* deeply ironic. Here again, Haneke denies us straightforward consolation—for perhaps that would amount to creating an unconscionably, all-too-easily consumed representation of the family's horrendous choice. This other music rises shortly before Evi dies, when Anna brings her sleeping pills diluted in milk, presumably for making her insensible to a lethal injection. Evi drinks the milk while she is watching television with her father. On television, Jennifer Rush sings the power ballad "The Power of Love" (see Figure 2.9) [1:31:15–1.33.49].

The song is tonally and structurally predictable, at odds with the great narrative disturbance of the family's imminent suicides. Rush's colorful, heavily made-up, "manufactured" appearance visually contrasts with the dominant dark hues of the scene around the television, much as the showcased range and expressivity of her voice contrasts with the family's flattened voices. And yet, for all this darkly ironic contrast, the lyrics of the song directly "speak" for what the family does not say. That the lyrics are within a commercially successful musical product does not negate their resonance. Indeed, the lyrics are thrown into new, sharp relief by their consonance with what is happening onscreen in *The Seventh Continent*. The lyrics (italicized below) dominate the scene in the following order:

As the sequence begins, Georg and Evi are sitting in near-darkness in front of the television. Evi is in a red tracksuit, the color foreshadowing her death.

FIGURE 2.9 The concept of "The Power of Love" is reduced to the image of a pop star performing manufactured emotions on a television set atop an uneven mess of indistinct things. But a deeper reading of the song allows for emotionally gripping, and deeply disturbing, interpretive possibilities.

> *When the world outside's too much to take.*
> *That all ends when I'm with you.*

Suddenly, as Anna slowly opens the door, there is light on Georg's and Evi's faces.

> *Even though there may be times,*
> *It seems I'm far away.*

The lyrics prompt us to understand that even as Anna slowly enters frame she is "far away." Anna sits in silent darkness on the other side of Evi from father.

> *But never wonder where I am*
> *'Cause I am always by your side.*

The lyrics match the action as Evi nuzzles in close to her mother's side.

> *'Cause I am your lady, and you are my man.*

Anna puts her arm around Evi, matching the rising intimacy of the lyrics.

> *Whenever you reach for me . . .*

The film cuts to show Rush on television, at her crooning height of expressivity.

> *. . . I'll do all that I can.*

The film cuts back to Evi handing back a glass of milk to her mother and her saying that it tastes "bitter." She has swallowed the sleeping pills all too quickly under cover of the music at an affective peak. The film cuts back to show Rush on television.

We're heading for something, somewhere I've never been.
Sometimes I am frightened but I'm ready to learn of the power of love.

The television is shown sitting atop trash and on an angle, so its image is skewed, just as every structural component of the song exists in clear but skewed relation to the reality of the diegesis: the song is about deep love, and this is presumably what Anna feels for Evi, and yet her decision to have Evi join her in death is a perverted form of love. On the lyrics "I'm ready to learn of the power of love," the camera slowly tracks in on the television, intensifying our sense of where the family is headed.

The sound of your heart beating . . .

The film cuts to show Evi now slumped in her mother's lap, the lyrics suggesting that her heart's rhythm has changed with the pills.

. . . made it clear suddenly.
The feeling that I can't go on is light-years away.

We see Evi rest her head, lying back against mother's arm, and the lyrics repeat an emphasis on romantic intimacy—

'Cause I am your lady, and you are my man.

Over these lyrics, Evi softly begins a prayer she habitually speaks in the film: "Dear Lord, make me meek, so that I in Heaven shall Thee meet."[23]

Whenever you reach for me.

Evi lies still against Anna, both Anna and Georg appear immobile. The film cuts to black.

Anyone who argues for the "coldness" of Haneke's cinema would benefit from considering this scene. The intersection between lyrics and diegetic action is so clear as to seem initially overdetermined, perhaps even trite. And yet the visible impassivity of Georg and Anna against the rising expressivity of Rush's lyrics and performance creates a profoundly unsettling sense of strain. Further, the song lends a feeling of romantic triumph to the suicidal decision that is horrifying when we dwell on Evi's loving compliance and stillness. Georg and Anna's unmoving faces are offset by Rush's face moving ceaselessly with her delivery of the song, intensifying this horror. In addition, Rush's performance of emotional openness betrays us by concealing the moment when Anna gives Evi the pills. The love in Rush's song thus takes on devastating connotations in this narrative context. At the same time, we

---

[23] Gregor Thuswaldner argues that Evi does not speak these words in a way to suggest genuinely full religious commitment, but as a "mere part of her predictable bedtime routine" (2010, 194).

cannot dismiss the strength of the song from a critical, ironic, or cynical perspective, for its every lyric resonates with what Georg and Anna have decided for their family. Rush's voice joins others that speak "for" the internal disturbance of the characters earlier in the film: including the radio newscaster whose reports stands in for the first conversation that Georg and Anna do not have; and the offscreen child's voice speaking for Evi when she pretends to be blind at school.

The scene featuring Rush's performance prompts the most complex, Brechtian response of the film, one that surely oscillates between detachment and engagement. At one and the same time, the scene invites us to condemn the banality of the music *and* to recognize its profundity, to perceive the tension between the music of love and the diegetic action of killing but to *also* understand their awful interrelatedness (after all, Evi's parents believe they are kindly saving her from the world). The scene requires that we recognize the self-consciousness of its construction from a critical distance, along with being caught up in and off guard by the awfulness of seeing a child begin dying at the hands of her own parents. Like the extract from Berg's concerto, the music is used in far-from-straightforward terms, prompting contrary impressions rather than obviously telling us what to feel. There is an undeniably mesmerizing, heartbreaking correspondence between the song and the characters' actions. And this sense of structural order *hurts* because it feels wrong: we cannot help knowing Evi will die, an ultimate kind of disorder.

Summary

The Seventh Continent features unconventionally heightened sound effects and complex music cues. The sounds of every scene relay a consumerist society in which comparative affluence masks a deep reality of humanity under threat: in particular, the noises of *things* dominate, animating objects so that they seem to have more power than people. The film is designed to sensitize its audience to every single aural detail. The characters seem oblivious to the noises they make and the sounds of many things around them, but the film sonically registers their every move in the world. If we are listening carefully to *The Seventh Continent*, we can newly perceive the immorality of a society that puts things before people, and the unnaturalness of people living like objects.

This analysis of *The Seventh Continent* establishes the main patterns of all Haneke's sound tracks, all of which discourage complacency and encourage critical distance, even as they make a "direct path" to our imaginations and hearts through emotive impact: the emphasis on absent sound and silences, heightened sound effects of everyday objects and actions, the non-sutured use of sound, the use of music as "noise," sound effects that are carefully "orchestrated," pared-down dialogue, abrasively depersonalized and often acousmatized speech, and the sparing use of music that is clearly meant to be heard. Having established such patterns, we are freer to combine such an auteur-centered approach with other theoretical possibilities in the chapters that follow.

3

Funny Games

AMPLIFYING VIOLENCE, THE VIOLATORS, *AND* THE VICTIMS

How can a sound track make an audience newly alert to their own consumption of violence? By what methods can a film amplify a victim's pain without exploiting their suffering? Is it possible to sonically stress the incredible power of those who kill without making them awe-inspiring? When does the *absence* of sound have profoundly unique meaning, even within a narratively generic context? This chapter is a genre-based analysis of *Funny Games* (1997), Haneke's most easily classifiable film as a family-in-peril thriller.[1] The action focuses on a family of three who are systematically manipulated and killed by two male adolescents with no more rationale for violence than the droogs of *A Clockwork Orange* (1971). Haneke has directly acknowledged the influence of *A Clockwork Orange*, though he finds it a "miscalculation" because Kubrick "makes the brutality so spectacular that you almost have to admire it" (Wheatley 2008, 19). Kubrick's film incorporates music that is shockingly and ironically incommensurate with much violent onscreen action, as when the protagonist sings "Singin' in the Rain" during the infamous home invasion scene. Haneke's sound track for *Funny Games* is sometimes similarly and horribly playful because the killers revel in what they do. But its overall sound track makes witnessing violence more consistently serious. The film demands our greatest sonic alertness to every victim's pain in the hope we will no longer see *any* violence as "fair game" for entertainment.

---

[1] Two versions of *Funny Games* exist: the original 1997 Austrian film and the 2007 nearly shot-for-shot American remake with an English-speaking cast. The sound tracks of the films are extremely similar in that they share the same prominent music cues and patterns of diegetic sound, along with featuring parallel visual details. That said, there are inevitable differences between the original *Funny Games* and *Funny Games USA*, especially given that their different casts speak in German and English, respectively. It is beyond the scope of this book to provide an in-depth analysis of the two versions in comparison with each other. Leland Monk (2010) provides a strong account of their differences. We limit our focus to the earlier version and its original impact.

A Red Warning

When *Funny Games* premiered at Cannes Film Festival, audiences were given tickets with red warning stickers (previously used only for *Reservoir Dogs* [1992]), as mandated by the 1997 festival director Gilles Jacob (Riemer 2000, 159). This created expectations it would be "a blood soaked nail biter,"[2] which the film knowingly plays against. As Catherine Wheatley argues, the opening thirty minutes seem "to conform to standard genre precepts" since the family under threat is a "familiar premise from suspense thrillers" (2008, 18). She specifically mentions *Cape Fear* (1991), *Fatal Attraction* (1987), and *The Hand That Rocks the Cradle* (1992) as representative precedents. Though Haneke's film does indeed revolve around a family under threat, it subverts generic narrative expectations. Thrillers showing the family at the mercy of a killer (like *Cape Fear*, both the 1962 and 1991 versions) often end with the reinstatement of the family patriarch's power and/or a final showdown that ensures the absolute destruction of the killer's power through death or at least incarceration. Instead, *Funny Games* shows the father, Georg, asserting his authority early on (demanding the killers, Paul and Peter, leave his home, and slapping Paul in the face), but soon becoming incapacitated when Paul smacks his legs with a golf club.[3] From then on, the killers take and retain control of the narrative's direction, and the final scene assures us they will create yet more similar narratives on their own terms without foreseeable end. Kartik Nair (2009) writes that more conventional thrillers show "nuclear families [. . .] rallying together" until they "find themselves rejuvenated in the process."[4] By contrast, *Funny Games* shows the family attempting to rally, and tantalizingly holds out the possibility of their triumph, until we see them all killed with unceremonial brutality. Because it thus denies us restitution and closure, Haneke argues that *Funny Games* is a "parody of a thriller." He also says it critiques "the cinema of stylized ultra-violence represented by Peckinpah, Tarantino and Oliver Stone" (Wheatley 2008, 19). Obviously and ironically, then, *Funny Games* relies on audiences drawing upon their previous experiences of violent cinema in order to understand what makes it unique. And *Funny Games* not only demands our aural alertness to its own specific processes, but also demands that we rehear all those other films that show the loss of human life with less care. The film's ultimate goal extends beyond

---

[2] Jonathan Romney uses this phrase, as quoted by Wheatley (2008, 18).

[3] The killers may or may not be named Paul and Peter: though they most often use these names that sardonically allude to the Apostles, they use other playful names for each other (including Tom and Jerry, and Beavis and Butt-head). We consistently refer to them as Paul and Peter for convenience only.

[4] The generic labels of "thriller" and "horror" are both used in the criticism of *Funny Games* to date. Regardless of its exact genre classification, Haneke himself says in a more "standard" film the source of conflict indirectly helps the couple: "There's an exterior threat and as a result the threatened couple is reunited" (Toubiana, *Caché* interview, 2005b).

cinema, asking for our greater attention to all human suffering that can too easily go unheard.[5]

This chapter builds on our discussion of *The Seventh Continent* because the films share many aural patterns. Given their entirely different sound department personnel, this underlines Haneke's artistic control. The patterns that *Funny Games* shares with *The Seventh Continent* include sudden aural changes *on* the cut, notable absences of music, amplified diegetic sounds, pared-down dialogue, sound registering as a form of violence, and routine actions that are sonically amplified. Though the diegetic sounds of *Funny Games* are mostly more subtle than those of *The Seventh Continent*, the film still places perceivable sonic emphasis on every movement of the characters within a domestic space. Like *The Seventh Continent*, *Funny Games* disrupts that space through numerous surprising moments of sonic impact that require we be unusually engaged. And like *The Seventh Continent*, the film demonstrates Haneke's awareness of the affective power of sound *over and above* the image.

Since we have established Haneke's sonic style through analyzing *The Seventh Continent*, this chapter builds upon that foundation with a genre-based approach. *Funny Games* contains many familiar semantic elements of a conventional thriller: the quiet, affluent, and isolated domestic space inhabited by a family oblivious to initial danger; the all-too-human threat; killers driven by their unstoppable, sociopathic desires; a sense of foreboding that creates dramatic irony from the outset; the extreme physical vulnerability of a female victim; an essential opposition between unknowable villains and ordinary victims; and inescapable violence. However, the film so relentlessly uses the shock value of sound that it never feels generic in the sense of being safely formulaic. Its sound track always disallows us the luxury of being able to predict how the action will unfold, thus giving us a destabilizing experience that intensifies every violent act. The film thus not only reaffirms Haneke's distinctive style as a radical, aural auteur, but also opens out the resonance of his work as it "talks back" to more mainstream cinema.

Disrupting Expectations, from the Beginning

Funny Games emphasizes the illusion of being in knowable territory, but only to upset our sense of security almost immediately. The film repeatedly reminds us that it refuses the "play the game" of a typical thriller, and thus implicitly

---

[5] In an interview with Serge Toubiana (2005c) for the Kino release of *Funny Games* (1997), Haneke connects the action of his film with real-life incidents: "I read many articles, especially after *Benny's Video*, about criminal acts committed by young people, always young people from good families, so without any social explanation. Always people from middle class families who committed crimes neither for revenge, nor to get rich, but only for the pleasure of feeling a sensation. This disturbed me. And that was what triggered this story."

critiques the genre as entertainment. The first scene establishes deceptive calmness through several tracking long shots of an SUV with a sailboat attached, driving through the Austrian countryside in summer. The shots position us as outsiders, passively watching from a distant position. As Willy Riemer notes, "the scene could be a commercial for a resort, for SUVs or sailboats" (2004, 96). At the start of the film, we hear operatic music fade in. We are led to assume this music is non-diegetic, given the long-shot view and the absence of an onscreen source: however, with a transition to shots from within the car, we are meant to perceive the music as coming from the onscreen CD player. The cut from outside to inside the car brings the first close-up of the film, after a near minute has elapsed [0:53sec]. This first close-up does not belong to any character, as we might expect from countless other films irrespective of genre. Instead, the first close-up shows a stack of CDs in the car, calling attention to Haneke's recurrent emphasis on objects that define characters as representative beings as rather than as sharply individuated people.[6] At this point, the signifiers of bourgeois privilege—the opera CDs stacked next to the SUV player—matter more than the family. The objects of music relate to numerous other signifiers of their relative prosperity—a lake house, a home security system, a cellphone (still a luxury item in 1997)—all of which fail them. Even the comfortably insulated space of the SUV, first sonically defined by canonized opera, is redefined as a place of death when the mother (Anna) later finds the family's murdered dog (Rolfi) inside it. The immediate visual emphasis on the stack of CDs also alerts us to the film's emphasis on the power of aural cues as much as, if not more than, images. After the first close-up, the opening scene emphasizes the parents' sonic control of their world through further close-ups of Anna's hands changing CDs (see Figures 3.1 and 3.2). She is playing a guessing game with Georg, in which they identify operatic extracts and performers for each other: specifically, recordings of "Tu Qui Santuzza" from *Cavalleria Rusticana* by Pietro Mascagni (featuring Jussi Björling and Renata Tebaldi), and "Care Selve, Ombre Beate" from *Atalanta* by Handel (featuring Beniamino Gigli).

Soon we witness the extreme fragility and temporariness of the family's security, which in turn imposes a sense of insecurity on us. Their smug privilege is represented by the opera game they play, and the parents knowing all the answers between them. But this game is very suddenly, and musically, disrupted. After the operatic cues have established an aesthetically pleasing sonic space, one that is diegetically controlled by characters safely insulted within their car, the non-diegetic combination of two thrashpunk songs by John Zorn ("Bonehead" and "Hellraiser," from the Naked City album *Torture Garden*) intrudes upon the

---

[6] Even if it becomes difficult for us to separate from the family's suffering, both in *Funny Games* and *The Seventh Continent*, it is not because of who they uniquely are but because of what the films force us to experience in parallel to their suffering.

FIGURE 3.1 The visual motif of hands that emphasizes depersonalization in *The Seventh Continent* is directly connected with a different theme of sonic control in *Funny Games*.

FIGURE 3.2 A close-up on Anna's hand selecting music for the first game of the film.

sound track [2:32].[7] Suddenly the characters' selection of music is thrown into relief by a *forte* cue from outside the diegetic space. As Brian Price points out, Zorn's music enters only after "Georg is unable to identify what he hears" during the guessing game (2010, 39). It thus sonically marks his limits, along with challenging us with unfamiliar sounds: ironically, Georg himself asks, "Is it new?"

---

[7] These tracks are from the album *Grand Guignol* and performed by Zorn's avant-garde project band, Naked City.

FIGURE 3.3 The title as it first appears, punctuating the entrance of Zorn's anything-but-funny music.

a few moments earlier, though in reference to the different, diegetic music he can hear. The intrusion of Zorn's music stresses the startling appearance of the film title "Funny Games" in blood red (see Figure 3.3). The tonal, consonant, harmonious, sonorous, cadence-driven, smoothly modulating, lyrical extracts of operatic music are violently displaced by Zorn's "anti-musical" music:[8] dissonant sound clusters, unpredictable rhythms, and abrasive timbres including shrill vocals "pierced with screams."[9] As Peter Brunette writes, Zorn's music is not merely "loud and assaultive, like a lot of punk rock, but nearly berserk, even insane," along with being "the psychological, geometrical opposite of the operatic arias in a hundred different ways" (2010, 52). That this aural shift is punctuated by the film's title "Funny Games," words that by themselves *could* connote the opposite of the hellishness evoked by "Bonehead" and "Hellraiser," throws us in the midst of a deeply unsettling indeterminacy of meaning. Though the disjunct between the between title and images here might seem somewhat playful, its extremity is undeniably disturbing.

Zorn's music begins after we have caught our first sight of the family, *and* after we have seen Anna and Georg playfully grappling for a CD cover when he is unable to guess the details of the music she has chosen. "Just listen," she insists, and they smile at each other as their son Georgie looks smilingly on from the back seat. The instruction to listen is within the diegesis but is also, at least retrospectively, the film's instruction to us, especially since Zorn's music shakes us into a state of new aural alertness just seconds later [2:32]. The family

---

[8] Landon Palmer uses the term "anti-musical" to describe Zorn's music (2012, 82).
[9] This is Riemer's phrase (2004, 97).

is visually unaffected by this musical intrusion, though we might read their expressions differently (Georgie, for example, suddenly looks pensive where before he seemed quietly happy): Anna and Georg continue to delightedly play their own musical game. Of course, we do not typically expect non-diegetic music to directly affect onscreen action, but a kind of "harmony" between the two is the dominant norm of mainstream cinema. Here, however, we cannot escape the danger signified by the strained relationship between what we see and what we hear.[10]

Along with perceiving the audiovisual tension within this opening, an arresting experience in itself (thus echoing Mother Courage's silent scream), we understand that the musical screams anticipate what will be the screams of the family in peril. We retrospectively understand that Zorn's music non-diegetically "breaks into" the beginning of the film to anticipate the way that, within the diegesis, murderous adolescents will break into the family space. In parallel to this, Zorn's music later disrupts the diegetic space of the film when Paul plays a CD in the neighbors' house where Georgie hides [56:57].[11] This particular music is in the neighbor's stereo so that Paul may start it at his theatrical convenience, as a terrorizing accompaniment to his stalking Georgie. This knowingly preposterous detail potentially reminds us of the artificiality in any other cinematic moments when music intensifies terror. Of course, by the same token, one might argue that Zorn's music *is* conventional in terms of creating and reinforcing generic expectations of extreme terror. However, the film still sidesteps creating a *pleasurable* generic experience through the extremity of this same music: it callously, sardonically, and ironically makes us all too uncomfortably aware of how things will go. Moreover, *Funny Games* does not allow us to enjoy the music of its killers: consider the violence of Zorn's songs in contrast with the pleasant music of Bach and Mozart that is (in)famously associated with Hannibal Lector in *The Silence of the Lambs* (1991), for example, or Beethoven's works associated with Alex in *A Clockwork Orange*.

Zorn's music is given more terrifying power as the first (and only) non-diegetic sound we hear in *Funny Games*: since it first comes from a place beyond the diegetic space, it has a particular kind of authority beyond what the

---

[10] The disjunct between the actors' performances and Zorn's music here resonates with Brecht's argument for the usefulness of having theatrical actors "play *against* the emotion which music called forth" (1964, 90). For Brecht, the lack of coherence between performances and music allows for an audience's productive engagement, rather than folding them into an experience of enervating affect. Ironically, in 1957 Brecht expressed dismay at the unlikelihood that sound films, "one of the most blooming branches of the international narcotics traffic" would be likely to favor such practice, notwithstanding some exceptions composed by his longtime collaborator Hanns Eisler (90).

[11] Zorn's music makes a third entrance at the end of the film, just after Paul finally faces the camera, drawing us into complicity with his plan for victimizing another family. The camera freeze-frames on his unblinking stare as the thrashpunk blares out and the main credits appear [1:42:04–1:42:56], followed by a silence that allows space for our consideration of the whole film. The silence is "louder" for coming directly after this music signifying Paul's unending triumph.

characters can know. Haneke speaks of Zorn's music as a kind of "*über* heavy metal, an extreme and ironic accentuation of that form." He says that "Zorn's style tends to alienate the listener in a sense that heightens awareness" (2003, 29). His conceptualization of Zorn's music parallels his tendency to take familiar genres and manipulate them with uncomfortable, ultimately unconventional extremes of aural representation. The intrusion of Zorn's music at the start of *Funny Games* is a knowingly rule-breaking moment, one that immediately disallows us the luxury of "losing ourselves" within a predictably suspenseful narrative.

The opening of *Funny Games* presents ultimate dualities in music: there are operatic excerpts "to underscore the normal, stable or functional" and there are thrashpunk songs that signify "the abnormal, unstable or dysfunctional."[12] In that sense, the music plays into thematic dichotomies at the heart of the horror genre as discussed by Timothy E. Scheurer (2008, 176–204).[13] Scheurer writes of the standard practice in scoring for horrors, including the use of title music that represents the collision of ideas and the communication of oppositional states of being that are reliant upon well-worn music associations. Dissonance, for instance, often equals the threat of monstrous disorder in a horror film (179–181). The dualities represented by the opening music of *Funny Games* might create the impression that Haneke buys into a stylistically conservative hierarchy of operatic/refined music in contradistinction to thrashpunk/avant-garde music. Roy Grundmann argues that Haneke "demonizes pop culture" only to give classical music "the benefit of the doubt" (2007, 7). However, Haneke says he is "very skeptical of the false conflict that already exists between so-called 'serious' music and music categorized strictly as entertainment" (Sharrett 2003, 29). The scene that revolves around "The Power of Love" in *The Seventh Continent* is a memorable example of his using "lowbrow" music most seriously. Further, Haneke's use of operatic music cues at the start of *Funny Games* is meant as a criticism of the film's central characters: Haneke says that their guessing game establishes their "deliberate isolation from the exterior world," and he explains that "in the end they are trapped in a sense by their bourgeois notions and accoutrements, not just by the killers alone" (Sharrett 2003, 29). Leland Monk calls the parents' game a "snobby" lesson for their son about "how to stockpile and profit from an accumulation of cultural capital" (2010, 428). More broadly speaking, "serious" art has negative associations throughout the intertext of Haneke's cinema. In several of Haneke's films made over a seventeen-year time frame (*Benny's Video* [1992], *Code Unknown* [2000], *The Piano Teacher* [2001], and *The White Ribbon* [2009], as well as *Funny Games*),

---

[12] These are phrases used by Scheurer when he refers to film scoring for the horror genre generally (2008, 177).

[13] Although the lack of fantastical narrative elements makes *Funny Games* more a thriller than a horror, Scheurer's descriptions still resonate with the film as it plays with thematic dichotomies.

the music of high culture is directly connected with the threat of violence.[14] Haneke himself relates the commodification of classical music "to the culture of Vienna and its construction of an illustrious musical tradition in order to focus attention away from Austria's role in the violent history of the twentieth century."[15] It is surely no coincidence that the original *Funny Games* is set in Austria (Cowan 2008, 122).[16] In addition, the use of music by Mascagni in both versions of *Funny Games* might be a corrective to potential elitism given the composer's association with Italian fascism and the composition of operas for Mussolini in particular, the infamy of which led to the composer's solitary and shameful death in poverty. To overlook this intertextual association would be to partake in the bourgeois complacency of privileging high culture that Haneke consistently critiques in his films.

Hearing the Victims and Villains

In parallel to the classical music, the voices of *Funny Games* are used in defamiliarizing and self-consciously unsettling ways. When the family arrives at their lake house, we do not see them enter the space right away. Instead, we hear their voices offscreen, a common device in Haneke's films that forces us to comprehend how characters vocally define themselves. (Recall that we hear Georg, Anna, and Evi's deadened voices long before we see them in *The Seventh Continent*.) As we see the family dog wandering into the house on his own, we hear Anna telling her son what he needs to do: take things upstairs, open windows, and unpack. When Georgie is slow to respond properly, she simply asks, "are you listening?" with the expectant authority of a parent used to directing her child's action. Once the killers enter her home, however, they take over Georg's and her own power to direct. While the parents lose vocal control, most obviously in their involuntary cries of pain, shock, or grief, the killers always maintain mastery of their own voices.

---

[14] Though *Benny's Video* clearly associates "the propensity to violence with the influence of aggressive "rock" music" (Wood 2007, 51), the same film shows the adolescent killer choosing to hear a Bach concert featuring "Liebster Jesu, wir sind hier" while he channel-surfs in a hotel room in Egypt, escaping the reality of his young victim being disposed of by his father back at home.

[15] We use the term "classical" in the loose sense here, to connote any "serious" or highbrow piece in a chamber, operatic, or symphonic form. This loose application of the term "classical" is to be distinguished from the formal use of "Classical music" that designates music of a particular period within the Western world (c. 1730–1820), and which exemplifies principles of order, tight harmonic and melodic logic, balance, and structure well represented by the works of Haydn and Mozart.

[16] *The Piano Teacher*, the film featuring the most music of all Haneke's works, is also set in Austria. The film includes works by Schumann, Schubert, Bach, and Beethoven, all of which might connote emotional warmth in a different narrative context. Instead, the music of this film is inextricably connected with the central character who is defined by her alienation from others, violent fantasies, and painfully sexualized repression. Thus any consolatory connotations or lofty aspirations potentially connoted by the music are thrown into cruel relief. We return to this central irony in the chapter on that film.

There is a comparatively moving vulnerability and intimacy in how Anna and Georg express their physical trauma in sonically amplified ways. After their son is killed, Georg bursts into a crescendo of uncontrolled crying and then sobs into Anna's chest while she holds him and coaxes him into slowing his breathing in time with her. It takes several minutes for her to bring Georg to this relative calm. They are shown from a consistently long-shot distance in a long take with closely miked sound that isolates Georg's cries and their breathing. His calming down feels like an excruciatingly slow effort [1:07:48–1:10:28]. By contrast, Paul (Arno Frisch), never loses his capacity to authoritatively command and control the sounds he makes. Throughout the film (with the exception of one moment where Anna nearly stops him),[17] Paul can make his voice change at will rather than involuntarily surrendering vocal control, and mostly maintains the even keel of his voice. Frisch's delivery of every line is well-enunciated, rhythmically controlled, and limited in range. The same often applies to how Peter (Frank Giering) speaks, though he is sometimes petulant-sounding or whiny as he defers to Paul's vocal authority. Occasionally Paul's voice become more animated, such as when he imitates a game-show host to declare "as they say on TV: The bets are placed!" [41:30–41:33]. He makes this repulsively-playful declaration right after claiming that the family will die within twelve hours. Since his tone is parodically out-of-keeping with his diabolical plan, the line becomes just another demonstration of his uncommon control. That said, his presence is always meant to be more odd than charismatically coercive to us.[18] Haneke told the adolescents playing the killers to perform "the comedy" and the actors playing the family to perform "the tragedy" (Brunette 2010, 65). This direction leads to a level of tonal strangeness that consistently enforces our alertness: narratively we are in familiar territory, but sonically we are not.

The *Funny Games* sound track takes the villain/victim dynamic to a new extreme. Where Anna has to tell both her husband and her son to listen, Paul repeatedly *ensures* that the three of them always hear him. He even assumes *our* being his receptive audience through directly addressing the camera. He first breaks the fourth wall by smilingly winking at us during the hot/cold game with Anna [28:22–28:24], a silent and tiny gesture that is violently suggestive (see Figure 3.4). Later he turns to ask us if we think the family has

---

[17] In an infamous moment before her husband is shot, Anna grabs the rifle and shoots Peter dead, but Paul then uses her television remote to "rewind" the film so that he can resume as planned. In this moment of Anna's near-triumph, the film presents plays out a fantasy of her becoming the "final girl." Carol J. Clover coined the term in her groundbreaking, feminist analysis of violent cinema: the final girl faces death alone, and she is the only one with the necessary strength to survive, whether by waiting long enough for a rescue or by killing the monster herself (1992, 35).

[18] Frisch shows his vocal range here much more than as the main character of *Benny's Video*, and this reinforces his violent power. In *Benny's Video* he plays a teenager who kills for the first time, in a curiously dissociated way, and he mostly speaks with a voice appallingly devoid of emotional engagement. In *Funny Games*, he is a seasoned killer, in full and self-aware possession of his ability to vocally shift the action.

FIGURE 3.4 Paul taunts us with a wink that assumes our complicity with him.

a chance—"What do you think? Do you think they've a chance of winning? You're on their side, aren't you? So, who will you bet with?" [40:48–40:55]. He thus taunts us with our own participation in the film. In the world of *Funny Games*, listening becomes a terrifying activity for us, as well as for the family.

Like all Haneke's feature films, *Funny Games* not only manipulates us through sound, it also demands our awareness of its own power to do so. Haneke has repeatedly vocalized his Brechtian commitment to making the constructions within his films manifest. With reference to Jean-Luc Godard's famous claim that film is "truth at 24 frames per second," he says that "film is a lie at 24 frames per second *in the service of truth*" (Porton, 51, my emphasis). This is a way of stressing the limitations of cinema to portray reality. Yet Haneke simultaneously implies the radical possibilities of making a film's artifice manifest to serve the ultimate goal of honesty. When Paul breaks the fourth wall to speak to us, the film self-consciously catches us out in the undeniable act of watching the suffering he causes: it is, at one at the same time, a moment of overt artifice and of startling candor. This is the potency of *Funny Games*—its sound track always disallows us a safe retreat from the reality of its victimized characters.

Patterns of Rule-Breaking

When Paul speaks to us, *Funny Games* most obviously manipulates our reactions. But there are many other patterns of aural manipulation that build a cumulative sense of ruthless, rule-breaking unpredictability. These patterns include the following: slight sounds have dangerous connotations; spoken words shift unpredictably in meaning (the word "game," for instance); the tonal properties of the killers' voices are incongruent with the actions they take; and pauses and silences are atypically prominent, forcing us to read into what cannot be sonically encapsulated. The overall impact justifies Haneke's belief in the shock value of sound. By examining memorable examples of each sonic strategy further, we can better understand the film's radically unsettling potency.

First, *Funny Games* builds fearful anticipation through many small sounds that become associated with great danger. For instance, the sound of Peter breaking eggs offscreen after he has troubled Anna for them is slight and momentary [12:22], yet the sound is retrospectively frightening in connection with his being able to stay too long. Being duped by or made to fear such seemingly ordinary sounds is part of what makes *Funny Games* deeply unsettling. Other small sounds are even more frightening, such as Paul flicking on the light switch in the room where he finds Georgie hiding at the neighbors' house [57:22], and his quietly saying "poof" when Georgie fails to shoot him dead with the rifle he wrongly assumed was loaded [58:16]. These two small sounds are amplified enough that we hear them clearly even while Zorn's aggressive music is playing in another room, strengthening Paul's unpredictably controlling presence. There is also the small sound of a golf ball when Paul and Peter return to the house after capturing Anna. Georg has just covered up his son's body with a sheet, a devastatingly quiet act of care in relation to his loud sobbing beforehand. Suddenly, the lake house door opens and Georg calls out, "Anna?," only to hear an unseen hand drop the golf ball. The object itself is tiny when it is first viewed from a long-shot distance, rolling through the door and slowly coming to a stop (see Figure 3.5). The quiet of the whole sound track, combined with the subtly amplified sound of the ball, stresses its significance [1:27:48–1:28:03]. We recall Paul letting the same ball roll near Georg's foot before having the family guess that he killed their dog. The sound on its own is enough, therefore, to "announce" the killers have returned, even before close-ups on Georg's face and the golf ball punctuate the significance of the object's return. That Peter and Paul's entrance is perceivable through this object is at once playful and awful: its hard, small sound is in place of Anna's vocal response to Georg, quietly signifying her (as well as Georg's) imminent annihilation. Through ordinary sounds that take on such awful meanings, the film invites us to connect its action with our everyday reality—we cannot simply dismiss what happens as belonging to a completely different, artificial or genre-bound world.

Just as ordinary diegetic sounds have surprisingly startling impact within *Funny Games*, words shift in terrifying ways. The word "game," for instance, comes to mean something like "an intensely controlled scenario during which killers determine nastily playful and changeable rules." The word is first spoken by Anna to reassure Peter and Paul that Rolfi jumps up to them because "he just wants to have a game." "Funny game," Peter flatly responds [17:45]. At this point, the word "game" has its familiar meaning, even if it is sarcastically used by Peter, and Anna

FIGURE 3.5 The rolling golf ball virtually disappears within the pale *mise-en-scène* but its subtly amplified sound dominates the sound track until it slowly stops: because the noise alerts us to the killers' offscreen re-entry, it seems even louder than it is.

does not yet recognize that she is in danger. Within a few minutes, however, the word means something else: "Listen young man," Anna says to Paul after he has loitered with Peter too long for more eggs, "I don't know what game you're playing but I'm not going to join in" [20:24–20:26]. Paul responds by simply asking, "what game?" and proceeds to ask why she's "suddenly so unfriendly." Because he maintains a relatively soft, polite tone, we begin to suspect Paul is playing a new kind of game, one that frightens Anna while it puts him at ease. Over the course of subsequent scenes, Paul initiates and leads a series of other, increasingly frightening games, including: a guessing game that leads the family to understand Paul has beaten Rolfi to death with Georg's golf club; the "hot cold" game for Anna to find Rolfi's body; the "family game" titled "Kitten in a Bag," in which Paul holds Georgie's head trapped in a cushion cover while humiliating Anna and Georg; Paul's variation on an "Eeny, meeny, miny, moe" game to choose which family member dies first; and another game he dubs "The Loving Wife" or "Whether by knife or whether by gun, losing your life can sometimes be fun," in which he makes Anna perform a prayer to choose how both she and her husband will die.[19] By the end of the film, the word "game" is connected with a string of horrendously life-changing experiences: discovering death, anticipating death, losing a child, being nakedly humiliated, living in grief, and dying alone.

---

[19] Moments after dropping the golf ball to announce his reentrance, Paul cries, in English, "It's play time again!" Like the word "game," the word "play" comes to mean something unpredictably terrifying.

Absent Sounds

The sonic power of *Funny Games* extends even beyond what we hear. Throughout the film, there are many pauses around the lines of dialogue that allow us to register every detail of it, and which invite our active engagement with its critique of violence as "entertainment." These sonically "empty" moments are full in that they are suspenseful, fearful, confusing, and unpredictable. The pauses around the words weight every detail of dialogue, even when the words are ordinary in themselves. The pausing invests each question and reaction with a strong sense of Paul's unhurried control, and his willingness to wait, even as it reinforces the impression of the family being forced into sonic compliance. The silences demand that we wait along with them for the revelations that hurt all the more for taking *too long*. Anna's search for Rolfi is most memorably punctuated with pauses between the banal words of the "hot-cold" game (Paul saying "cold . . . cold . . . colder . . . cold . . . cold . . . warmer . . . warmer . . . hotter . . . cold . . . cold, cold, cold . . . cold . . . really cold . . . cold . . . warmer, hot, boiling!"). These pauses painfully draw out her process of finding the dog until she is suddenly all too close to his dead body [27:31–28:42]. Paul repeatedly shouts and sings the word "*cold*" in particular, signifying his playful sadism as well as his near-boredom and emotional detachment from watching Anna search for her murdered pet. Though *The Seventh Continent* uses much pausing, and there are many blackouts with silence, the quiet moments within *Funny Games* are more persistent and frightening. Since there is yet more noticeable quiet in *Caché* and *Amour*, we should consider the structuring importance of absent sound more fully.

The intentional absences of sound in *Funny Games* generate "an anxious expectation, a palpable desire, for what is missing" (Walsh 1992, 79). Comparatively speaking, in sound track studies, there is little work focused on the meaning of aural absences. In this context, Timothy Walsh's article entitled "The Cognitive and Mimetic Function of Absence in Art, Music, and Literature" is a useful reference. As Walsh writes, "absence often commands an attention that far surpasses the potential of anything present" and "[g]enerally speaking, absence can be registered only when the *expectation* of something is thwarted or deferred" (79). When Walsh writes about the palpable power of absence, he does so with reference to various works of art, music, and literature in which there are pieces notably left out or missing: for instance, he refers to the missing arms and left foot of the Venus de Milo, a statue we might imaginatively reconstruct (70).[20] He refers to the interstices of modernist literary works (such as James Joyce's "The Dead") that sometimes matter more than

---

[20] Walsh describes it as a statue that takes shape "amidst a background of emptiness made more than usually palpable" (1992, 72).

anything verbally included. And he mentions musical compositions in which structured silences (such as the "thousand and one manipulations of rests and pauses" featured in Haydn's work) are as important to form as the notes played (83). What Walsh is analyzing here amounts to more than "the deconstuction-ist tendency to see absence as a condition 'always already' underlying *all* texts and evenly distributed through language" (69). Instead, Walsh is writing about instances where something is "more missing" than in the immediately sur-rounding artistic context or in other comparable works of art (69). Certainly, the many absences of sound in *Funny Games* are conspicuous.

Walsh argues that the absence of a sound can become "paradoxically a positive force, a state pregnant with unrevealed significance" (82–83). He then provides a positive, anti-deconstructionist, and psychoanalytic reading of absence. His essential argument goes like this: since we are born into uncer-tainty and limitations, and since we grow to understand the inadequacies of language to communicate, we might see our own consciousness reflected in the notable absences within artistic works. Artistic works with notable absences can thus, for Walsh at least, becomes a subtle form of mimesis.[21] The absences of sound in *Funny Games* do help establish and reinforce the affective authenticity of the family's horrific experience, but they do not offer consolation of the sort discussed by Walsh. Most of the quiet moments in *Funny Games* build toward an experience that is initially unnerving, eventually harrowing, and unsettlingly unfinished rather than cathartic or epistemologically consoling. Indeed, to be cathartic or epistemologically consoling would be at odds with Haneke's overt Brechtian emphasis on deconstructing generic experiences. More positively speaking, the absent sounds necessitate our active engagement by placing an onus on us to make meaning from them. This is part of, to apply Walsh's words once more, "insuring that a living quality of uncertainty, of untapped and unrealized potential, resonates perceptually around and within the work" (70).

One scene of such perceptual significance revolves around the killers forc-ing Anna to strip down. Paul suggests playing this perverse "game" because Peter and he argue about whether or not she has any body fat [46:58–47:58]. The action itself references countless moments within other films where female bodies are critically scrutinized as well as voyeuristically shown. However, *Funny Games* makes the process of seeing a woman strip down extremely uncomfortable because there is no music or other sound to detract attention from the agony that Anna feels. While Paul holds a cushion case over Georgie's head (making him the "Kitten in the Bag"), he uses sound to control her: we hear Georgie's offscreen squeals of pain when Paul squeezes the cushion case as well as Georgie's shallow, anxious breathing behind the fabric, sounds that visibly disturb Anna into compliance. Paul forces Georg to deliver a line to

---

[21] This is a paraphrase of Walsh's overarching arguments (with particular attention to 77–8, 88).

FIGURE 3.6 The close-up on Anna after she has stripped down honors her distress, denying us a sexualized image.

Anna: "Get undressed, my darling." During the consequent undressing, Anna says nothing. All the same, we cannot help perceiving her sonic presence: most of the scene is so quiet that it seems possible to hear the tears running down Anna's face, along with her gulps, tortured breathing, and the movements of her clothes. Several close-ups show Peter, Georgie in the cushion case, and Georg looking in her direction in turn. When the film cuts back to Anna unclasping her bra and taking off her underpants, only her head and neck are shown (see Figure 3.6): in another film, this would be titillating, but here we are surely grateful to be spared seeing more, not least because the sound track is quiet enough for us to register every painful physical detail of Susanne Lothar's performance. "Bravo!" Paul ebulliently exclaims, "What did I say? Not an ounce of flab. Now, let's get dressed again."[22]

As Thomas Leitch writes, "every film comes with telltale traces of other films it could have been."[23] At this point, *Funny Games* implicitly references all violent films that revel in a spectacle of a female victim's flesh before her death. Even when the woman triumphs, she is often physically exposed along with a

---

[22] The impact of Anna's stripping down is reminiscent of scenes from *Salò, Or the 120 Days of Sodom* (1975), a film of decisive influence on Haneke (Coulthard 2011b, 183). *Salò* features a character named Eva (one of Haneke's recurrent name choices), who is selected as a captive by fascist libertines. The selection process involves an older woman presenting Eva's naked body to several male officials, saying "a delicious little ass, I've never seen finer; a pair of little breasts to revive a dying man." Though Eva is thus presented as a desirable sight, the scene is far from titillating, along with being austere in the absence of music. When she tearfully kneels before the men who smilingly assess her, the already drawn-out action reaches a new level of abhorrence.

[23] Leitch says this with regard to adaptations of novels to film that are necessarily selective interpretations, and which implicitly refer to possibilities outside themselves (2007, 17).

bombastic sound track, as in the classic sci-fi horror *Alien* (1979). In the final sequence of *Alien*, the protagonist and last survivor Ripley (Sigourney Weaver) has stripped down to a skimpy camisole and underpants when she becomes aware of the alien onboard her emergency aircraft. Her near-nakedness before she slowly slides into a spacesuit to kill the alien is impossible to miss, and strangely undermining of her androgynous power up to that point. Along with the film thus emphasizing her vulnerability in the scene, we cannot help noticing the contours of her body as the most human flesh and familiarly organic matter we see in *Alien* (especially by contrast with the film's gruesome alien and robot bodies). However, lest we become too distracted or perturbed by Ripley's near-nakedness, the thickening aural texture pulls attention from her body: there is a relentless sound of ticking, along with wind, and the mechanical noises of the ship as she manages its controls, and then the sudden intrusion of Jerry Goldsmith's unnerving non-diegetic music when the alien becomes visible. As Ripley gradually shifts herself into her spacesuit, the sound track emphasizes her physical aloneness and vulnerability: now Goldsmith's score drops out, abandoning her in her moment of greatest need. To calm herself, she breathily sings, "You Are My Lucky Star" (an ironic quotation from the Classical Hollywood musical *Singin' in the Rain* [1952]) until she can only gasp for air at progressively higher pitches before she fatally shoots the alien. This sonically signifies a familiar connection between sexual and violent narrative climaxes. Ripley's scream and the alien's last screech make up the film's "orgasmic" moment. In sum, the scene sexualizes Ripley, builds suspense about whether she can physically survive, and gives us aurally enforced, absolute closure at her hands. In *Funny Games*, by contrast, we have no choice *but* to focus on the female protagonist's agonized stripping-down without suspenseful hope of her possible triumph, and in the *absence* of sounds that would mediate or detract from watching her. The telltale aural traces of other films that *Funny Games* might have been include a doom-laden score that anticipates our fear and encapsulates Anna's distress, or some noise onscreen that might signify emotional release (such as Paul's laughter or Georg's sobs), or Anna's own voice that might assure us of her refusal to be victimized.

From a feminist perspective, the sonic emphasis on stripping down the female body as a cruel event has radical implications. *Funny Games* ensures that we hear every sonic detail of Anna's physical discomfort and grief, whereas generically violent films usually highlight sudden screams over and above the aural minutiae of drawn-out, small, and painful movements. *Blow Out* (1981), a horror-thriller that is exceptionally self-conscious about the coercive power of sound, climaxes on the screams of a woman mixed with fireworks during a massive Fourth of July celebration. A more recent, revisionist horror, *Cabin in the Woods* (2012), peaks on a scene in which the female victim's screams are drowned out by the sound of party music: while her assault is shown on a massive screen within a party scene, the upbeat energy of "Roll with the Changes" (performed by REO Speedwagon) ironically and cruelly clashes with the violence that the partygoers fail to see. Despite their different stylistic strategies, both these films apparently agree with Alfred Hitchcock's oft-cited, infamous claim that "blondes make the best victims" (Dowd 2012). *Funny Games*, by contrast, explores the cost of believing this.[24]

The Culmination of Aural Disturbance

In *Funny Games*, the only experience of quiet to provide any room for relief comes after Peter murders Georgie. In this particular quiet, the film most explicitly asks us to feel the impact of everything the family suffers, along with giving us time to process it. We need this time after the biggest aural shock. Several minutes before killing Georgie, Peter casually channel-surfs while Georg and Anna sit in stunned silence: Georg is still incapacitated from his golf club wound, and Anna is immobilized after being bound by the killers with masking tape. Having failed to awaken Peter's conscience through her most passionate pleading, she now has no reason to speak. Peter selects a program showing uninterrupted car racing [58:46]. The car racing suggests indomitable will, ceaselessness, circularity, and automation—all sinister properties associated with the killers who have killed before, and who find their next victims by the end of the film. More immediately, the car racing creates a monotonous baseline of sound that makes the gunshot that much more startling.

Georgie has temporarily escaped to the neighbor's house, but Paul soon enters the scene, having recaptured him all too easily. We stay with the family long enough to witness Georgie running to his mother's lap in despair. They cry together in relief *and* desperation, for they are back together but still under the killers' control. Unmoved, Paul leaves Peter to play "Eeny, meeny, miny, moe" with the rifle while he makes a sandwich. Haneke's having directed the actors to play comedy and tragedy against each other is crushingly obvious here. The tonal mix creates an overwhelmingly unpredictable, rule-breaking sense of

---

[24] Lest we mistakenly assume that the scenes of female victimization in *Funny Games* do not resonate with contemporary Hollywood cinema, we need only consider a recent thriller like *No Good Deed* (2014). Within this film, a mother of two must defend herself against a convicted murderer in the absence of her husband. One scene shows her would-be killer forcing her to strip and redress at gunpoint, actions that are played for the nauseatingly titillating possibility that he will rape her until he says, "don't kid yourself," the strangely sardonic punchline of the scene. In the same scene, she repeatedly rebukes her would-be killer for playing a "*game*" with her. Near the end of the film, she manages to kill him herself, becoming another fantasy final girl who, unlike Anna from *Funny Games,* is extraordinarily able to take control of the situation. *No Good Deed* presents itself as a façade of progressiveness because it stars black actors (Idris Elba and Taraji P. Henson), yet it plays out many well-worn clichés of family-in-peril narratives, not least through its conventional sound track, including an overwrought score by Paul Haslinger, copious stinger sound effects, and the noises of a literal storm that signify danger.

danger. The film cuts to show Paul casually entering the kitchen, the camera maintaining a long shot on his controlled movements, even when the gunshot rings out and we then hear Georg's and Anna's sobs and shouts of pain. Most films would, of course, cut on the gunshot to show its impact but here "the sound track compels us to imagine what the camera refuses to show" (Saxton 2008, 105). Price writes that we are therefore asked "to think about the relation between bourgeois domesticity and violence, a late-night sandwich amid the sounds of someone else's agony" (2010, 42). Haneke's intentions are perhaps bigger than this too. The director says:

> The sound track gives spectators more freedom to imagine their own picture; the image itself is rather a handicap in that it limits the scope of imagination. Since nowadays only experimental film uses this fact, it plays no role in conventional cinema. It is therefore, I believe, not all too difficult, to jolt spectators out of their attitude of consumerism. (Haneke 2000, 174)

Haneke's generalizations are admittedly problematic here—surely images of some conventional cinema can still have the capacity to shock or excite our imagination, though perhaps in different ways from experimental cinema. Nevertheless, his emphasis on an anti-consumerist theme is of decisive importance here. Though *Funny Games* repeatedly invokes that which we have "imbibed" before (especially thrillers that revolve around threatened families), it never allows us to enjoy its action. Where *The Seventh Continent* critiques consumer culture on a macrocosmic scale through its emphasis on numerous objects, the anti-consumerism of *Funny Games* is focused on genre films as dangerous products. The scene of Georgie's death makes this most apparent—and the ironic detail that Paul is preparing food for his personal consumption during the scene gives the point an unsettlingly domestic groundedness. The sheer ordinariness of Paul's action serves to both defamiliarize *and* affectively accentuate the violence (see Figure 3.7). It forces us to consider what we "eat up" in genre films that dispense with human lives more freely.

To return to the scene itself, just after the gunshot that kills Georgie, Paul pauses for a second in the preparation of his sandwich. The film then allows time for us to see him resume his activity before cutting back to the living room [1:02:19]. Surprisingly, the cut is not to show Georgie's body. Instead, the film cuts to blood streamed across the car racing on television: the blood represents Georgie's body while the car racing represents the killers' will (see Figure 3.8). The sight of the blood silently "screams out" against the relentless car racing. Now we hear the killers talking offscreen, and then unexpectedly leaving.[25]

---

[25] Here, Paul says (offscreen), "You're an idiot Fatty. You don't shoot the person you've counted out, but the one that's left over! What's wrong with you." His lines convey a disgusting arbitrariness in Georgie's death. We are denied a visual confrontation with Paul's face as he speaks these lines, which only makes what he says more appalling.

FIGURE 3.7 Paul pauses on making his sandwich for just a moment after Georgie is shot in the very next room. The attentive viewer may notice the Mickey Mouse fridge magnet, a detail that sardonically reminds us that *Funny Games* refuses to be entertainment in the escapist sense.

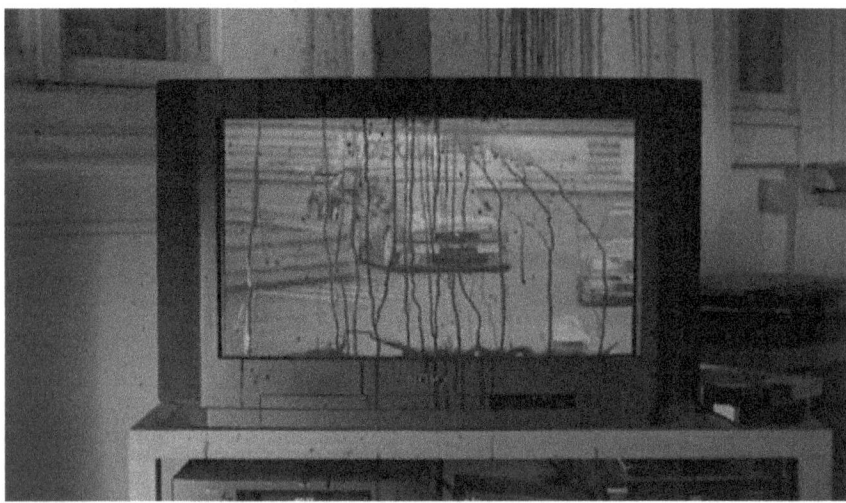

FIGURE 3.8 The blood streaked across the television prompts us to imagine the destruction of Georgie's body, and it "screams out" against the noise of the car racing.

After we hear the door close behind them, the film cuts to show the whole living room scene: Anna kneeling with her legs and arms bound; Georgie lying dead on the floor next to her, with blood splattered on the wall above him; and Georg's legs just immediately visible behind a couch as he lies incapacitated by pain and grief (see Figure 3.9). For over a minute, there is no more noticeable movement, other than the car racing on the television.

FIGURE 3.9 The long take after the killers temporarily leave forces us to dwell on the reality of young Georgie's death, while the continued sound of the car racing suggests the killers' unstoppability.

The car-racing noise is now like the aural erosion of the drill in *The Seventh Continent,* a sound that has become part of the environment. The irritating constancy of the car-racing noise leads us to look deeply into the image, and to search for a visual change. The car-racing sound that results from break-neck movement clashes with the almost-stillness of the image, just as the killers are able to leave the house while the parents are left unable to move: the film thus emphasizes unthinkable ruthlessness versus unbearable loss. The long take aligns us with Georg and Anna, making us to pause on the reality of Georgie's death. Where countless other films move quickly on from a moment of death (whether by a cut, or with a counter-attack within the scene), the sound and the shot hold us in the experience of shock. *Funny Games* demands our emotional involvement by making us sit "with" Anna and Georg for as long as they need before they can speak or move. The rhythm of the film is therein extremely different from other films about killing, such as the satire *Natural Born Killers* (1994), in which Haneke argues that striking montages interrupt our full comprehension of each act of carnage (Sharrett 2004).

After over a minute of our being forced to contemplate the space where a boy lies dead, Anna hops over to the television and uses her tape-bound hands to awkwardly switch it off [1:04:28]. The little click of the television button seems big because the car-racing noise finally stops. Again, a tiny and ordinary sound has profound impact. The ensuing relief of quiet that follows is short-lived—soon Anna must help Georg to move and his sounds of agony take over the sound track. But, for a few moments, *Funny Games* allows us peace in the absence of the killers *and* the sound of race cars that represents their will. After several minutes of car racing, the sudden quiet created by Anna's hand temporarily restores her sonic control. In this quiet, Anna simply says to Georg, "they've gone. [A long pause, with Georg's stifled sobs offscreen.] Do you hear? They've gone!" Yet again, the film self-consciously commands us to listen, and now to Anna again rather than Paul. We are thus given a profoundly moving, Brechtian experience that prompts us to align ourselves with the parents, but which also positions us to be aurally alert to the film's newly shocking representation of victimization. In particular, we perceive how much this scene differentiates itself from others that are focused on victims, especially in the absence of a rousing musical score.

Hearing Haneke versus the Killers

Because *Funny Games* uses its unconventional sound track in such disarmingly Brechtian ways, some critics have understandably accused Haneke of terrorizing his audience. In an article tellingly titled "Cat and Mouse: Haneke's Joy in the Spectator's Distress," for instance, Alexander D. Ornella argues that "the victims are not only the family who is doomed to die but also the audience because Haneke denies them any cathartic moment whatsoever" (2010, 166). Similarly, when Stephen Holden reviewed *Funny Games* for the *New York Times* he called it "a sophisticated act of cinematic sadism" (Sterritt 2010, 257).[26] Such critics conflate the director with Paul and Peter, implying that his intention is to victimize his audience much like the killers victimize the family. We *are* aligned with the disempowered family because we are subjected to so much sonic disturbance. The sound track prompts our alertness to everything we hear as if from the family's perspective: we register the car-racing sound, for instance, as it impacts on the family, not as it is casually chosen by Peter. The film provides us with an even deeper illusion of closeness to the family through the closely miked emphasis on their physical and vocal expressions of grief and pain. This aural intimacy forces us into an emotional position of resistance to the killers, even when they seem most comedically in control. In addition, along with the killers driving the narrative forward, we *might* sense the auteur controlling us in accordance with his preestablished aurally enforced agenda. However, we should avoid making too-easy correlations between the family and the film audience, the killers and Haneke: though hearing *Funny Games* means being subjected to awful sounds and threatening quiet much like the family, Haneke guides us to understand much more than they, *or* the killers, can perceive. Just as *The Seventh Continent* demands that we hear sound effects and music beyond its characters' comprehension, the sound track of *Funny Games* exceeds its diegesis, not least through

---

[26] A. O. Scott's review for the U.S. remake was no less critical: he called it "A Vicious Attack on Innocent People, on the Screen and in the Theater" (as noted by Brunette [2010, 71]).

the many implicit allusions to films that are more aurally conventional. Further, while there is no evidence of either killer's genuine introspection, Haneke's film is structured to prompt *our* introspection while perceiving his directorical radicalism. The killers give no rationale for their actions beyond saying, "why not?," whereas Haneke is vocal about his directorial intentions. He made *Funny Games* out of a belief that violent cinema is "only a good sell when it is deprived of that which is the true measure of its existence in reality: deeply disconcerting fears of pain and suffering" (Grundmann 2010b, 576). So the film gives us an intensely destabilizing experience in accordance with Haneke's anti-mainstream objectives, one that is parallel to the family's disturbance, but *also distinct from it* as a metacinematic experience. By alluding to many family-in-peril thrillers, while using sound in many unconventional and genre-defying ways, *Funny Games* always points to a perspective beyond the film. We are therefore not encouraged to simply align ourselves with the victims, but to consider other representations of victimhood that we more typically witness, and to stop playing the game of going along with them.

So *Funny Games* is not about terrorizing us so much as demanding that we hear its characters' suffering and consider our participation in that. By extension, the film is damning of those who fail to hear others' pain in the world at large. More than once during tense moments of the narrative, there is a sudden cut to show the outside of the house, where there is nothing but the sounds of nighttime stillness along with crickets [1:13:08, 1:20:59]. These are sudden experiences of the world beyond the house that is oblivious to the agony happening inside it. The film therein visually recalls a scene from *Halloween* (1978) that shows a quiet suburban street of closed doors, suggestive of an entire neighborhood that is unknowingly closed off to human suffering. The female protagonist (Laurie) repeatedly calls out and bangs on doors for help while running from the killer, but none of her neighbors respond. *Funny Games* more urgently asks us to perceive the danger of being oblivious to violence because its victims *all* die, whereas *Halloween* has at least the triumphant final girl. The film most obviously emphasizes the danger of failing to hear when Georg almost manages to make his cell phone work in the killers' absence: he calls a friend (ironically named Peter, like one of the killers), who cannot hear him and who thus unknowingly leaves him victimized. The implication is that not hearing can be a form of violence in itself.

Summary

Hearing *Funny Games* means perceiving how and why it deprives us of familiar "entertainment value."[27] Like *The Seventh Continent*, the sound track of *Funny*

---

[27] Consider that when Anna herself asks why the killers do not kill her family right away, Peter simply says, "Don't forget the entertainment value. We'd all be deprived of our pleasure" (50:51–50:52).

Games features numerous concentrated moments that are akin to the Gestus in making strong cognitive *and* affective demands of us. The film's perturbing use of sound is a crucial component of its deconstruction of thrillers and its critique of mainstream violent cinema more generally. Haneke's principle—*and* principled—objective is to restore shock value to the image, and he does this through incorporating numerous sonic shocks. The violent musical collision of its opening sets the tone, reminding us of the ideological, thematic, narrative, and emotive power of music to transform cinematic experience *even when* the visuals are themselves designed according to rules of generic convention, continuity, and/or familiarity. The experience of *Funny Games*, like *The Seventh Continent*, is painful. Haneke himself says, "I violate spectators into autonomy" (Grundmann 2007, 12). But there is more than hurt in perceiving his films—there is the exhilaration of being awakened to the power of new, sonically driven cinematic possibilities.

4

Code Unknown

SONICALLY REPRESENTING SOCIAL DIVISIONS, DIVERSITY, AND HOPE

Why does our hearing multiracial, multinational, and multilingual voices matter? How can cinema help us hear the racial politics that often go unspoken? What kind of music signifies progressive hope without sounding trite or too easy? When does hearing necessitate moral action? How can not speaking be a form of immorality? What strengthens humanity despite the hostile noises and oppressive silences of the world? These are the questions that guide this postcolonial analysis of *Code Unknown*. The film provides us with multiple storylines, all of which represent divided peoples and strained communication. The sound track is crucial for thematically and ironically connecting all the film's characters, no matter what different realities they embody. *Code Unknown* is even more surprising for its emphasis on joyfully collective music that holds the possibility of limitless unity. It is Haneke's most socially optimistic film.

A Polyphonic Experience

In keeping with Haneke's musical approach to creating cinema, we can understand *Code Unknown* as a polyphonic work: it features several interweaving "melodies" (or stories). It is also one of Haneke's rhythmically challenging films: most scenes are punctuated by blackouts that interrupt them, often when conversations are in progress, and at sporadic intervals. This is a visual reminder of *The Seventh Continent*, but the rhythmic complexity is more extreme due to the more elaborate narrative structure.[1] The quiet voices of both *The Seventh Continent* and *Funny Games* lead us toward seemingly inevitable conclusions in

---

[1] *Code Unknown* thus parallels *71 Fragments of a Chronology of Chance* (1994), a film shaped by multiple storylines. The opening sequence from *71 Fragments* includes several television news stories (about conflict in Somalia, and Haiti, and in resistance to U.S. troops), followed by a montage of

straight lines, whereas the overlapping and louder voices of *Code Unknown* suggest many directional possibilities that are indeterminate. Likewise, the sonic texture of the film is more representative of different perspectives and places. Where *The Seventh Continent* and *Funny Games* focus on white, German-speaking, middle-class families in Austria, *Code Unknown* includes scenes from France, Africa, Kosovo, and Romania, as well as dialogue in several languages: French, Malinka, Romanian, German, English, Arabic, and French Sign Language.[2]

From the beginning, *Code Unknown* prompts us to consider the interconnectedness of diverse human lives. Wendy Everett defines it as a "fractal film" because it is "structured by various interwoven narratives." As she explains, "these narratives are connected through a seemingly random starting point, after which the characters develop apparently randomly, in unpredictable and dynamic ways that demand a creative reading on the part of the spectator" (163). In the first posttitle scene of *Code Unknown* we meet a white adolescent named Jean who commits a casually violent, but culturally significant, act; it is the "seemingly random starting point" for all that follows. Jean has left his father's farm to visit Paris where his brother Georges lives with his white girlfriend, Anne. After buying Jean a pastry, Anne gives Jean the keys and the number "code" for entering her apartment before she goes to work.[3] As he walks up the street, Jean throws his pastry bag at Maria, a Romanian illegal immigrant begging in Paris. A Franco-African character named Amadou witnesses the indignity of Jean's action. He vocally, and then physically, confronts Jean who nonchalantly refuses to acknowledge any wrongdoing. After police then intervene, Amadou is taken away for questioning and Maria is deported. Her forced return to Romania seems cruel because she is a victim of circumstance. The callousness of Jean's action, and the lack of comeuppance for him, sets the tone for a film that foregrounds injustice.

"Talking Back" to a Culture of Silence: A Postcolonial Perspective

From the first scene of conflict, *Code Unknown* resonates with fundamental themes of postcolonial scholarship:[4] the stakes of representing diverse peoples;

---

characters in disparate situations, sonically stressing the social fractures of a broken world. Like *Code Unknown*, the film is focused on the silences and cries of characters that are most vulnerable, including an illegal immigrant boy, a sick baby, and a disturbed girl being introduced to her new foster parents.

[2] The film was financed by production companies from three countries, further underlining its multicultural significance: Arté France Cinema, France 2 Cinema, Canal+, Bavaria Film (Germany), a Romanian production Company (Filmex Romania), and the Romanian government (Brunette 2010, 71).

[3] In an interview with Michael Cieutat, Haneke explains the genesis of the film was his observing that in Paris he "couldn't go anywhere without knowing the code number of a building." He compares this to not being equipped to handle the feelings of a novel without an introductory preface that explains its "code" (Brunette 2010, 71). So, the director anticipates our being locked out from the film's meaning, at least until we can make enough sense of it emotionally.

[4] Ironically, as Rada Iveković points out, there is "no academic field called 'postcolonial studies' in France: instead, postcolonial topics are 'distributed' across disciplines and the concept of postcolonialism is only 'being constituted at present and probably since the suburban riots in 2005 in France'"

the consequences of people negatively perceiving racial and ethnic Otherness; the importance of understanding *and* representing social fragmentation, contrary to an illusion of coherence and homogeneity according to the dominant (white) order; the political imperative to acknowledge the marginalized position of racial minorities, especially by emphasizing their having been silenced or their being unable to speak the "right" language; and the acknowledgement that there is no such thing as a "unified (single) nation-state" any more than there is a "unified (single) citizen-subject" (Hayward 2006, 296). Above all, as Susan Hayward reminds us, postcolonial theory stresses that "there are other multiple voices to be thought about, listened to" (298).

Our hearing diverse voices in *Code Unknown* resonates with much postcolonial scholarship. The phrase "having a voice" is frequently used with reference to the long-standing ways in which marginalized peoples' voices have been oppressed or lost, and the related importance of our hearing what they have to say with greater historically contextualized awareness. The editors of the authoritative anthology *The Post-Colonial Studies Reader* (Bill Ashcroft, Gareth Griffiths, and Helen Tiffin) point out that "the silencing of the postcolonial voice to which much recent theory alludes is a metaphoric rather than a literal one" (2006, 3). That said, references to voices, speech, silencing, the heard *and* the unheard abound throughout this anthology of influential postcolonial texts: Homi Bhabha writes about the "noisy" command of colonists in relation to the "silent repression of native traditions" (43); Stephen Slemon refers to the "cultural institutions that continue to police what voices will be heard" (102); James Clifford stresses the contingent selectivity of any "articulation" (181); Gayarti Chakravorty Spivak explains that intellectuals must avoid presuming to know the suppressed "subaltern voice" (32);[5] Trinh T. Minh-Ha imagines the postcolonial woman's voice that "dissolves on the walls of silence" (246); Ketu H. Katrak discusses the importance of voices that defy the rules of so-called 'proper speech' (241); and R. S. Sugirtharajah cites Gloria Anzaldúa who summarizes postcoloniality by asking, "Who has the voice? Who says these are the rules?" (538).[6] Even a cursory glance at this anthology's sonic references invites us to make a leap that film scholars seldom do: while many note the figurative importance of voices being heard, comparatively few consider

---

(2011, 47–48). In France, the field of study known as postcolonial studies in English is therefore often perceived as "foreign," "inadequate," and only "reluctantly accepted" (48). She uses this important example to illustrate the reality that no language can "say it all" (56), a point of some relevance to *Code Unknown*'s representation of numerous miscommunications in several languages.

[5] As Hayward reminds us, Gramsci "coined the term ['subaltern'] to mean the silenced history of those subjected to the ruling classes" (2006, 280).

[6] To take more recent examples, we might consider Malala Yousafzai's internationally recognized "Raise Your Voice" campaign for girls' education and Leonardo DiCaprio's speech in defense of Indigenous peoples after winning a Golden Globe for his role in *The Revenant* (2015): with reference to how big-time business has oppressed native peoples he said, "it is time that we heard your *voice*."

the literal components of sound tracks that enable subaltern, diverse, and/or Othered peoples to gain aural prominence.[7]

The very fact that five languages are spoken by main characters within *Code Unknown* is noteworthy beyond providing superficial sonic color. The sound track "talks back" to histories of suppression, along with ensuring we hear various ways of conceptualizing the world and the numerous "codes" that human beings use to unlock its meanings. The voices of *Code Unknown* sound out strongly against *Caché* (2005), Haneke's later film about the post-colonial realities of contemporary France. In *Caché*, the voices of the minority Algerian characters have little screen time in comparison with the white main characters played by major stars Daniel Auteuil and Juliette Binoche (the latter being featured in both films as characters named "Anne"). When Auteuil's character (Georges) wrongly accuses an Algerian of kidnapping his son, police almost immediately take the man (Majid) and his unnamed son into custody. *Caché* shows them within a police truck making no sound as it rattles toward the station, with their faces in near-darkness. The film cuts before we see them being taken in for police questioning, but Georges later tells his wife that "the kid started yelling" and "that got his Dad going," after which he explains that the two men were held in jail for the night. If we perceive the innocence of these accused men along with the social context of their brief imprisonment, particularly in relation to Georges' white prejudice and privilege, we can appreciate the significance of their protesting voices *even as we do not hear them*. The two actors playing Majid and his son, Maurice Bénichou and Walid Afkir, are featured in one of the last scenes of *Code Unknown*, inter-amplifying the cultural resonance of and thematic connections between the two films.[8] But where the later film focuses on the awful silences around what is suppressed by zeroing in on the losses of just these two men, *Code Unknown* foregrounds *multiple* minority voices that should be heard on film more often. Several scenes revolve around extended speeches by characters representing racial minorities—Amadou, Amadou's mother, and Maria in particular. Their speeches are thematically linked by confronting power struggles: Amadou tells his white girlfriend about his Malian father's travels by ship, including his outwitting a captain who withheld the passport he needed to secure a job; Amadou's mother speaks of her difficulty with assimilating herself within French culture in relation to her son's unfair treatment by police; and Maria confesses her revulsion at a begging Gypsy only to later find herself begging on the Boulevard St. Germain, and disgusting a businessman who threw twenty

---

[7] Speaking more broadly of representing different peoples, Robert Stam argues that all art is not so much mimetic as political: it is "a delegation of voice" (2000, 667). This figurative way of speaking is so common that we can easily forget about the literal importance of listening.

[8] The scene shows a climactic confrontation involving Binoche's white character (Anne) and the two Algerian men in the confined space of a subway train. We return to it toward the end of this chapter.

francs at her because she was too dirty to touch. The film thus sonically allows us to perceive something much bigger than a monolithic reality according to one familiarly white point of view. As Haneke himself says, "A total reality can never be seized in the cinema or in real life. We know so little!" (Brunette 2010, 77). Referring back to Wendy Everett's discussion of fractal films, "the multiple 'realities' implied by [the characters'] parallel or intersecting stories," as well as the shifting identities of the characters themselves, mean that *Code Unknown* offers "neither stasis nor closure, but merely ongoing change and process" (2005, 163). This open-endedness deepens the film's representation of postcolonial truths: rather than closing down meaning according to one perspective or character's trajectory, the interweaving narratives of *Code Unknown* reverberate without a foreseeable end.

Lest this might read as if *Code Unknown* is naively optimistic about the possibilities of all peoples being heard, and about their lives extending open-endedly beyond themselves, consider that the film begins with a pre-title scene about the *difficulty* of communication. The first sounds of the film are very quiet: a child makes physical movements without speaking or props. There is a blank white screen behind her pale face: the visual equivalent of silence. The empty space offsets her physical presence, and the outline of her dark hair in particular. As she creeps back toward the wall, her own shadow moves closer and closer toward her. She takes small cowering steps into this darkness as she attempts to communicate what others cannot understand (see Figure 4.1). She sinks to her knees and then suddenly stands to indicate the end of her "performance." The film cuts to another white child's face, then another, and then another who signs the word "Alone?" while making a small clicking sound. The girl silently shakes her head. A black girl signs "hiding place?"[9] A white boy guesses "gangster," which makes the first girl smilingly shake her head: the word "gangster" evokes a generically familiar world that is far from the immediate ambiguity of her performance. A white girl then guesses "guilty conscience" before two more shots show other children sitting silently. This pause from guesses is like a musical rest before the "note" that follows, the sound of another white girl who signs "sad" with a gut-wrenching gesture of tearing at her face [2:01–2:02]. The sound she makes is a low, quiet scream that is arresting in the context of the exceptional quiet that precedes it (see Figure 4.2). Then an Arab boy guesses "locked up." His is the last guess before the title appears onscreen: "*Code Unknown*" [2:18]. This last juxtaposition clearly suggests that we are imprisoned by the codes we do not know, or the failures of communication that we cannot resolve. But the film has already established other important emphases from a postcolonial perspective. In particular, two children of color provide guesses that resonate with real histories of oppression

---

[9] We later learn that this girl is Amadou's little sister, so she becomes more explicitly connected with a storyline about injustice and the struggle to belong in France within a family of (Malian) immigrants.

FIGURE 4.1 A young girl cowers against a blank wall and her own shadow, a "performance" that other children struggle to understand, establishing *Code Unknown*'s theme of strained communication.

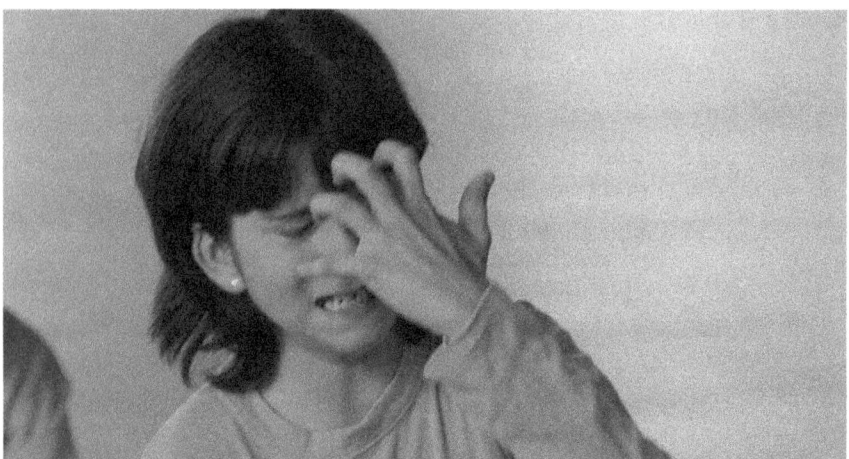

FIGURE 4.2 The girl who signs "sad" seems to tear at her own face, a gesture of immediate poignancy.

that are often suppressed: "hiding place" and "locked up." In relation to the perturbing gestures of the girl whose cowering, retreating gestures are difficult for her audience to understand, these words stand out because they evoke visualizable situations that are racially politicized. We will explore the concept of suppressed colonial realities much further in our analysis of *Caché*. With *Code Unknown*, we focus more on various forms of communication in relation to social diversity and division within contemporary France. Because the opening scene features multiracial children attempting to understand some nonverbal communication, the film immediately suggests positive possibilities of patient interpretation. It positions us to guess at meanings with humility, like the children sitting on the floor. [10]

Paris, France: Past and Present

Code Unknown focuses on diversely disempowered peoples, and on everything they say or physically communicate during scenes of long duration. By privileging their suppressed voices, including the quietly meaningful sounds of deaf-mute children, the film resists the actual silencing of minorities in France. It was released after a period of increasingly restrictive French legislation with regard to the rights of all foreigners (Jelloun 1999, 27). More specifically, it can be interpreted as responding to the rising popularity of the National Front: just three years before *Code Unknown* was released, the National Front had its greatest success at legislative elections, receiving more than 15 percent of the vote in metropolitan France and securing its place as the nation's third leading political party.[11] As the Moroccan writer Tahar Ben Jelloun writes in his ironically named book *French Hospitality: Racism and North African Immigrants*, the "Front has made use of the immigrants, insulted them, scorned and humiliated them without restraint, shame, or scruple. And what right of reply do they have against that flood of hatred? [. . .] The language of the Front is indistinguishable from that of any other fundamentalist group. It contains no thought, only reactions; no vision, only slogans and clichés" (1999, 26). The importance of resisting the all-too-familiar language of xenophobia is Jelloun's emphasis here, within his text as well as in his act of writing against the ideology of racism. Similarly, *Code Unknown* implicitly talks back to the innumerable films before it that feature the "structured absences" of minority peoples.[12]

The sonic power of *Code Unknown* also matters in contrast with the prevalent and widely acknowledged culture of silence around issues of race in

---

[10] The opening scene of *Code Unknown* is ripe for poststructuralist analysis because the meaning of the utterance is not controlled by the enunciator of body language. But this is more than a formal exercise in showing the indeterminacy of the signifier. The scene shows how easy it is for a message to be misunderstood or for an audience to get it wrong. This has deep implications from a postcolonial perspective of understanding the cultural relativity of truth. It also resonates with Mikhail Bakhtin's work on dialogic discourse, which Dominique Maingueneau defines as follows: "speech is assigned to specific places but its elements are constantly disseminated" (2011, 114).

[11] Though this election was followed by a split within the National Front that weakened its power significantly, it has largely regained power. Both Adam Chandler and Nicholas Vinocur provide analyses of the party's more recent rise in popularity: in 2015 the National Front received well over 6 million votes (Chandler 2015) and "currently counts in its ranks 11 town mayors, two senators, two National Assembly deputies, 72 departmental councilors and [. . .] 358 regional councilors—triple the number it had before" (Vinocur 2015).

[12] For a full discussion of Robert Stam and Louise Spence's definition of "structured absences" (the marked but often "invisible" lack of racial minorities onscreen), see their original article of 1983,

France: the best current estimate of legal immigrants is around eight million but it is impossible to be certain because "it is forbidden by law to collect statistics referring to racial or ethnic origin" (*The Economist* 2009).[13] This is a policy reflective of France's so-called egalitarian ethos, an assimilationist ideology that makes charting racial inequalities extremely difficult. As an anonymous writer for *The Economist* asks, "How can a country decide if ethnic minorities are thriving when it refuses to acknowledge they even exist?" Crystal Fleming, the author of a major forthcoming book on racism and the legacies of slavery in France, critiques the institutionalized "colorblindness" that is enforced at the highest levels: "Instead of formulating anti-racist policies and collecting anti-discrimination statistics, [France] contents itself with anti-racist discourse and magical thinking" (2015).[14] In 2011, the United Nations issued a report condemning the country for its "racist climate" and lack of "real political will" to address racial discrimination (Fleming 2015). However, France continues to develop policies of "colorblindness" that obfuscate the truth of its racial politics. "In 2013, French politicians took steps to remove the word 'race' from its laws, apparently guided by the magical belief that changing words is enough to fight racism" (*France 24*, 2013).[15] This suppression extends to how history is taught as well: according to Fleming, "the history of colonialism itself is mostly a *non-lieu de memoire*: barely taught in schools, mostly forgotten and marginalized in the nation's collective memory." Though *Code Unknown* does

---

and Walker's summary (2015, 93–94). Aude Konan (2015) writes about the lack of French films that focus on minority characters: "every ten years or so, a French film is released, with the goal of portraying the real lives of Black French people. The characters always go through awful struggles and live in what filmmakers believe is Black people's natural environment: 'les cites.'" These films are full of good intentions but completely lack any kind of relatability, because they are made by people who are not Black, and not even working class." The films Konan cites include *La Squale* (2000), *Fatou la Malienne* (2001), and *Bande de Filles* (*Girlhood*, 2014), and she provides her analysis in the context of some staggering statistics ("half of the French population [admit] that they have a racial prejudice," for example). By contrast, Ginette Vincendeau (2015) argues that the tide has shifted since the new millennium, or around the time of *Code Unknown*'s release, and provides a range of references to French films that represent multiculturalism from various perspectives. In parallel to this, Temenuga Trifonova (2007) positively situates *Code Unknown* within a European tradition of representing complex European identities in the last two decades of the twentieth century. He contrasts "European cinema's double-voiced, multi-leveled or polyphonic discourse" with "Hollywood's dramatic or monologic discourse," which is "by its very nature alien to genuine polyphony."

[13] As stated on the *French-American Foundation* (2014) site: "France has maintained its official color-blind approach to race relations in spite of high numbers of ethnic minorities on its territory. It is still forbidden by law to collect statistics referring to racial or ethnic origin, and it is therefore difficult to determine how certain communities are faring compared to others."

[14] Fleming describes her forthcoming book, *Resurrecting Slavery*, on her personal website: "At the heart of the book is a puzzle: How does a nation that officially frames itself as blind to race make sense of its racist and racial past?" (http://www.stonybrook.edu/commcms/cas/faculty/facultyprofiles/fleming.html).

[15] The author of this bill, MP Francois Asensi, recently argued that "in eliminating the legal category of race, the Assembly has helped our country move forward on ideological and educational levels" (*France 24* 2013).

not engage with specific governmental policies, statistical realities, or assimi-lationist policies, its emphasis on aural heterogeneity (as opposed to one lan-guage), along with visible color (as opposed to color-blindness), matters in a real, broadscale context of racial insensitivity and enduring prejudice against minority peoples within mainstream French society.

When it comes to immigrants, France has a long history of forcing assim-ilation. "They are bleached, stripped of their identity and culture, in order to become the 'true French'" (Konan 2015). That *Code Unknown*'s action mainly happens in Paris, the multicultural capital, is important in this context.[16] As Dominique Maingueneau writes, "when the term 'multiculturality' is used, one thinks immediately of differences within populations and, alongside these, the misunderstandings and power relationships between groups that live together within one space" (2011, 105). The film does not romantically suggest that all people can understand each other—quite the opposite—but in privileging dif-ferent peoples *and* their languages, the film subversively represents the French nation. Further, *Code Unknown* gestures toward future *possibilities* through the many unfinished storylines, the numerous sounds and conversations that are interrupted, and the full title of the film itself (*Code Unknown: Incomplete Tales of Several Journeys*).

Though *Code Unknown* speaks to the present and the possible future, it is still haunted by the past. Postcolonial theory demands that we consider the presence of the past within the present, and against the colonist ideology of "progress." The film prompts us to consider how different time frames overlap with and influence each other in relation to themes of enduring prejudice, intol-erance, and cross-cultural miscommunication. Many conversations are loaded with subtexts about past oppressions, tensions, and conflicts among peoples of different racial backgrounds: Georges, for example, gives a monologue about being taken prisoner by a Taliban fighter in Afghanistan while he was doing photojournalistic work [1:28:14–1:29:12]. The fighter repeatedly asked Georges, "What can I do for you?," a question that sparked hope in Georges until he real-ized it was the only English phrase that the fighter could say and that he did not evidently know its meaning. Georges relays this experience through a voiceover letter to Anne while we see a montage of photographs that he has surrepti-tiously taken of strangers on the Paris Métro. The montage includes the face

---

[16] Although all constructions of national identity are in constant flux, Brigitte Jandey explains that French identity is largely defined in terms of "whether or not one adopts the traditional values of the Parisian upper class" (2011, 57). In addition to birthrights (including ancestral lineage), and "feel-ing French," Jandey stresses the importance of being *perceived* as French—this last aspect of identity is, of course, inevitably subjective and reliant upon other people's points of view. Jandey mentions that second-generation North African migrants are frequently perceived as "foreign," for example. She then considers the importance of not having an accent (for example, North African) or speaking French "properly" (with the "standard Parisian accent") that determines the ability to identity as French with-out contestation (64, 65).

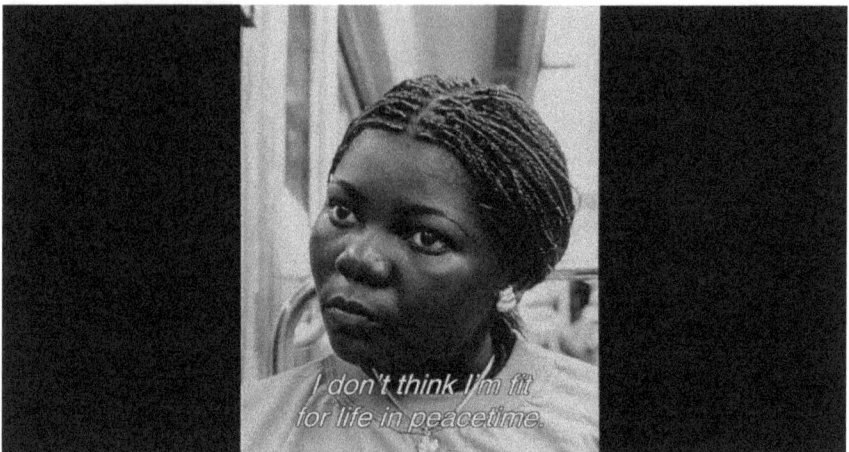

FIGURE 4.3 As Georges speaks, we see faces of color that are dissociated from him. Examples such as this throw Georges' disaffection into relief, reminding us of the luxury he enjoys as a white person of privilege.

FIGURE 4.4 Our seeing the faces of minority peoples (including this unnamed Indian woman), while Georges voices his separation from a life of peace subtly underlines his complacency—being able to call himself "unfit for peace" is a *choice* for Georges, whereas conflict is an inescapable fact for the racially marginalized characters of *Code Unknown*.

of a black woman as Georges follows his recollection by saying, "I don't think I'm fit for life in peacetime" (see Figure 4.3). The film then shows the face of an Indian woman before he says, "At least, what you call 'peacetime'" (see Figure 4.4). Here, Georges is speaking of the recent past: his visit to Afghanistan near the end of Taliban rule. However, the black and Indian faces we see along with his lines about not being fit for peace imply the legacies of much longer, wider histories of racial oppression. Here, Michel Chion's deceptively simple concept of "synchresis"—"the forging of an immediate and necessary relationship between something one sees and something one hears"—is complex (1994, 5).[17] The strangeness of our hearing Georges' monologue along with seeing faces that are disconnected from his story requires that we find coherence where the film resists it, suggesting possibilities of interrelation that are tenuous at best. As Georges' story reminds us, words only have meaning as they are comprehended (the Taliban fighter did not understand "what can I do for you?," so the question became useless). By extension, the film only holds meaning if we can make sense of its complex "language." *Code Unknown* demands more of us than simply looking at the images Georges has taken of strangers without their permission, and with which he fails to verbally engage; it demands that we look beyond the surfaces of such multiethnic faces, along with reminding us that understanding each other is a fundamental part of human (and humane) survival.

Adam Tate argues that Georges' photography recalls that of Dorothea Lange because the images of faces display "remarkable insight into each subject" (2011, 58).[18] He claims Georges' photographs are an effort to "'rehumanize' those in his environment," and that Georges "attempts to reframe his gaze from his own environment and gain a humanistic and sympathetic understanding of his fellow citizens" (58–59). Such claims sidestep the fact that Georges photographs his subjects without their permission, and that he seems oddly dissociated from them through the voiceover.[19] Furthermore, he tells his story in the voice that belongs only to *him,* coming from a different time and place than his subjects.

In the aforementioned voiceover about the Taliban fighter, Georges alludes derisively to the "value of the non-transmitted message" but then pronounces that "what matters is the end result." Yet Georges himself provides no "end results," only images that lack verbal context or explanation but which invite *our* making an "end result" of interpretation.[20] The entirety of *Code Unknown*

---

[17] Chion's term is often simply used in relation to the welding of image and sound (the "added value" they give each other), but he stresses those "points of synchronization" or "synch points" where the effect of synchresis is unusually significant, "rather like an accented chord in music" (1994, 5, 58). Here, the "added value" is largely in the tension between the photographs representing minority peoples and Georges' self-important voiceover.

[18] Though the photographs are presented in *Code Unknown* as Georges' own, they were actually taken by Luc Delahaye for his *L'autre* series of ninety portraits. He used a hidden camera on the Paris Métro from 1995–1997, and published them together as a book in 1999.

[19] In a different, more damning scene, Georges speaks of witnessing genocidal horrors without being distraught: while eating a fine restaurant dinner, he describes documenting the war in Kosovo.

[20] Georges' photography is sonically connected with negligence, *and* more troublingly with deliberate violence. The very next scene shows him with a camera under his shirt, turning toward a mirror to ensure it is well concealed, and preparing to press the picture-taking clicker he has attached with a hidden cord. At the moment Georges is about to take a picture, the film cuts to black with the sound

arguably works this way, resisting any grand narrative or ultimate statement that can be decoded, although it is more engaged with its subjects than Georges is with his. This is the film's most important strategy from a postcolonial point of view: it opens a dialogue that is both incomplete and unending, opening up the past *and* interrogating the present, and always requiring our aural alertness as we read beyond appearances. This connects with how the film repeatedly disallows presumption. We cannot assume complete knowledge of any character in *Code Unknown*, especially those we see in different contexts that entail new identities: Anne is an actress who literally plays several roles; Maria is a family woman at home in Romania and a beggar in France; Amadou is an oppressed Malian (in Anne's words, "the black kid who hassled Jean"), and a percussion *leader*; and the children of the opening and closing scenes are deaf-mutes but they are also, ironically, the most communicative people we meet.

Along with resonating with present-day racial politics, and shifting contexts for understanding diverse people, *Code Unknown* alludes to historical racism. For example, there is a striking motif of yellow that may allude to the stars worn by Jews during the Nazi regime, implying that contemporary Paris remains haunted by the Vichy regime and/or still infected by the poison of anti-Semitism.[21] Yellow is not only an important visual motif but is also vocally mentioned several memorable times: in the first scene proper, after Maria has fled from the police who stop the altercation between Jean and Amadou, a bystander identifies her as "the one with the yellow bag"; Anne auditions for the role of Maria in *Twelfth Night* who tricks Malvolio into a ridiculous display of his legs in *yellow* cross-gartered stockings for Olivia; when Maria returns to Romania she speaks of needing a "carte jaune" (or, "yellow card"), a record of vaccinations that is a medical kind of passport; a friend of Amadou's mother criticizes his sister for having a "yellow crew cut" in the context of saying that Amadou spends too much time with "white girls"; and after Amadou is forcibly constrained by police, his mother tells an elder about a nightmare in which she saw "yellow lights twinkling in the distance," along with unidentifiable "shapes coming toward the house." This color is more spoken about than visually shown, thus vocally connecting characters who represent diverse nations, cultures, and ethnicities. Perhaps the color connection suggests that all the characters are potentially vulnerable: even Anne, the beautiful white actress (played by the one major female star, Binoche), is shown belittled by a long shot when she speaks of yellow.

---

of a gunshot: the next scene opens up on Jean's father having killed a cow, which we hear slump to the ground as the new scene begins, an action connected to his rage after Jean runs away from home. So, the gunshot we hear, a noise in place of Georges' act of taking the picture, is the sound advance of a callously violent act that comes out of great distress [1:10:48–1:10:49].

[21] Although Jews form less than 1 percent of the population, compared with 10 percent for Muslims, they are the target of fully 40 percent of the country's ongoing racial violence (Harriss 2014).

Listening, and Not Listening

Anne delivers a deliriously strong audition of Maria's speech about successfully duping Malvolio. She laughs with infectious hysteria. But the six people in the large auditorium, presumably there for casting, do not audibly respond to her. Instead, they silently observe her and sometimes whisper to each other while Anne appears alone and far away on the illuminated stage. Her relatively closely miked voice brings us spatially closer to her, but the perspectival diminution of her body visually underlines that she is disempowered as well as ignored. Here and elsewhere, listening is an important action in *Code Unknown*. Along with ensuring that we hear its sound track in complex, sometimes contrary, relation to its visuals, the film repeatedly shows characters in the act of listening *or* choosing not to hear. The people who *should* be listening to Anne's audition have their backs to us, positioning us as if we are an extension of them as her audience, and visually underlining their lack of vocal response to her high-pitched, virtuoso performance. When Anne becomes aware of their inattention, she stops performing and steps forward to the front of the stage as their whispering continues. They are oblivious to her having broken role. Her long pause, and the inaudibility of her audience's words, prompt *us* to listen more attentively. She holds her arm up against the light on the stage and simply asks, quietly and somewhat plaintively, "Anyone out there?" Her sudden change in tone, from delirium in performance, to distress in "reality," is startling. Yet there is no diegetic response to her before the sudden blackout that ends the scene. The very next scene opens on Amadou speaking the end of a sentence: "to start a new life" [1:14:14–1:14:20]. The context for Amadou's words emerges through the ensuing scene—his father has left his family in Paris to return to Africa, and his sisters are asking him questions about their father's decision. We can assume that his father saw no future for himself in France, especially after we witness a passenger in his taxi treating him with intolerant aggression.[22] Given Amadou's trouble with police, and his younger brother's struggle after a bully accuses him of distributing drugs at school, their father's leaving represents a choice to opt out of a society that is institutionally hostile toward immigrants. We can understand this choice, although the personal cost (abandoning a family) is huge. That said, the film's editing optimistically asks us to consider the possibility of progressive change on a massive scale. If we put the words that end the previous scene together with the very next words that begin this scene, we get the following question: "Anyone out there to start a new life?" (see Figures 4.5 and 4.6). The deliberation with which Haneke cuts off and

---

[22] In an earlier scene, Amadou's father interrupts his passenger's ride after receiving a phone call about a family emergency (probably about Amadou's being taken into custody by police). The scene withholds the passenger's face to throw emphasis on his unmediated aggression toward Amadou's father, even though he has aurally witnessed the urgent call, and even though Amadou's father gently explains he can drop the passenger off at a nearby taxi stand, without any charge.

FIGURES 4.5 AND 4.6 "Anyone out there?" asks Anne, holding her arm up to her face to shield her eyes against the stage lights as she appeals to anyone in the audience (including us, by visual implication). After a two-second blackout, the film cuts to a new scene with Amadou speaking to his sisters about their father's choice to leave France "to start a new life."

begins scenes mid-conversation throughout *Code Unknown* prompts us to connect the pieces of dialogue here. Perhaps the film is asking whether we are willing to participate in making a different kind of world, "a new life" for all, but this is clear only if we listen well enough to make a very particular connection. So, our listening leads to a big invitation, but only if we are ready to hear it.

Just as listening leads to massive possibilities, not listening or choosing not to act on something heard is harmful in *Code Unknown*. The clearest example of this is the tragedy of the young girl whom Anne hears being abused but whom she does nothing to protect. This girl is not only the most intriguing sonic presence of the film: from a postcolonial perspective, she has a crucial role. She stands for the pain of many disempowered peoples, and for all those whom the

FIGURE 4.7 Anne pauses her ironing, and mutes the television because she hears the little girl crying next door: she makes no sound but her alarm is manifest.

more privileged characters *hear* but fail to help. Her story begins with Anne ironing in her apartment with the television turned up loudly [27:36–31:06]. The show she watches is not clear, but it is punctuated by suspense-evoking music that suggests ominous possibilities in a clichéd way. Anne soon hears her neighbors over the television: the girl screaming and her parents scolding and shouting at her. She mutes the show to hear more clearly, and then pauses her ironing until the commotion quietens (see Figure 4.7).

Anne looks perturbed, as though her heart is beating quickly. She seems to register the real significance of what she hears as the child's crying and the parents' shouting crescendos. These voices temporarily command her attention more than the aural artificiality of the television. After a long pause as precisely scored as music, she resumes ironing with the television still muted, and the child's crying dies down. We hear the amplified sound of the water and steam as Anne moves the iron around each item before quietly folding it and putting it aside. She stops for a drink of wine, a deliberate effort to inoculate herself from what she has just heard. Then she puts the television volume back up before ironing again. The sound of the water in the iron may be an oblique reference to life in the womb as we hear it along with the little girl crying. This makes Anne's choice to carry on despite what she hears all the more disturbing.[23]

---

[23] This scene is a strong sonic and thematic parallel to a heartbreaking scene from *Time of the Wolf* (2003), Haneke's dystopian drama focusing on characters struggling to survive in an intensely hostile world of limited resources. *Time of the Wolf* makes us witness a young child's *preventable* death due to unmedicated sickness: several relatively privileged characters ignore her mother's pleas for help after her condition becomes increasingly critical. The film shows the child being laid in state as an indistinguishable mound on the earth while her family mourns: the absence of faces within the frame forces us to dwell on the gut-wrenching pain in her mother's and sister's anguished cries offscreen [1:05:29–1:08:24].

In a later scene, Anne receives a note about the little girl being domestically abused that seems to be written by her elderly neighbor, Mrs. Becker. The note is signed by "a defenseless child," which, as Anne points out to Georges, seems more like the phrasing of an adult than a ten-year-old girl. Mrs. Becker emphatically denies all knowledge of the note when Anne asks her about it, with the ironic result of arousing further suspicion about herself, but Anne takes no further action. *Code Unknown* makes us therefore understand that at least two people hear a child being violently attacked without saving her. Georges also plays a part in this negligence when Anne tells him about the note [59:52–1:04:40]. They are shopping together at the supermarket, and Georges responds with the nonchalant observation that Anne either believes the girl or not. Anne responds by nodding sarcastically and asking, "It's that simple, huh?" She and Georges stand still when he then stops moving the cart, an important physical gesture that throws particular weight on what he says next: "No, it's just how it is." Here Georges voices a resignation to inevitability that is the antithesis of a Brechtian commitment to change. Then he says, "If you believe her, call the cops. If not, forget it. Or talk to the girl's parents." His calm tone is at odds with the Anne's anxiety, even though she fails to be proactive herself. That said, it matters that Georges has not been an aural witness to the girl's pain. After Anne becomes increasingly hostile, and criticizes his detached response, Georges defends himself by saying, "I've never heard her cry. I don't even know her." The film thus stresses an important connection between hearing and being compassionate. Their conversation then quickly devolves into a couple's quarrel during which she feigns having had an abortion, perhaps in order to shake Georges out of complacency. Their passionate kissing at the end of the argument and their resuming movement around the supermarket is a distraction from the child in crisis: a different way of not hearing.

Lest we feel great sympathy for Anne given Georges' inability to match her concern in this scene, we should consider the later scene where she re-records dialogue for post-production on another film. This scene involves the near-death of a child that dwells more upon the distress of Anne's character/his mother than on the negligence that leads to his being in danger: she cavorts with her husband in a pool, laughing and kissing him while their son climbs a concrete wall of a high-rise apartment complex. When Anne is re-recording dialogue with her co-actor they, and especially she, break into hysterical laughter, belying the seriousness of the scene's subject.[24] The post-production scene reminds us to be aware of the intentional constructedness of everything we hear in *Code Unknown*. This reminder is compounded by Haneke's providing

---

[24] Even though the ADR scene shows only the playful part leading up to the boy's death, there is something perturbing about Anne's hysterics given the content of the film scene as we know it unfolds. Her lonely laughter in the comedic audition for *Twelfth Night* sounds very different from this giggling during post-production on a scene of near-tragedy [1:34:38–1:38:55].

the offscreen voice of the director who is frustrated with Anne's hysterics during the ADR recording. Such emphasis on post-production control is an important defamiliarizing strategy, forcing our active comprehension of the film's artifice as well as its social truthfulness, just as the characterization of Anne prompts another Brechtian response hovering between detachment and engagement.

The tragedy of the little girl ends with Anne and Mrs. Becker attending her funeral. The shock of seeing mourners gathered around the child's grave is strangely perturbing because we never see her or her coffin. The scene begins with the ceremony under way [1:25:06], and the minister's line, "we believe that little Françoise has already entered into your Kingdom." This is the first time we hear the little girl's name, so it creates a different potential attachment to her unseen presence. That said, "Françoise" is a common enough name in France that the cries of the girl we do not see could be potentially attached to *many* children, and by extension many *people*, whose pain is ignored. The existence of Françoise that is purely through sound is Haneke's most haunting use of offscreen space. Haneke often denies us the full view of a violent event, as in the shooting of young Georgie in *Funny Games*. In *Code Unknown*, this pattern within his oeuvre is taken to a polemic extreme: Françoise is the completely acousmatized presence as the always disembodied victim. The film never visually reveals who she is, nor who she might represent, nor the extent of the pain she endures. The lack of her image makes her story a most potent appeal to our imaginations and hearts. Eventually, even Françoise's aural presence is reduced to nothing through her offscreen death. Moreover, the sound of traffic at her funeral competes with the minister speaking sentiments that are hollowed out by their incompleteness, the ritualized familiarity of his delivery without apparent conviction, and the lack of specific detail about who the child was: after saying he believes she is in God's Kingdom, he simply closes with "In your goodness grant that we might one day share with her in eternal life. Through Jesus Christ, Amen." No one else speaks, as if there is nothing to say about her individual existence. We then see the lined-up mourners respond by following the minister's lead, each dropping a shovel's worth of dirt onto Françoise's offscreen grave. Anne and Mrs. Becker line up to whisper words we cannot hear to Françoise's parents before they leave the graveyard. The rest of the scene shows them walking past many gravestones as the traffic continues and the camera tracks with them as if waiting for them to speak. The camera slowly moves closer as it tracks, shifting from a long to a medium shot. The closer proximity allows us to see that the old woman has a drop of water dangling from her nose. The physicality of her slightly messy crying matters in the absence of speech: there is an obvious tension between her physical expression of grief and her lack of words. The only interaction between Anne and Mrs. Becker is that they walk together and Anne helps the old lady slightly over a bumpy part of ground. But the traffic continues relentlessly and sometimes loudly, a grim suggestion that the world is oblivious and ceaselessly indifferent to the death of a child, a thematically loaded echo of the race car noise in *Funny Games*.[25] The scene cuts to black, punctuating this truth with sudden quiet [1:28.13].

The funeral scene shows that Françoise's parents are white, so we might reasonably assume she is as well. However, *Code Unknown* uses her acoustic presence to signify much more than a single Caucasian person in need. She may remind us of the group of children in the opening scene, but where these other children can see each other without being able to raise their voices, Françoise raises her voice without being seen. By being heard offscreen and never shown onscreen, she is cinematically marginalized. In crying for help, but not being saved, she stands for the many peoples of contemporary France who are heard but not *seen* in the figurative as well as the literal sense. She is an indirect allusion to the "invisibility" of sidelined peoples. She may remind us of the less obvious, but no less structured, absences of minority peoples onscreen. Her presumed whiteness more certainly reminds us of the essential vulnerability of *all* children, just as the film's opening urges us to dwell on the importance of multiethnic deaf-mute children in their struggle to communicate beyond physical limits. Françoise attempts to reach her neighbors, or at least stop her parents' violence, by screaming through walls, but even her strong screams do not lead Anne to action. Instead, she becomes an opportunity for Anne's privileged choice to ignore agony. This is a strong parallel with one of the roles Anne plays in a film-within-the-film titled "The Collector": a well-to-do woman who chooses to block out all sounds of the street (as discussed more fully below). Conversely, *Code Unknown* wants us to *hear* all different kinds of speaking, languages, and communication. This imperative to hear every living being is the culturally loaded dream of the film. The heaviness of postcolonial realities weighs heavily on this dream, but it is borne of a sincere commitment to inspiring compassionate change.

The Noise of the World, and the Death of Noiselessness

Along with urging us to consider what change is possible, *Code Unknown* repeatedly implies the indifference of the world to human suffering. This is sonically stressed by a motif of traffic noises mixed with dialogue. At Françoise's funeral, the sounds of moving vehicles compete with the minister's lines, and take the place of dialogue when Anne and Mrs. Becker do not speak. The scene

---

[25] The aural motif of traffic noise as it relays the callousness of the world to those who are most vulnerable is similarly important in *71 Fragments of a Chronology of Chance*. For example, an early scene features a homeless adolescent boy (an illegal immigrant) eating from a trash can by the road while numerous cars drive by. A couple within one car, stopped for a traffic light, watch him critically until he moves on down the street and his footsteps become inaudible against the traffic [11:44–12:22].

of Amadou's mother crying in distress after her son has been beaten by police is also underscored by traffic [24:32–27:06]. The noise becomes noticeably louder as Amadou's mother cries and the elder to whom she speaks murmurs unsubtitled prayers, underscoring her desperation in the context of an oblivious city. The sounds of a jet engine revving up dominate the scene where Maria is forced by police onto an airplane home to Romania [22:32–24.30]. We cannot clearly hear the airline stewardesses' speech beyond "Bonjour" to the boarding passengers, nor can we hear an air traffic controller talking over the sound of the noisy plane engine, nor the steps of two police officers and Maria walking on board. Ironically, the sound mix *does* make it possible for us to hear the quiet chinking of chains when one policeman undoes the handcuffs on her wrists before he pushes her onto the plane (see Figure 4.8). When we hear amplified noises like the handcuffs over the engine, we must instinctively grasp they are louder than they "should be," which weights them with symbolic meaning beyond naturalistic representation. Here, the sound track underlines the vulnerability of every human life as it is subject to all the "noise" of the world, and as it should be free.

Noises repeatedly threaten human voices in *Code Unknown*, but completely blocking out sound is shown to be dangerous too. This becomes clearest when Anne performs a scene from "The Collector." In this film-within-the-film, a realtor shows her character around an upscale apartment [40:10–43:02]. The realtor leads her into what was "once the music room." When she asks why the room has no windows, he explains that "They were walled up and paneled over. For the acoustics, I guess." The dialogue thus makes a connection between the luxury of musical enjoyment and a desire to tune out the rest of the world.

FIGURE 4.8 A policeman undoes the handcuffs on Maria's wrists as she boards the plane. The lines of the *mise-en-scène*, including the eyelines of the extras in this scene, lead us to the handcuffs, reinforcing the impact of our hearing them even though they are not clearly visible in close-up.

(This anticipates the doomed life of the protagonist in *The Piano Teacher*, as we explore in the next chapter.) The music room more critically symbolizes the insidious danger of rarefied aesthetic pleasure that inoculates the upper class from the reality of the street. The unnaturalness of such inoculation is the subtext of the extreme quiet in this scene from *Code Unknown*. The realtor closes doors to the room, blocking out the quiet traffic present from the scene's beginning, and then asks Anne, "You hear the silence? Quite amazing with all the traffic outside." We already know that "hearing the silence" in Haneke's cinema is important. In this case, silence signifies the danger that Anne's character has walked into by entering the music room that separates her from everyone else. The realtor leaves for a few moments, and Anne opens a new door that reveals a solid brick wall. Now her place of privilege is revealed to be a prison. She turns around dramatically to the camera as the door crashes into the wall, punctuating her terror.

Lest we become caught up in the victimization of Anne's unnamed character, Haneke's offscreen voice interrupts the filming to say, "She can't look straight into the camera" and his assistant then says, "her mark fell off during the pan shot of—." The film suddenly cuts to a new take, beginning with Anne's character looking out a window, shortly before she enters the music room. The noise of traffic outside resumes, along with the realtor giving her details of the apartment: he says, "Almost 30,000 square feet, 28,000 to be precise. Yet the trees and hedges ensure complete privacy." The emphasis thus falls back on how her character chooses to close herself off from the rest of humanity (a critically ironic parallel to Anne's failure to act on Françoise's behalf).[26] The scene soon segues into lines that we have already heard in the previous take. The specific repeated lines are as follows:

ANNE'S CHARACTER: "Does the central heating work?

REALTOR: "It was completely overhauled 4 years ago. We can see the
    boiler later, if you wish. Now we come to what was the music room.
    This way. A superb room. The paneling provides excellent acoustics."

---

[26] There is a compelling intertextual relationship between Anne's character in this scene and the lead role Binoche plays as Julie Vignon in *Three Colors: Blue* (*Trois couleurs: Bleu*, 1993). After suffering the loss of her husband and five-year-old daughter in a car accident, Julie chooses to withdraw from the rest of the world. However, sounds repeatedly force her back into the land of the living: she is disturbed by her own phone late at night, her door bell, a street fight, and repeatedly stunned by strong memories of her husband's music (indicated by many sudden, non-diegetic, *forte* fragments of his work). By the end of the film, she has reinvested in life: she bequeaths her husband's property to his mistress and her unborn child, and completes her husband's unfinished symphony. This symphony "For the Unification of Europe" culminates with a soprano singing 1 Corinthians 13 in Greek ("If I speak in the tongues of men or of angels, but do not have love, I am only a resounding gong or a clanging cymbal. . ."), backed by chorus and orchestra. The music rises over a montage that includes Julie making love with a man who has patiently waited for her attention throughout most of the film, amplifying her decision to reciprocate his affection. The film's climax portrays love, affection, music, and union as all interrelated on a personal and macrocosmic scale. It is the inverse of "The Collector" in *Code Unknown*,

Such repetition is striking in Haneke's cinema because of its rarity. Danijela Kulezic-Wilson usefully considers moments where speech is musically treated through rhythmic patterns, becoming an "element of 'audio-visual scoring' that is not a purely narrative device" (2015, 62). She explores the paradoxical effect of repeating particular lines, which can communicate both monotony and development (65). In other words, repetitions can suggest both stasis *and* shifting meanings through recontextualization (65). Through the repetition of these particular lines from "The Collector," *Code Unknown* tells us of what is unchanging in Anne's character (monotony) versus how the film wants *us* to change or hear things differently (development). The film's message is clear: the traffic of the world may sound oppressive, but completely withdrawing from that noise is a kind of death. We can choose to listen, and live, differently.

Unity through Drumming

Complete withdrawal from the sound of the world can be deadly, but *Code Unknown* foregrounds one kind of sound that evokes the vitality of life: the drumming of several deaf-mute children from the opening scene, joined by many others. They give us an extraordinary example of sonic connection in contrast with many characters who fail to hear each other, both literally and figuratively. Haneke explains that the main theme of *Code Unknown* is "the difficulty or the impossibility of communication. At all levels. Private, in the family, at different social levels, in countries." He then stresses a contrast between the limits of language and the possibilities of music in terms of unifying humanity. As Haneke explains, "with words, one is amongst all the difficulties of language." Being a concert pianist was his first professional dream, because his love for what music can do exceeds language: he says, "apart from sexuality, the most efficient form of communication is music. Because one breathes together. This is something practically unheard of in verbal communication." Though *Code Unknown* features dialogue in more than half of its scenes, it consistently stresses Haneke's "idea of not knowing the code of one's interlocutor.[27] Again, the film resonates from a postcolonial point of view because it discourages any presumptions we might have about knowing any languages, and by extension any cultures, with complete assurance. By contrast, the deaf-mute children embody the tentative, beyond-linguistic, and "most efficient" musical communication of a new generation. Given they can neither hear nor speak, we know that their drumming in time

---

which shows a woman withdrawing from the world, isolating herself, and being confronted with her death within an acoustically confined, nonmusical space.

[27] The quotations from Haneke in this paragraph come from the documentary *Michael H.— Profession: Director* by Yves Montmayeur (2013).

with each other demands an exceptionally strong level of intuitive, physical, and rehearsed union. This union has its roots in the distant past, for rhythm is the most fundamental element of music. Because musicians can never unite through rhythms that are metronomically perfect, a group playing any rhythm together must be attuned to the subtlest changes in pace that come down to fractions of a second. This level of robustly physical connectedness is moving in the context of a film that repeatedly shows bodies being hurt, violated, or regimented, including: Jean throwing the trash at Maria, Jean's father shooting his cattle dead after his son runs away, Anne hearing Françoise being physically abused by her parents, Amadou and Maria being forcibly controlled by police, and montages showing Georges' photographs of violent war crimes. If there is a way out of solitude and pain, and a universal code that can be known, the film suggests that it is a musical, bodily one. But lest we think this too easy an "answer" to the conflicts among and within divided peoples, consider again that this hope is embodied by children who are unusually vulnerable. Consider, also, that this is not the established classical music that we imagine Anne's character in "The Collector" wants to hear and/or play in her music room. This is music that relies purely on non-scored percussive collaboration by the most unlikely of performers. So, the children embody both hope *and* fragility. The fact that Amadou is one of their leaders is significant too: because we witness Amadou being taken away by police when Jean is left free, we know that his leadership could easily be cut short. *Code Unknown* thus provides us with a sense of unity that is most precious because it is both physically difficult to achieve and probably impermanent.

The two drumming scenes are sonic surprises, and not only because of the social coherence suggested by them—they *feel* different from anything else in Haneke's cinema. The first drumming scene occurs between the film showing Maria having been deported back to Romania and Georges returning home to Anne after photographing crimes against humanity in Kosovo [33:27–34:29]. Neither of these characters could be perceived as being at peace, whereas the children who play drums together achieve the peace of musical togetherness. We can clearly see the child who signed "sad" during the first scene drumming near Amadou's younger sister, in the front row. They play with confident exuberance, along with many other children and adults. Everybody drums together indoors. So, the explosion of joyful musical sound is visibly and acoustically contained, but nevertheless bombastic (see Figure 4.9). The drumming re-enters the film after a scene showing Anne being harassed by an Arab adolescent on the subway, a confronting experience that points to long-standing racial and class divisions [1:40:03–1:46:35]. The unnamed adolescent vocally leads the scene while his friend laughingly looks on, sardonically referring to Anne as "one of those beautiful rich people. You know, high society," and to himself as "just a little

FIGURE 4.9 The first drumming scene is a surprising explosion of musical sound, albeit within a contained space.

Arab."[28] Haneke holds us within a discomfiting long take throughout the scene, aligning us with Anne. She refuses to vocally respond but is visibly distressed—she moves about the train to create some space around herself, holds her own body in discomfort, and averts her eyes from him and the other passengers. The adolescent suddenly spits at Anne, thus turning his malicious speech into something tangible that makes her reflexively flinch. After an older Arab man stands up to face him confrontationally in Anne's defense, the adolescent leaves the train at the next stop, only to re-enter the scene offscreen by shouting an inarticulate noise at them. His shout overlaps with the stinger of the subway horn. Anne and the older man are startled enough that they involuntarily jump in their seats. The scene thus places negative emphasis on the physical impact of sound (see Figure 4.10).

The subway scene ends with a typically sudden cut to black but with an atypical sound advance: the return of the children drumming [1:46:35]. This is the only time when there is no marked break between scenes, subtly suggesting the possibility of moving forward in a newly powerful way. When a two-second blackout cuts to the next scene, the drumming is in full swing, and it is happening outside, with a large crowd gathering around to hear it. This suggests that the hope implied by the earlier indoor performance has gained strength as well as outreach (see Figure 4.11). A train goes by on a bridge above the drummers, connecting the scene to the previous one. Yet we now witness a completely different example of sound being physically felt. Where the adolescent's

---

[28] At one point the adolescent Arab refers to himself as part of the "racaille," a word meaning "scum" that was infamously used by the French president Nicolas Sarkozy some years later "to describe troublesome Arab youth" (Brunette 2010, 85).

FIGURE 4.10 When the "little Arab" spits at Anne, he turns his hateful words into something tangible.

FIGURE 4.11 The drummers finally play outside, embodying a collective dream of liberation. As the train passes them overhead, it reinforces the momentum of their music as well as implying that its symbolic meaning travels far.

impromptu shout made Anne and an older man jump in fear and off-guard on the subway, the drumming is a joyfully catchy expression of embodied social energy: the crowd around the percussionists physically respond by swaying, nodding their heads, and dancing.

The drummers keep playing over the film's final montage, starting with a tracking shot that focuses on Maria attempting to find a new place to beg on the streets of Paris. As she moves up and down the street, cautiously sitting down outside a florist's shop only to be pressured away by the presence of two men, the noises of traffic stress the anempathetic character of the city. We see many other pedestrians walk past or around her without paying her any attention, but their movements are noiseless, just as Maria's conversation with the two men is inaudible. The drumming continues over a blackout and cut to show subway steps from the street level, with Anne ascending, presumably after the train ride we just saw. The camera tracks her moving up the street, with traffic still audibly present until she enters the code for her building to re-enter it. Just one second later, a new scene shows Georges arriving outside Anne's building and approaching the outside door, attempting to gain entry and then realizing she has changed the code so he cannot. He hails down a cab before the cut to black, followed by the end of the drumming [1:54:02–1:54:04]. *Code Unknown* implies lost humanity through the soundless human presences of this sequence. This is compounded by the aural erosion of yet more traffic noises, similar to the drilling that we heard in *The Seventh Continent*. That said, the drumming is louder than everything else here, and the implication of the mix is therefore ultimately uplifting: the sound of togetherness is greater than the sounds of division, machinery, and individual directionality—or, at least, this is the most hopeful possibility, despite there still being no place for people like Maria to rest.

Christopher Sharrett refers to the percussion of *Code Unknown* as "noise" rather than music.[29] He questions the power of the percussion by arguing that "communication happens only at an atomized, insulated level, an act of communion within a minisociety at the margins of a larger, vicious civilization" (218). Girish Shambu (2006) provides a positive contrary argument—for him, the percussion suggests "a pre-verbal state of pure, ecstatic communion/communication using the sound and rhythms of tribalistic drums." Though his words ("pre-verbal," "tribalistic") imply a lack of sophistication at odds with the extraordinary ability of the children to play with confidence despite their disabilities, and a simplicity about the process of playing that sidesteps the nuances of achieving musical cohesion, he rightly emphasizes how much their playing matters in relation to the communication struggles that dominate *Code Unknown*. Further, even if the group of children is only a "minisociety," they represent a new generation and a diverse population. Their final drumming is exceptional in that Haneke's films seldom make much use of sutured sound.

---

[29] By contrast, Sharrett stresses the significance of another musical element of the film's opening sequence: the "rhythm and blues street artist, whose exemplary performance goes unnoticed by the key characters just as they are about to unleash the terrible chain of events representing the film's vision of social collapse [. . .] Rhythm and blues—one of the liberatory music forms of the world, evolved from the experience of slavery and the betrayal of Reconstruction in the United States—is shown here to be ripped utterly from any social/historical context" (2010, 218). Though the characters' seeming inability to hear the rhythm and blues may indeed be disturbing as Sharrett suggests, *Code Unknown* uses the percussion scenes to suggest the possibility of a new, different, and commandingly subversive music that is embodied by people on the margins of society.

Because the music continues over a montage, the film suggests that what the children play—and, by extension, the hope they embody—transcends any or all of the other characters' storylines.

The children repeat the same percussive pattern over and over again without losing a sense of momentum or intensity. This connects with how the film narrative finally comes full circle: *Code Unknown* ends with another deaf-mute child performing a concept for other children to guess. We see him against the same white wall of the opening, making sounds that are not speech. His hands sign in several different ways: fluttering, swimming, pulling at his chin, extending from the mouth as if to suggest words and/or song, and touching and crossing his body. As Thomas Elsaesser writes, "The next generation, whatever their handicap, the film seems to say, is still capable of playing the game of communication, however fraught it is with misunderstanding or plain incomprehension" (2010, 71).

A near-contemporary film with *Code Unknown, Touch the Sound: A Sound Journey with Evelyn Glennie* (2004), can help us better understand the deaf-mute children as physical embodiments of uplifting sonic power. In *Touch the Sound*, Glennie explains her life-affirming experiences as a near-deaf percussionist who delights in sound because she can "feel it through [her] body." She speaks of hearing as "a form of touch" and of her body as a "resonating chamber" for every sound. When "a so-called hearing person" asks Glennie how she can possibly hear anything, she says, "I hear through my body, through opening myself up." Her words suggest how we can perceive what the percussionists do in *Code Unknown*: along with creating collaborative music, they seem to open themselves up on every level. The film does not require that we pity them—it affirms what they achieve by making us hear their music played *forte* in two impactful scenes. At the same time, the children represent disadvantaged people given France's reputation as one of the least progressive countries when it comes to the rights of the disabled. Julia Kristeva has written critically of how disabled people are often not acknowledged as such in French society for fear of vocally announcing their difference: this kind of silence parallels the assimilationist tendencies of the government's race-related policies.[30] Because the deaf-mute children of *Code Unknown* are of various ethnicities, they embody the potential vulnerability of us *all*, even as they give us the most robust music. Their

---

[30] Sam Haigh writes that in comparison with the United States, the United Kingdom, Canada, most other European countries, and Scandinavian countries, France "has historically lagged behind in terms of disability law and provision" (2011, 136). Haigh charts the shift from policies of exclusion to those of "integration," asking whether the latter promote "equality or participation" or whether they create another "form of erasure" with regard to recognizing people with disabilities. Haigh also points out that the "able-bodied population" generally fear that "disability may strike their lives at any time" (145). In this context, he describes Julia Kristeva's very public campaigning against prejudice toward disabled persons, including her argument that "vulnérabilité" should be added to the Republic's creed of "liberté, égalité, fraternité" (Haigh 142; Kristeva 2003, 10).

confident performances, as well as their conceptual games via body language, are the film's most optimistic representations of social effort. The children's communications with each other are particularly moving in light of their severe physical *and* cultural limitations.

Summary

From the first to the last scene, *Code Unknown* reminds us how much our efforts to communicate matter. By contrast with the deaf-mute children who book-end the film with their extended efforts to physically "speak," many hearing-speaking adults of the film fail to speak or listen with patience, good will, or moral kindness, and sometimes with awful consequences. Françoise's death is the most startling result of the failure to keep listening that would lead to speaking out and saving a life. Georges explicitly connects sound with compassion when he explains his indifference to Françoise by saying he never heard her. By extension, *Code Unknown* demands that we hear many different kinds of voices, silences, and noises because it wants us to engage with diverse lives. This is how the sound track addresses the fraught cultural politics of contemporary France.

Code Unknown does not offer us the utopian possibility of communication that transcends racial, cultural, and physical bounds, for it ends by reminding us of what we cannot know in a child's ambiguous body language. Haneke himself speaks of the scene as "sad" because neither the children nor we can be sure of what the boy is trying to say "in such a delightful and enthusiastic way." At the same time, Haneke stresses the importance of making the film open-ended, referring to it as a kind of "ski jump" that invites our making an interpretive leap.[31] So, the camera finally places us in the position of the children involved in another guessing game. The following silence, over the closing credits, leaves yet more space for interpretation, pointing to an unending process of trying to understand.

---

[31] For Haneke, all filming is about making good ski jumps: "you have to build a good jump, but viewers have to take the leap, and how far they go depends on how good your ski jump is." He makes these points in the documentary about *Code Unknown* included with the 2015 Criterion Blu-ray release.

5

The Piano Teacher

MUSICAL BEAUTY WITHOUT TRANSCENDENCE

How can we understand a sound track's power as an "adaptation" of multiple texts, genres, and musical works? What makes a sound track inspired by a novel newly impactful? By what strategies can a sound track both revise and repudiate generic cinematic norms for representing female perspectives? When can cinematic music that matches a woman's emotional life be more than melodramatic? How can the most beautiful classical music be a sinister representation of the status quo? These are the fundamental questions that drive this analysis of *The Piano Teacher* as an adaptation of several artistic forms.

Contemporary adaptation studies move away from the so-called fidelity model that dwells on how well a given film adapts a single text. Where the term "adaptation" used to be reserved for analyzing text-to-film translations (such as the numerous film versions of Shakespeare's plays), it now refers to any number of allusive possibilities that come together within any single feature.[1] These possibilities include how a film interacts with multiple histories, and how it combines multimedia modes of representation as it reframes preexisting stories. The concept "adaptation" has itself been *adapted* to refer to all manner of recallings, reworkings, and recontextualizations.[2] The concept is

---

[1] For a representative example, Thomas Leitch considers those multiple cinematic and literary influences that bear on the resonance of a given film's details. More specifically, he analyzes the multiple forms of Robin Hood's story that build up his mythological outlaw status, and which are always in excess of any single representation: "The outlaw of Sherwood and his merry men open an intoxicating prospect to theorists who are willing to challenge the abiding authority of canonical literary sources" (2008, 28). In making this argument, Leitch problematizes the traditional "high-low" approach to literature versus film, along with challenging the fidelity model of more conservative adaptation studies. We parallel his approach by considering multiple aurally driven, cinematic forms of representation that preceded and that influence Haneke's *The Piano Teacher*, rather than Jelinek's novel alone.

[2] For more on this overarching trend, see Walker's editorial introducing the "Roundtable" of essays by leading scholars in adaptation studies for the inaugural issue of *Literature Film Quarterly* (*LFQ*) online (2017): www.salisbury.edu/lfq.

malleable enough that we can meaningfully use it to help us fully hear the multidimensionality of the sound track for *The Piano Teacher*. Though the sound track most clearly and directly uses details and patterns from an original novel by Erika Jelinek,[3] it also recalls and reworks the sonic conventions of several well-established film genres, and recontextualizes well-known classical works of music. In addition, *The Piano Teacher* is a vital part of the Haneke intertext as one of his most notorious works, though its infamy is a disservice to its compassionately feminist vision.

The Piano Teacher revolves around the pain of its central character named Erika. There is much to say about how Haneke's emphasis on the sounds of her world, along with the music and silences that define her, parallel the sonic details of Jelinek's novel. But in the adaptation from novel to film, Erika's story becomes bigger through its many resonances beyond this primary source. For example, Haneke calls the film "a parody of a melodrama."[4] Such a claim might seem preposterous when we compare the extreme brutality and stylistic austerity of *The Piano Teacher* with the affective consolations of Classical Hollywood melodramas. Yet we shall find many narrative elements within *The Piano Teacher* that ironically offset the film's radically non-Classical aural logic: where the films of Douglas Sirk feature music that bathes us in affect in accordance with his female protagonists' exquisite suffering, for example, Erika is denied a sound track that "sides with" her straightforwardly. Indeed, it is the broken music and silences of *The Piano Teacher* that create the strongest, most persistent sonic impressions, in parallel to the protagonist's divided and lonely self. The film's subject matter rewards further genre-based analysis in comparison with other musician-based dramas, especially through its atypical focus on a female musician. In addition, *The Piano Teacher* resituates and adapts the meaning of specific musical compositions, most notably Franz Schubert's *Winterreise* song cycle. By analyzing *The Piano Teacher* in relation to the multiple texts that it both directly *and indirectly* engages with, we shall better understand its far-reaching significance.[5] Like a piano chord played hard, with

---

[3] Willy Riemer details how Jelinek's novel has been adapted in other ways with strong aural dimensions: a composition by Patricia Jünger for speaking voice, singer, percussion, and tape, first broadcast by Südwestfunk in 1988; a stageplay directed by Barbara Mundel and Veit Vokart in 1989 at the *Komödie* in Basel; and dance theater performed by *Mind the Gap Tanztheater* of Wuppertal in 1989 (2007, 273).

[4] Haneke refers to the film as parodying melodrama in Yves Montmayeur's documentary *Michael H.*, though without specific attention to the film's sonic refusal to comply with melodramatic conventions. Parody in *The Piano Teacher* is a serious business, despite its darkly comedic elements. Drawing on the work of Linda Hutcheon and Gary Saul Morson, Julie Brown explains that parody can be more about transforming and recontextualizing a subject than being humorously derivative (2005, 169).

[5] This chapter breaks with well-established psychoanalyses of *The Piano Teacher*. As Jean Ma writes, Erika herself "cries out for a psychoanalytic interpretation as a paradigmatic case study of repression, exhibiting symptoms of neurosis, psychosis, narcissism, and frigidity" (2010, 520). Slavoj Žižek provides a brief but memorable Lacanian analysis of how the film foregrounds Erika's unfulfilled desire in connection with Real terror (2012, 24–26), and Jean Wyatt (2005) devotes an article to the

the damper pedal pressed down for its maximum vibrating strength, the sound track of *The Piano Teacher* is an experience of lasting reverberations that fill more than one space.

Jelinek's Novel as Source Text

The primary inspiration for Haneke's film, Jelinek's novel *The Piano Teacher* (*Die Klavierspielerin*, 1983), features numerous disturbing conceptualizations of music, and many symbolically loaded references to silence, as well as affective sonic details that define the protagonist's troubled world. We begin with its dominant aural patterns as the basis for understanding what Haneke's adaptation does. First, music is frequently mentioned as a general term though individual works are seldom described in detail. For a story that revolves around a pianist, specific musical details are often *strangely absent*. Specific formal elements of musical works are scant, though the novel includes meandering explanations of the disturbance that Erika reads into them as a result of her own mental and emotional turbulence. In other words, the descriptions of musical works point back to Erika, rather than prompting us to revel in them as having their own uncompromised artistic logic. Moreover, the tawdry and violent sexual encounters that Erika experiences are described in much more detail than the music she plays or teaches. Canonical composers are mentioned by name numerous times, but the absence of much sustained attention to their works takes us back to the limits of Erika's disturbed subjectivity: we can never get "lost" in her music because her pain is always bigger than it.

In Jelinek's novel there is no lovely "art for art's sake." Music can have a frightening presence, and *the* "city of music," Vienna, is a relentlessly hostile place (12, 19). Erika's musical expressivity *could* have made for a narrative of relative female freedom, but Jelinek's text is an important feminist statement about "the subjugation of women" (Johnson 2009, 117). Music that is equated with rarefied or high-brow Art (often spelled with a capital "A") provides no outlet or escape for Erika: instead, it "pursues you everywhere" (Jelinek 1988, 29). Similarly, "Culture" is referred to as a "seething gruel" that will never finish cooking (189). Erika's music spreads "like poison gas into every nook and cranny," an allusion to Austria's alignment with the Nazi regime (26). When she plays Mozart, his "spirit shrieks as if from an infernal abode" (35). Erika sacrifices herself to music's terrible power: she "spices the soup" of her playing with "heart's blood" (14), and her body is described as being like "one big refrigerator, where Art is well stored" (21). Through such descriptions of Erika, Jelinek's

---

relationship between the protagonist and her mother, especially as Erika is the vehicle by which Mother attempts to fulfill herself. These are incontestable explorations of what *The Piano Teacher* forces us to confront with disarmingly overt intentionality. Our sonic reading of the film is about meanings that are more subtextual, but just as significant.

novel connects the civilized musical history of Vienna with hellishly debilitating pain. Her novel thereby undercuts widespread, lofty perceptions of the city as "capital of the European classical tradition" (Ma 2010, 512), particularly as home of the Vienna Boys' Choir, the Vienna Philharmonic Orchestra, and the working lives of Haydn, Beethoven, Mozart, and Schubert. Ultimately, Vienna is turned into a revolting personification of death: "Its buttons are bursting from the fat white paunch of culture, which, like any drowned corpse that is not fished from the water, bloats up more and more" (12). The city is dirty, dangerous, misogynistic, and violent. Erika seeks out people on the periphery, in the darkness, away from tourists, and in the slums. She takes herself to the seediest places: a peepshow, a porn shop, and a muddy forest where couples have sex.

Just as Jelinek's novel rejects reverence for Vienna as a place of high Art, the association between music and salvation becomes absurd within it. Indeed, music is inseparable from profound mental instability. Erika herself rejects "health" as a "transfiguration of [the] status quo," derisively citing "that profoundly healthy Brahms" (71). She prefers the work of two composers who were mentally disturbed: Schumann, who wrote of experiencing "Torments of the most terrible melancholia" (Geck 2012, 31); and Schubert, who probably suffered from a mild form of manic depression (cyclothymia), evidenced by his erratic productivity and changeable moods (Gibbs 2000, 95). Erika views such composers as "closest to my bruised heart" (71), dwelling on Schumann as he descended into darkness: she says, "He yearningly tries to catch the fading echoes, he mourns the loss of the most precious thing: himself" (71). In relation to Schumann's loss, she reveals to her most precociously talented student (Walter Klemmer) that her own father "lost his mind and died in the Steinhof Asylum" (71). Walter is a dangerous presence in Erika's life, but she uses this story as an effort to "flay some feelings" out of him (72). In the absence of unproblematic connections to the people in her life, Erika seems to seek solace for her absent father in the canonized "Fathers" of classical music, a point visually represented in Haneke's film by portraits of Schumann and Bach that are prominently displayed on the walls of her rehearsal rooms at the Conservatory.

In Jelinek's novel, music is also about powerplay over pleasure. Music is frequently connected to specific hierarchical dynamics: the pecking order at the Conservatory; the teachers' selection of students to teach and to be concert soloists; Erika's autocratic way of controlling her pupils' interpretations of music; and the power that Erika's Mother exerts over her daughter's life in the name of musical aspirations for her. Just as Mother controls her daughter's body like a "stubborn, easily deformable, living instrument" (36),[6] Erika wields her knowledge of music like a weapon. Instead of lifting her spirits, music raises "her fist" (16). When she duets with Walter, "they take turns at outdoing

---

[6] We use "Mother" as a given name to echo the novel and how Erika refers to her.

each other's fury at the ignorant, the uncomprehending" (70). She even uses her pedagogical position to aggressively assert greater authority than what is musically notated, implying that she knows more than the composers: "Don't hold every note as long as the score tells you to," she scolds Walter, "not every note is marked as it ought to sound" (188). Yet musical scores imprison her too: "Those five lines have been controlling her ever since she first began to think." Along with Mother, "this grid system . . . has hamstrung her in an untearable net . . . like a rosy ham on a butcher's hook" (190). Jelinek's novel is filled with such lurid metaphorical descriptions of music's power, which cumulatively create the impression of a force that can never be truly understood because it always evades final conceptualization. The metaphors about music relay an unending struggle to adequately describe the pain of Erika's life.[7]

Shortly before the end of the novel, Walter rapes Erika. Before he takes control of her through "brute force" (268), she pleads with him to "remember the differences between sonatas" (267). Erika's attempt to assert her own musical authority is sadly absurd here: it holds no sway when "Klemmer is laughing his head off at the flesh he has twisted" (267). Her words indirectly resonate with Theodor Adorno's work on sonata form. (Adorno is absent in Jelinek's text but mentioned, in passing, by Erika to Walter in Haneke's film.) In his writings on Beethoven in particular, Adorno uses violent metaphors to describe the work of the sonata: he invokes "the childhood image of the sonata as a battle involving a march, an opposing march, and a collision leading to a catastrophe" (Miller 2009, 8; Adorno 1998, 81). He describes "the main theme [of a sonata as it] *descends* on the music with the anticipated force of the whole; against this the individual subject, as the second theme, *defends* itself [emphasis in the original]" (Miller 2009, 23; Adorno 1998, 81).[8] Similarly, the novel knowingly and emphatically denies us the comforts of enjoying the evocations of fine music without feeling compromised, which in turn resonates with Adorno's criticism of music that inoculates humankind from the true atrocities of the world.[9] Erika bitterly acknowledges, "art is credited with many things, especially an ability to offer solace. Sometimes, of course, art creates the suffering in the first place" (23). *Occasionally*, Jelinek's novel contains platitudes about

---

[7] For more on Jelinek's extraordinarily elastic, subversive, and controversial use of language, as well as her own radically elusive feminist identity, see Carlotta von Maltzan (2002).

[8] Timothy D. Miller (2009) provides an extended analysis of violent metaphors in Adorno's conceptualizations of music, and he selected these representative quotations.

[9] Adorno's writings advocate for music that resists the so-called culture industry, the mass-produced works of creativity that not only normalize violence in insidious ways (for instance, the cartoonish characters like Popeye who are repeatedly injured to the point that they encourage us to accept violence as an inevitable element of life) but also suppress the full consciousness of violent impact: he is, for instance, extremely critical of Stravinksy's *Rite of Spring* for the way it victimizes a woman. As Miller writes, "In its recounting of a young girl's sacrifice to the gods of Spring, Adorno sees a distortion of art's subjectivity: the identification 'not with the victim, but with the annihilating authority'" (Miller 2009, 41; Adorno 2006, 109–110). *Rite of Spring* is a representative example of the music that

aesthetic gratification, such as the reference to music as "the celestial power" and the assertion that "Nothing offers so much pleasure as a magnificent performance by the finest virtuosi" (6)—both of which are given in the context of Mother's control over Erika, and both of which evoke generalized assumptions. But there are so many revolting and haunting descriptions of music that any such pronouncements ring hollow, not least because they are incorporated without being attached to any specific character who believes them. Overall, then, Jelinek's text obsessively references music in order to deconstruct its affectively positive and edifying associations.[10]

The absence of heartening music is compounded by Jelinek's unusually strong emphasis on silence. Because she makes so many references to silence, it is worth citing a range of significant examples to convey their incremental impact. Erika views silence as a form of empowerment, in many problematically self-defeating ways. Her body has not revealed its "silent secrets" for many years (108), and her door knob is "mute" to Walter when he touches it (125). Erika knows to move "silently, as light as a feather" when she voyeuristically seeks out a couple having sex (141). Mother and Erika "aim silence at each other" during a confrontation (157). Walter uses "a significant silence" against Erika's patronizing claim that "practice makes perfect" (159). When Erika wants control over Walter sexually, she repeatedly orders him to "keep silent" (179, 180, 182). Mother punishes Erika by withholding comments on a movie because "the daughter can't talk to herself" (210). In a letter to Walter detailing her violent sexual fantasies, Erika instructs him to make her silent by stuffing nylons "into my mouth as deep as you can and gag me so cunningly that I can't emit the slightest peep" (218). Then she silences herself: when Walter asks if she wants "a slap in the face," she "does not give herself permission to speak" (218). Mother makes a woman almost "voiceless," by turning down the volume on her television, so she can eavesdrop on Erika with Walter (221). After Walter has read her letter, Erika reiterates a desire to be silenced: "To keep me from whimpering in pain, please stuff nylons and panty hose into my mouth, gag me with pleasure" (223). Mother assaults Erika with questions, in response

---

Adorno sees as perpetuating the modern era's assault on the individual (Miller, 45), always falling short of realizing the ultimate goal of music to represent the "complete liberation of the human subject" (Chua 2006, 11; also cited by Miller, 36). For more on Adorno's work, his affiliation with the Frankfurt School, and his arguments for the moral obligations of art in the aftermath of the Holocaust, see Freedman (2012).

[10] Though noises are much less frequently mentioned than music through the text, there are several that accost Erika, including the television that Mother controls, turning up the volume as a form of angry protest against Erika's insubordination (210), and the telephone that "shrieks" when Walter calls Erika (261). The most startling noise is a "shriek that slices the air in half," after a female student squeezes the glass that Erika planted in her coat pocket (170). The novel gives such emphasis to sounds of oppression, threat, and pain that the *absence* of any soothing or aesthetically pleasing sound is obvious.

to which she "remains silent" so that Mother will become more frenzied with rage (232). After Erika sexually attacks Mother, Mother asks Erika if she has gone crazy and "no answer follows" (234). But then Mother "remains silent, as if nothing happened" (235). The day after Walter rapes Erika, Mother is again "unusually silent" (275). Silence does not mean peace any more than music. Silence, like music, is about powerplay and conflict within every major scenario. Silence is full of poignant and troubled meanings—it is suggestive of repression, desire, manipulation, violence, disappointment, alienation, and aloneness. The meanings of silence shift just as the conceptualizations of music change, contributing to the novel's overall pattern of stressing a quixotically dangerous sonic world.

Silences, Pain, and Confrontation

Much like Haneke's other films, and in parallel to Jelinek's text, the adaptation of *The Piano Teacher* includes many discomfiting silences. Being subjected to these silences is more palpable than reading about them, even despite the impact of Jelinek's emphasis on numerous moments of withholding sound. Silences are thematically significant but are no more actually present in the act of reading Jelinek's text than the music she alludes to. By contrast, *both* music and silence gain a presence in Haneke's adaptation, yet the film still strongly parallels Jelinek's text because neither silence nor music brings peace or lasting relief. The adaptation achieves a remarkable intensification of the sonic descriptions within Jelinek's text through giving us a direct experience of aural impact.

The palpable silences of *The Piano Teacher* begin with the first opening credits [0:25sec–1:00]. (Yet again, Haneke denies us non-diegetic music when we would typically expect it.) The second set of opening credits comes after a preliminary scene establishing Erika's conflict with Mother. The setup begins with Erika returning home late from work, having purchased an expensive dress: Mother views both her tardiness and material indulgence as acts of punishable rebellion, tearing the dress from Erika's grasp, in response to which Erika viciously strikes her. The latter opening credits then appear silently onscreen without musical accompaniment, much like the first, but now interrupting a series of fragmented lesson scenes. As each student plays, Erika passes on Mother's restrictive judgment by barking critical instructions of interpretation over the music [7:42–9:24]. With each cut back to the diegesis from the credits, a different set of hands is playing, visually representing a new lesson, and changing music along with Erika's constant criticism.[11] The

---

[11] The specific extracts played by Erika's students are from Chopin's Fantaisie in F minor, Op. 49, Haydn's "Une Sonate plus simple," and Schubert's "Im Dorfe" from the song cycle *Winterreise* (discussed more fully below)—the first two are played by anonymous hands, whereas "Im Dorfe" is played

breaks into silence offset the hard tone of her voice. Carl Freedman argues that the aesthetic beauty of the "impeccably-pronounced French" in *The Piano Teacher* makes it "extremely pleasurable to listen to" even though it is "painful to watch" (2012, 20).[12] However, if we carry out a process of what Michel Chion calls "masking" (listening to the film without its visuals), it is obvious that the actors' voices often sound harsh.[13] Erika (Isabelle Huppert), in particular, frequently speaks in an officious, quick, and staccato way. The timbre of Huppert's voice is markedly different from her everyday speaking style that can be comparatively warm, delicate, and soft (as heard in the documentary *Michael H.*, or when she plays a desperate widowed mother protecting her children in *Time of the Wolf*). In *The Piano Teacher*, her clipped speaking matches the fragmentation of music. Her vocal criticism of her students establishes the pressured narrative context in which all music is made. The repeated return to silence further reinforces the fragility of musical power, the implication being that every act of creativity can suddenly lead to naught—music is there and is then suddenly gone, a person is present and then suddenly replaced. The expository sequence abruptly ends with a shot of Erika standing at a rehearsal-room window, silently eating a sandwich while she looks outside with her back toward us [9:27] (see Figure 5.1).

A grand piano dominates the frame, dwarfing Erika's small, thin body. We cannot miss her lack of sonic presence next to it. The only dominant sound is the low drone of traffic: a sound that returns most forcefully at the end of the film, and to which we will therefore return. Felix W. Tweraser stresses the ironic tension between the suggestion of transcendence in Erika's looking out the window, and the traffic noise coming through it (2011, 198). Erika's wordlessness conveys her isolation, along with her symbolic smallness (next to the grand piano), and her separation from the world outside (represented by the traffic). All these details cinematically recall elements of Jelinek's novel—the oppressiveness of music, the connection between music and powerplay, the hostile noises, and the absent speech that is thick with destructive implications.

---

by Anna Schober (and then Erika). The separation of music from the first two performers' identities places emphasis on Erika's controlling voice rising over the sounds they make. For a full rundown of the music used in the film, in relation to the cues written into Haneke's original screenplay, see Brown (2005, 180–187).

[12] Freedman dwells on the strangeness of the French dialogue given that the action focuses on native-speaking German characters in a German-speaking city. He argues that the French language has a "dominance in the linguistic sphere" that is comparable to the status of "Austro-German music"— French was "the most common language of educated Europe after the decline of Medieval Latin and is recognized by many Germans as having a cultural standing loftier than that of their own mother tongue" (20). So, the perceived musicality of French speaking is problematized in parallel to the revered music of *The Piano Teacher*.

[13] As Chion explains, the act of masking means "discovering the sonic elements and the visual elements separately, before putting them back together again," which in turn "will dispose us most favorably to keep our listening and looking fresh" (1994, 187).

FIGURE 5.1 Erika stands alone at the window after exerting authority over her students. Her musical prowess is undermined by her physical smallness next to the grand piano she uses for teaching.

Such long takes featuring Erika's silence in Haneke's film—as opposed to the frequent and passing references to her silence within Jelinek's novel—most consistently amplify the limits of her life. Silences certainly oppress her, even though she uses her own silences to oppress others. Mary Dalton and Kirsten Fatzinger point out that "breaking through silence has been a prevailing empowerment metaphor for women" in late-twentieth-century feminist analyses, because "power exists in naming and claiming one's experience" (2003, 36). So, Erika's frequent inability to break past silence is an important part of the film's feminist credibility. That said, Haneke uses silence to create a productive space for interpretation as well. With all his films, silence carries the expectation that we will imagine the meaning to "fill it in" or, at the very least, sit with the questions that remain unanswered in the absence of sound. In *The Piano Teacher*, the silent breaks during the second opening-credit sequence invite us to consider the oppressive role of the teacher, the disturbance of music being taken away (from us, and from the students through Erika's didactic criticism), as well as the suturing comforts that more conventional films provide for us via sonic continuity and predictably used non-diegetic music to "set the scene."

Haneke's appeal to our imaginations is more startlingly obvious in Erika's final silence, when she walks away from the Conservatory after stabbing herself. The moment when Erika silently drives the blade into her chest is akin to the shock of Mother Courage's silent scream—in both cases, there is the image without the sound of pain we would expect. Though Erika grimaces right before she thrusts the knife into herself with astonishing force, she gives herself no vocal relief (see Figure 5.2). Before this final action, Erika has been waiting

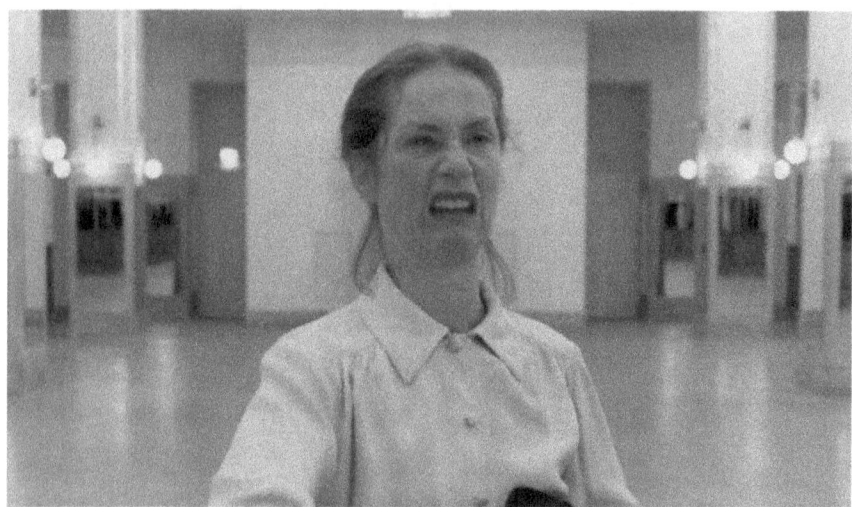

FIGURE 5.2 Erika grimaces horribly just before stabbing herself, visually anticipating pain without then aurally expressing shock.

to see Walter arrive at the jubilee concert. He arrives amid a throng of intermittent noises as other audience members enter the foyer through squeaky doors, their footsteps and excited chatter echoing through the space. Walter rushes past Erika, calling out to her as he rambunctiously arrives with a group of other students. Erika silently stands still while he calls out to her: "My respects, Professor, I can't wait to hear you play." Then she turns her body toward him, a voicelessly eloquent gesture of submissiveness. After Walter enters the concert hall and passes by Erika with his group, the noisy ebb and flow of concert attendees arriving is suddenly over: the thickening sonic texture is reduced to near-silence as Erika stands alone [2:01:03–2:02:01]. The sudden removal of sound is as confronting as the straight-on shot of her—in other words, the camera's unflinching stare is a visual equivalent to the aural starkness. Erika quietly reaches in her purse, rummages for the knife, and stabs herself while still looking in the direction where Walter left her standing [2:02:02–2:02:11]. With forceful effort, she removes the knife, and puts it back in her handbag while a patch of blood appears on her chest. She noiselessly raises her hand to the wound while looking around for a few moments, giving us time to absorb what she has done while she experiences the initial physical shock. This violence is doubly shocking because we see it *onscreen*—much more often, Haneke shows climactically violent actions from an outsider's viewpoint (as with the camera's position outside the car in which Maximilian kills himself at the end of *71 Fragments*), or he allows us to hear violent actions while they occur offscreen (as in the murder of young Georgie in both versions of *Funny Games*) (Speck 2010, 172–173). Here, we are forced to witness the act of violence but, in a reversal of the usual pattern of Haneke's work, *without* the sound we would expect. The impact is therefore most intensely defamiliarizing in relation to the auteur's intertext.

Shortly after Erika stabs herself, there is a hard cut to outside the concert hall and the *forte* sound of traffic [2:02:23]. The form of the film thus "breaks"—a stylistic parallel to Erika's fresh wound. We see Erika approaching the foyer doors to walk out, with the patch of blood on her blouse still visible from a long-shot distance—a visual emphasis on lasting damage. The film cuts to an extreme long shot on the main doors as Erika is walking out and the traffic noise carries on relentlessly [2:02:44–2:03:10]. She walks up the street as the cars go past. She seems oblivious to them as they are to her. This ending evokes the scene in *Funny Games* where the sound of race cars dominates for several minutes around the tragedy of young Georgie's death, and the traffic motif of *Code Unknown* that communicates the dangers of a dispassionate society.

When Erika stabs herself and walks away from all the other people near her, she makes herself into a strange kind of alienated martyr. In this moment, *The Piano Teacher* is a not only a haunting physical representation of the climax in Jelinek's book: it is a radically parodic adaptation of melodramatic conventions. Oliver C. Speck writes about the prototypical martyr of a melodrama who might suffer "a fate 'worse than death' or [decide] that this life is not worth living," but who nevertheless earns the status of making a meaningful self-sacrifice (2010, 163).[14] Consider the lead character of *Imitation of Life* (1959) for an extreme example of this within a racially charged context: Annie Johnson, the completely self-sacrificing African-American mother whose own daughter (Sarah-Jane) cruelly rejects her in the hope of passing as white. Annie's tragic death, and Sarah-Jane's heartbreaking remorse at her mother's funeral, is honored with a diegetic Gospel choir performance while Sarah-Jane cries out in agony, throwing her body against the coffin ("Mama, Mama, I didn't mean it, I didn't mean it, Mama, do you hear me, I'm sorry, I'm sorry Mama, Mama I did love you"). Sarah-Jane's grief is offset by the stunned silence and hushed whispers of mourners lined up the street, and an onscreen brass band procession that plays the funeral procession elegy while Frank Skinner's non-diegetic, heavenly evoking score underlines the pathos of the scene with female voices rising in poignantly high pitches. By contrast with all this, the aural follow-up to Erika's attempted suicide is an extreme quiet, the sound of traffic that passes her by, and complete silence for the end credits.

This final part of *The Piano Teacher*'s sound track challenges us to stay with the awful shock of what we have just witnessed, in the absence of any musical enhancement, catharsis, or aesthetic consolation. The "deafening silence" of the end credits harkens back to a scene midway through the film,

---

[14] Though Speck is writing about characters who commit suicide in particular, and "whether Erika's self-inflicted wound will prove fatal is left uncertain" (Freedman 2012, 22), his claim is generally applicable to Classical Hollywood melodrama.

when Erika confronts a pupil she has caught looking at porn magazines. After he has apologized and she threatens to contact his mother, she demands that he explain why he is sorry. "I'm listening" she barks at him with such bitterness that it seems like a threat. When the pupil fails to respond right away, she retorts that "the silence is deafening!," and soon demands his exit. The last silence of *The Piano Teacher* during the end credits is even more "deafening" than this, and our listening to that silence is more extended and full of implication. The silence between Erika and her shamed pupil is a dead end between them, whereas the final silence of the film invites us to dwell on the meaning of Erika's last act. This final silence is potentially about many things—it is about underlining what the world fails to notice (a woman like Erika's suffering), what she could not say to Walter and all the others around her, and what Walter and her mother could not hear or comprehend. The silence refers to the voice Erika does not have, the absence of her music in the concert, her repression, her suppressed truth, and the agony of her having no vocal nor other relief. Ultimately, this last deafening silence is the agony of there being no answer to, or solution for, her pain.

In Jelinek's novel, Erika's stabbing herself brings no sense of relief. Having turned herself into a spectacle of violence, she is walking home by the end, indicating that she will return to the life that traps her. Haneke's film seems less conclusive than this, for the final image of Erika walking away from the Conservatory implies she may have new agency beyond resigning herself to the same life. Beth Johnson reads Erika's stabbing herself rather optimistically as a form of resistance to being a subject of "the patriarchal system represented by the Conservatory" (2009, 128). Similarly, Julie Brown argues that the ending contains "the possibility of Erika's healing," particularly because she is walking away from the Conservatory concert (2005, 168). That said, Erika's silence in the final scene leaves us without any clear-cut sense of her movement away from what hurts her, along with denying us cathartic release. The final silence connects with Erika's many other silences, most of which point to the character's suffering beyond that which can be musically or verbally expressed.

Chion has written at length about how silence can be paradoxically empowering for a character because it lends them a degree of inscrutable authority (as with the young deaf-mute adolescent boy in *Out of the Past* [1947], for example [1999, 96–97]). However, Erika's muteness in many scenes of *The Piano Teacher* does not empower her except insofar as it makes us potentially work harder to understand her. Her muteness implies what evades and what oppresses her, as well as underlining the deep levels of repression that come with her sadomasochistic desires: in contrast with Jelinek's text, her silences always seem less about conscious control than having to hold herself in. She feels what she is not meant to feel, so she cannot speak. When she does eventually attempt to express what she wants to Walter through the letter, her own words become his warped justification for raping her. She lies silently on the floor as Walter

FIGURE 5.3 While Walter rapes her, Erika only whispers "please stop" once. Her face is a fixed expression that suggests passive resignation as well as death-in-life.

pushes his body into her (see Figure 5.3). He chooses to interpret her silence as submission, but the camera's steady focus on her unmoving face prompts us to perceive it as a death-in-life. Erika's silence, and the lack of non-diegetic music to heighten or underscore the action, makes the scene especially raw. This gives the film a special claim to reality too: rather than providing us with a fantasy of the female protagonist's strength or support, it makes us confront her unending powerlessness. The mentioning of silence in Jelinek's text is now the *experience* of a lost voice, and the palpable absence of sound that is the depths of Erika's despair. The combination of the fixed camera with the absence of consolatory music reveals her agony with unmitigated clarity. Haneke will not soften any part of her suffering for us. This is a hard-nosed form of compassion.

Music to Be Feared

The Piano Teacher is connected to all Haneke's other feature films through its numerous silences. That said, the silences are "louder" due to the abundance of music in many scenes leading up to when Walter rapes Erika. Music is used sparingly in every other Haneke film, with the exception of *Caché* where there is none at all (the impact of which we explore in the next chapter). Haneke's adaptation of *The Piano Teacher* includes music by several of the composers that Jelinek's original character is enamored of: Bach, Beethoven, Chopin, and Schubert. The film title alone immediately creates expectations of aesthetic gratification, even if that is only to be encapsulated by the music as opposed to the characters' experiences. But *The Piano Teacher* eclipses musical beauty with the stark reality of Erika's lack and loss. It's as if Haneke says, "Here I give you the music I've always avoided, but I won't let you rest easy with it."

Where Jelinek's text emphasizes absent music, Haneke denies us conventional *uses* of music that would allow us to luxuriate in aesthetic pleasure. In so doing, Haneke provides a logical cinematic equivalent to the novel—given that much of the narrative revolves around piano lessons, the absence of music in the film would be implausible. However, our hearing the music Jelinek alludes to or describes in terms of Erika's psychological disturbance never brings us uncomplicated respite. Amazingly, Huppert stresses that music contains heavenly associations within the film, arguing that "it's enough to listen to a Bach concert [. . .] to make you understand that you are in the vicinity of something completely sacred (*Michael H.,* 2013).[15] She holds that *at all times* the film "is underscored by both the attraction to the sublime and, at the same time, the attraction to the obscene, to the shameful." She claims that these extreme tendencies (the "transcendental" and the "abject") "coexist in all humans" and that Erika is a product of this (*Michael H.*). Her arguments provide a neat binary that the film does not consistently provide. While *The Piano Teacher* repeatedly gestures to that which is sublime and/or transcendental through the incorporation of much-revered, canonized works of classical music, *every piece* of music is either abbreviated or cut off. Though this is fragmentation is an unavoidable part of most films featuring lengthy works of classical music, *The Piano Teacher* makes the pattern unusually obvious through many *sudden* cuts during musical performances. The film thus interrupts the solace that comes with hearing *any* familiar, harmonious, respectable, celebrated, technically impressive, and emotionally uplifting music.

Much like Jelinek's novel, Haneke's film always denies us unironic, or uncritically represented, retreats into music. One moment alludes to the special spiritual edification traditionally associated with highbrow music: the host of a private chamber recital (featuring Erika) portentously offers her guests a buffet "after sampling spiritual nourishment of such quality." But the host makes her offer in the context of our seeing her lavish apartment where several waitstaff are attending an elaborate buffet—a visual setting of excessively and anachronistically smug privilege. Walter himself speaks to Erika of such recitals as a dying part of the past. More troublingly, the location of music within a

---

[15] Willy Reimer mentions that at the 2001 Film Festival in Cannes, where *The Piano Teacher* won the Grand Prix, and awards for best actor (Benoît Magimel) and best actress (Isabelle Huppert), Huppert had a "pronouncement lettered on her back: "Si Dieu peut remercier quelqu'un, c'est bien Bach car Bach a prouvé l'existence de Dieu" [If God could thank someone, it would have to be Bach, since he has proven the existence of God]" (2007, 270). Riemer sees the physical marriage of "the sublime discourse of classical music" with "the allure of naked skin" as an "apt emblem" for Jelinek's novel, parallel to Erika's joy in music as opposed to her pain in unhappy sexual experiences (278). He thus sidesteps the manifold ironies in the text's allusions to music's sublime properties, let alone the ways in which Haneke's adaptation disallows our easy enjoyment of any aesthetic beauty.

domestic space that blocks out all sounds of the street could be read as a negative critique of Art that is separated from social reality.[16] Further, even if Erika plays assuredly well at this same recital—showcasing her composed control of technically ambitious work—there is still the discomfiting impression that the music is an ordeal for her to play.[17] As Erika moves her fingers precisely at the keyboard, under the visual scrutiny of Walter's admiringly dissecting gaze, it seems like there are too many notes for her to get through.

In other scenes, Erika herself seems frightened of music, and not only the piano pieces that Walter plays with enviable command to the delight of her Conservatory peers (though she dismisses his performances as more showy than substantial evidence of his promise). One piece by Schubert seems most compelling *and* disturbing to her: "Im Dorfe" ("In the Village") from his celebrated song cycle *Winterreise* (*Winter Journey*). *Winterreise* is based on poems by Wilhelm Müller and it focuses on the perspective of a lone man who suffers unrequited love. In "Im Dorfe," he is alienated by sounds of the world ("dogs are barking, rattling their chains") and other people who are oblivious to his suffering: while they replenish themselves with sleep, he asserts that he is "finished with all my dreams." The song ends with a question that, in the context of Schubert's entire song cycle, is as haunting as any of Haneke's silences: "Why should I linger among the sleepers?" Though the song is indisputably in D major, there is an unavoidable heaviness in the text, as well as the "oscillating piano motive that represents the barking dogs and rattling chains that are the only sounds in the dark of night" (Brown 2015, 9). Ian Bostridge describes the motive as a "sort of rumbling" that communicates an overt "sense of threat" in connection with challenging the "self-satisfied bourgeois world" (376). Though Schubert "was not an agitator or revolutionary," Bostridge claims he was "trapped within a way of living which so often frustrated his ideals. He rattled the bars of the cage" (Bostridge 2015, 375). Whether or not the music represents the composer's mindset, it certainly reflects Erika's internal life in *The Piano Teacher*. Though we only hear snippets of *Winterreise*, the film prompts us to refer to the whole, much as the extract from Alban Berg's Violin Concerto prompts the same in *The Seventh Continent*.[18]

---

[16] This point resonates with the scene we discussed from *Code Unknown* where Juliette Binoche's character auditions for the role of a wealthy woman who wishes to immune herself from the sounds of the street: the woman is considering an apartment with sound-proof walls, a plan that is critically used against her when she becomes the ideally placed victim for her would-be attacker in that same space.

[17] During this recital Erika plays a duet with an older gentleman (the fugue from Bach's Concerto for Two Keyboards, BWV 1061), but the film focuses more visual attention on her presence than his, ironically suggesting her comparative power.

[18] Similarly, Robin Wood argues that one cannot completely understand *The Piano Teacher* without access to the entirety of *Winterreise*, and he draws a parallel with the fragment of Berg's music in *The Seventh Continent* (2002, 59).

In featuring repetitions of "Im Dorfe," as well as extracts from two other songs from *Winterreise*—Der Wegweiser ("The Signpost") and "Der stürmische Morgen" ("The Stormy Morning")—Haneke provides us with the closest thing to a leitmotif structure in his films to date. The opening of "Im Dorfe" is first played by Anna Schober, the student who suffers most from Erika's pedagogical aggression, and whose position at the piano is literally taken over by her.[19] After scolding Anna with questions—"Do you have no ear for what coldness is? Or maybe you're just sloppy?"—we see Anna's body move away to be replaced by Erika's at the keyboard. This is the last in the aforementioned series of fragmented lessons, intercut with the second set of opening credits [8:24–9:22]. The initial absence of their faces, until after Erika has begun playing, conveys the kind of dispassionate coolness with which she asserts her dominance. When Erika begins the piece herself, she plays in a much more calculated way, ending each of the opening iterations of the main piano motif with precisely clipped notes that require the swift removal of her hands from the keyboard. Her implication that coldness is a feeling to be thus *played* resonates with the whole of Schubert's song cycle: Müller's poetic text repeatedly stresses the coldness of the world as the speaker perceives it, both in tangible terms of the natural world, and in symbolic terms of others being closed off to his pain. Erika's emphasis on playing the piano to evoke coldness aligns her with Müller's speaker. The fact that she speaks the singer's lines from "Im Dorfe" over both Anna's and her own playing further reinforces this alignment.

Schubert's song cycle is among the most poignant and revered of his well-known works.[20] Ironically, *The Piano Teacher* shows Erika at a sex shop when "Im Dorfe" reenters the film. She is watching a pornographic video in a private booth, and deeply breathing into a discarded tissue containing a stranger's ejaculate [25:49]. "Im Dorfe" begins moments before the film cuts from the sex shop to show Erika supervising Anna's practicing the song with the baritone. The sound advance thus connects Schubert's music with a primal sort of sexual act that is represented as repugnant and desperate. The image of Erika reduced to basic bodily desire, as opposed to her being a conduit for great Art, makes the singer's first line comically *and* tragically ironic, an extreme kind of discordance: "I've reached the end of dreams."[21] The baritone necessarily

---

[19] Freedman notes how Anna Schober may be Jewish because her facial features seem "made up to seem stereotypically Semitic," by contrast with Anna Sigalevitch's appearance in other films, and that Walter (Benoît Magimel) looks "stereotypically Aryan" by comparison (2012, 21). This connects with his reading of the film in relation to Adorno's most famous aphorism against Art for Art's sake: "To write poetry after Auschwitz is barbaric" (18).

[20] As sublime as the music makes a death-in-life that comes with unrequited love, it is associated with actual death in several ways: Schubert was reviewing proofs of some of the songs just weeks before he died, Müller died before he heard the songs, Müller's poems were dedicated to the composer Carl Maria von Weber who had died by the time Schubert read them, and Schubert knew that he was dying of syphilis as he wrote the music. For more on all this, see Service (2010), and McKay (2009).

[21] There are many other darkly comic elements of the film: for more on its mixed tone, see Brown (2005).

"I've reached the end of dreams."

FIGURE 5.4 The baritone sings about reaching the end of his dreams directly after we see Erika watching a pornographic video and breathing in a stranger's ejaculate, ironically connecting her dirty private life with the canonized music of unrequited love.

contorts his face to hold the vocal line with few breaks for breath (see Figure 5.4). Unlike the piano part that is first shaped by the dominant motif alternating with rests, the vocal line contains much longer phrases that carry over the piano's rests: musically, this offsets the brokenness of the piano part with a legato vocal harmony, and it makes significant demands of the singer's stamina. The strain we see on his face is a visual reminder that, despite its beauty, the song is about pain.[22]

All of Müller's poetic text for Schubert's songs resonates with Erika's private grief. Taking the twenty-four songs in turn, each one presents us with crystalline impressions of a turbulent natural world, and each one reveals part of a never-ending struggle through the grief of unrequited love. Celia Sgroi's English translation of Müller's poems (2005) relays numerous poignant details, rather like the numerous references to music and silence that accumulate within Jelinek's text.[23] The song cycle is a journey through darkness with a mocking wind, a burning heart and frozen tears, dead flowers and depths of night, snowflakes "thirstily" absorbing tears, an untamed river and a raging torrent,

---

[22] Walter interrupts this rehearsal of "Im Dorfe" and, after Erika angrily sends him away, she instructs her students to carry on with "Der stürmische Morgen" before he has even left the room—the music punctuates the emotional "storm" that he brings into Erika's life, and at this point it rather playfully underlines his power over her.

[23] When referencing Müller's text as included in Haneke's film, we quote the exact subtitles by Simon John for the Kino DVD. Any other words from, or descriptions of, this text refer to Sgroi's translation.

crows hurling chunks of snow and ice, deepest mountain chasms, an inhospitable road and burning limbs, ravens shrieking on the roof, sluggish feet, a questioning heart, fear of the grave, a crow circling the speaker's head, falling hopes like autumnal leaves, a sky of fiery red flames around tatters of clouds, light that is mere illusion, snowy mountaintops, a graveyard, snow flying in the speaker's face, stubborn suns in the sky, and an old man barefoot on the ice. The whole cycle honors the single speaker's perspective and, as hard as this is, it therefore never veers away from his need to express. This is an aesthetic world away from the repression that Erika embodies. So, she maintains a strange relationship with the music: it does and does not represent who she is.

Though the despair of Schubert's singer repeatedly evokes Erika's state of mind, his baritone voice could literally belong to Walter, thus pointing to the cathartic release that she never has. Moreover, Erika is largely focused on teaching the music to Anna Schober, rather than anticipating the performance of it herself. Anna memorably plays it in rehearsal when Walter has soothed her nerves after a bout of diarrhea makes her shamefully late [57:12–58:07]. Erica watches Walter cajole Anna from afar, until she hears Anna's delighted laughter reverberate across the auditorium. The point of audition stays with Erika, and we can guess that Anna and Walter share a private joke at her expense.[24] Nevertheless, Erika stays to hear some of the rehearsal. Anna's laughter sounds like nothing else in the film, and it amplifies the lack of uncomplicated joy in every other scene of *The Piano Teacher* [56:35–56:40]. She then plays her part without mistakes, though with less assuredness than Erika demonstrates in the expository lesson sequence ending with "Im Dorfe." Still, there is a perceptibly new boldness to Anna's playing, which is partly attributable to Walter's jovial presence by her side (as page-turner, as well as comforter).

In comparison with Erika's clipped playing style, Anna's comparatively soft approach to playing "Im Dorfe" (letting the notes linger a little over rests, rather than abruptly cutting them off), and the mellifluous pleasantness of the baritone's voice, belies the troubling suggestiveness of the song's poetic text. Equally, though we cannot help hearing the beauty of the baritone line, we have just witnessed the unnamed singer (played by Thomas Weinhappel) almost refusing to rehearse with Anna when she tearfully arrived late—so, there is a callousness about him as the physical source of the song. Nina Hutchinson (2003) even argues that the baritone's "egocentric disregard" for Anna's anxiety reflects "everything that is perverted and unforgiving about the institutional Viennese music academy, and perhaps the aims of repressive culture in general." It is therefore all the more ironic that he sings Schubert's affective music

---

[24] Chion gives two meanings for "the point of audition" as an aural parallel to the visual point of view: "a spatial sense," and "a subjective sense" (1994, 90). Both these senses apply to this example—we hear Anna's laughter as if we are in Erika's physical space, along with being invited to hear the joke as she is emotionally offended by it.

so capably and coercively. "Im Dorfe" is about a man who perceives the world as an extension of his suffering, and in this scene Erika recognizes the song as an extension of *her* pain, along with watching Anna enjoy a comparatively easy intimacy with Walter at the piano. An atypically long medium close-up allows us to perceive the tears that she can barely suppress while she listens to the music (see Figure 5.5). We watch her absorbing the song:

Dogs are barking.
Rattling their chains.
People are sleeping in their beds.
Dreaming of what they don't have,
Replenished of good and bad.

With the line "Dreaming of what they don't have," Erika slightly winces, her eyes moistening with what seems like a sudden comprehension of the song as a reflection of herself. Moments later, after the next strangely equivocal line "replenished of good and bad," she suddenly leaves the rehearsal, turning her back to camera and thus to us—a visual motif of the film that makes sonic cues all the more significant for giving us "access" to her. Because Erika has remained quite still in a formidable effort to control her response to the music up to this point, her sudden movement is all the more striking. She descends stairs to the cloakroom, sits up on a bench with her back to camera, and rubs her ear (see Figure 5.6). The visual message is that she has to soothe herself immediately after what she has heard, both physically and symbolically. Though her back is to camera so we cannot see her face, her gesture is thus eloquent. Moments later, she commits her most viciously premeditated act. She sits contemplating the coats for a few moments before breaking a

"*Dreaming of what they don't have,*

FIGURE 5.5 Erika is moved by "Im Dorfe," though she visibly restrains her reaction.

FIGURE 5.6 Erika rubs her ear, as if trying to remove the aural traces of "Im Dorfe."

glass and planting the broken pieces in Anna's coat pocket. After the sonorous beauty of "Im Dorfe," the sudden sterility of the sound track is marked here—Erika's footsteps, stretching, breathing, and placing the glass in Anna's coat are all relatively thin sounds that echo quietly in the uncarpeted space of the cloakroom. This relative quiet is broken with the unnervingly brittle sound of Erika's foot pressing down on the glass. This brittle sound signifies her conscious choice to harden herself.

The film suddenly makes another cut back to the rehearsal of *Winterreise* [1:00:46], and the song "Der Wegweiser," which relays the singer's even greater alienation from the world around him. Where "Im Dorfe" has the singer questioning his own slowness in leaving the village, "Der Wegweiser" has him wandering far from all inhabited places to seek out his own road of no return. Erika's re-entrance with the latter song marks the significance of her violence against Anna that newly separates her from everyone else, and perhaps from us too. With the line "Why do I avoid the roads where other travellers go?," she stealthily reenters the auditorium behind the performers and the camera pans with her movement across the seated area: her movement as the lone "traveller" visibly contrasts with the other, still audience members. With the next line ("Seek out hidden paths through snowbound rock outcrops?"), the camera pans so that it moves behind the singer whose back fleetingly, and ominously, dominates the frame with darkness (see Figure 5.7).

Erika sits alone in the middle, with empty seats all around her. So, the lyric of the song underlines what she hides that sets her apart from everyone else. The next line stresses her inability to feel remorse: "And yet, I've done nothing to make me flee my fellow men." The film cuts back to show the baritone's face on this line, underlining its immediate irony. The song makes a temporary but

"Seek out hidden paths

FIGURE 5.7 Erika takes her place back in the auditorium, physically choosing to isolate herself from the rest of the audience.

striking change from F minor to F major, suggestive of the singer's foolhardy bravado or his need for reassurance before returning to the lonely path. The jarring use of "nothing" to imply its opposite connects this moment with how "nothing" is used in Haneke's other films (anticipating our analysis of *Caché* in particular). Finally, the singer asks a question: "What is this foolish desire driving me into the wilderness?" The film cuts back to Erika, stony-faced as she was before the rehearsal, showing she has regained mastery of her public appearance. Ironically, the singer's emphasis on "foolish desire" emphasizes the reality that she can never be released from her misery (consider that the quintessential, Lacanian definition of desire relies upon the premise that the longed-for object can never be fully possessed or else desire ends).[25] The film then suddenly cuts yet again, before the end of the song, to show Walter ardently attempting to involve Erika in a conversation in the auditorium foyer [1:01:54]. Erika looks offscreen in an agitated manner, presumably in anticipation of seeing Anna's injury. The sonic texture of this new scene privileges Walter talking to Erika, but soon becomes thick with the sound of other students and conservatory faculty moving in the same space. Their conversation is interrupted by Anna's echoing scream. The scream is a sound advance before the cut to show Anna. Then we see her staring at her bloody hand (see Figure 5.8). Though Anna is shown in a long shot that makes the blood relatively indistinct, her scream and subsequent

---

[25] Desire is the never-ending continuance of lack that breeds it. To quote Žižek: "the [Lacanian] realization of desire does not consist in its being 'fulfilled,' 'fully satisfied,' it coincides rather with the reproduction of desire as such, with its circular movement" (1991, 7). For more, see Walker's *Understanding Sound Tracks through Film Theory* (255).

FIGURE 5.8 Anna stares at her own bleeding hand: her scream makes the pain of the wound on her hand palpable, even when we cannot see it from a long-shot distance.

gasps of pain, while other concerned students cautiously approach her, make her seem physically closer. This, in turn, makes Erika's verbal coldness all the more indefensibly shocking: she flatly and quickly tells Walter "the sight of blood makes me ill. Go to her. Be her brave protector" [1:02:09–1:02:21].

The clear mirroring of Erika's state in Schubert's *Winterreise* during this sequence ironically parallels innumerable sound tracks that relay characters' inner lives. Schubert's *Winterreise* tells a story of inescapable poignancy, mortality, alienation, despair, vulnerability, grief, and lost hope that matches Erika's personal journey. She projects herself onto the music, but the film does not encourage us to empathize with her in turn: consider that Anna suffers from Erika's most callous act just after Erika has nearly wept to "Im Dorfe." Consider, also, the callousness with which Erika leaves after Anna's injury, along with the film's amplifying the sound of Anna's pain. So, *The Piano Teacher* is haunted by what it could have been, parallel to the ways that Erika is plagued by the dreams she has lost. Much like the film reconfigures details and patterns of Jelinek's text, it places Schubert's songs in a newly disturbing narrative context. It uses the songs to suggest the kind of journey that Erika may be taking in her head, a story of never-ending desire and pain, *and* to evoke the kind of production that it refuses to be: unlike Schubert's music, *The Piano Teacher* makes it impossible for us to revel in any beautiful expressions of grief. We cannot help perceiving the danger of Erika's psychological brokenness signified by the broken glass, and paralleled by the sonic breakages of hard cuts as well as the fragmented rehearsal of the song. These pieces of the film combine to disallow us the luxury of losing ourselves in any affect. The Romantic music is de-Romanticized.

Parodying Melodrama

Just as *The Piano Teacher* recontextualizes and ironizes Romantic music, it works against the most seductive sonic conventions of Classical Hollywood melodrama. Within that genre, music typically relays the lead female's subjective and emotional experience by recalling the heightened excesses of Wagnerian and other nineteenth-century operatic works. The music for melodramas is dominated by lush, orchestral, and string-led extremities. Such music is so recognizable that Claudia Gorbman has famously argued that it identifies the woman on screen for us, making her a perceivable presence even if we are not looking at the screen: "It is as if the emotional excess of this presence must find its outlet in the euphony of a string orchestra" (1987, 80).

At first glance, any connections with Classical Hollywood melodrama might seem tenuous, but the story of *The Piano Teacher* incorporates numerous semantic elements of the genre: it focuses on dire circumstances, evokes implosive intensity with every scene, uses the domestic sphere as a key place of psychological disturbance, dwells on its protagonist's excessive desires and feelings that can barely be understood by others, features themes of female sexuality as well as sexual violence, and uses the central family to represent social realities on a broad scale (Erika and her mother represent the repressed hostility of Vienna specifically, and the nastiness suppressed within apparently civilized contexts more generally).[26] But just as *The Piano Teacher* raises the possibility of being melodrama at every turn, it thwarts our expectations of what we will therefore experience. This is clearest through the melodramatic scoring that it knowingly withholds from us.

Reflecting back on *Imitation of Life*, when the female protagonist of a Classical melodrama is martyred, victimized, chastised, and/or socially condemned, music often rushes to her side. Non-diegetic scores, in particular, console us with a reinforcement of her feeling, giving that same feeling a level of vindication. This even happens in male-centered melodramas of the 1950s like *Bigger Than Life* (1956). Consider, for example, the scene in which the female protagonist, Lou, sees off her increasingly pathological husband, Ed, to hospital. In a scene from the exposition, Ed has become prone to psychotic episodes and extreme pain due to his overuse of the cortisone treatment prescribed by his doctor. Before he becomes despotic as a result of this medication, and tyrannically threatens to kill his young son Richie, Ed acknowledges he needs medical help. As a friend drives Ed away to be hospitalized, Lou stands with Richie, watching him

---

[26] For more on defining the broad concept of melodrama and so-called women's films (beyond the scope of this chapter), see Hayward (2006, 236–248). For more on a Brechtian application of melodrama to Haneke's work, see Metelmann (2010). And for a different genre-based interpretation of the film as it revisionistically resonates with horrors and pornographic films, see Gural-Migdal and Chareyron (2009).

FIGURE 5.9 Barbara Rush expresses her deep distress, but in a visually contained, beautiful way that is heightened by Raksin's music.

leave. Suddenly she realizes she has forgotten to give Ed his slippers, so she rushes back into the house to fetch them. She then watches Ed leave, before she can give him his slippers, with a grief-stricken face (see Figure 5.9). This small domestic detail signifies the comfort and warmth that Lou wishes for her husband, and her dogged devotion to him, despite his newly erratic behavior. Though the narrative therefore stresses the subservient position of a woman determined to love her husband whatever his condition and however he treats her and their child, David Raksin's musical score for this scene puts Lou's emotional life first, punctuating her distress with a moving musical expansion of Barbara Rush's performance. Her lines are simple enough: "Oh, his slippers!" she cries to Richie, and "Ed!" she feebly calls out to the car leaving the curbside. Her face is trembling with *contained* emotion, as is typical of the era during which *Bigger Than Life* was made. The woman's face, even in distress, is expressive but never contorted or visually crumpled to the extent that it becomes ugly. Raksin's music, however, fully expresses Lou's feeling. By masking this scene we can see that Rush's visual performance is one of sadness and agitation, but also one of deep, visible control. However, the combined impact of seeing her face *with* Raksin's non-diegetic music reveals the film's overall emphasis on her feeling. The specific cue that we hear during this scene incorporates variations on a musical theme associated with Lou and Ed's marriage, and this is all the more moving as we are watching Lou suddenly alone with her son while Ed is driven away from her [15:44–16:44]. As Lou turns away to go inside, and Richie quietly closes the door, the strings surge with a poignant crescendo, underscoring her loss.

Raksin's cue serves several particular functions that are representative of scoring for Classical melodramas. The music:

- speaks for the woman and becomes her "voice";
- signifies the woman's excess of emotion beyond what she actually says;
- enfolds us in a wash of overwhelming affect that coercively encourages us to emotionally respond to the woman's plight, even if this might be against our will;

- risks the possibility of being heard as risible extremity because it refuses to downplay the woman's feelings;
- places us within a generic space and primes us for a generic form of surrender;
- amplifies the emotive power of anything we see onscreen *and* anything implied by it (here, the desperation Lou feels as she says goodbye to her deeply disturbed husband in the presence of their young son);
- lends a level of orchestral grandeur to the woman's suffering;
- contains certain formal properties, such as a thickening texture and rising dynamics, that can be immediately recognized for their poignancy;
- provides catharsis in that the woman's interior life has some outlet, even if she cannot fully or diegetically express herself.

In short, though the woman feels inadequate and alone, the music of melodrama allows us to perceive an expressive world that fully recognizes the scale of her feeling *and* the significance of her experience.

In the first book-length study of music for Classical film melodramas, Heather Laing writes of women who are both empowered yet trapped by the conventions of scoring for melodramas. Because the music tends to be non-diegetic while it honors the socially enforced limits upon the woman's free expression, such music suggests that only by stepping outside the world (or at least the film's diegesis) can the woman be fully represented—for Laing, the female protagonist of melodrama is thus "the most powerful and the most powerless" (2007, 24). However, Raksin's score for *Bigger Than Life* succeeds as a somewhat subversive elevation of the woman's presence. Even if Lou is disempowered onscreen, the music encourages our acknowledgment of all she feels and enforces our respectful sympathy with her. The same could be said for the music in the most celebrated female-centered melodramas directed by Douglas Sirk—along with *Imitation of Life, Magnificent Obsession* (1954) and *All That Heaven Allows* (1955) feature thickly textured orchestral music by Frank Skinner with such elevating purpose.

The music from *Bigger Than Life* might seem too obviously representative, so much so that everything it does is easily taken for granted. But listening to *The Piano Teacher* teaches us how to hear such music better. By withholding this kind of music from us, even as it narratively resonates with many melodramas that precede it, *The Piano Teacher* forces us to confront a comparatively harsh truth of the female protagonist's aloneness.[27] This is clear through the

---

[27] For more on *The Piano Teacher* as it manipulates generic melodramatic norms, including themes of repression and female masochism, and visual inversions of expectation (with a "restrained palette" rather than "lavish color," for example), see Wheatley (2009, 118–120, 125). Loren and Metelmann also explore ironic visual contrasts between the films of Douglas Sirk and *The Piano Teacher* (2013, 74–75), as well as *The Piano Teacher*'s interrogation of melodramatic binaries (especially between male scopophilia and female masochism) (2013, 77).

FIGURE 5.10 Walter playfully prepares to leave Erika, stretching his body with physical confidence that emphasizes his new, surprising dominance within the scene.

ending of a scene that ironically parallels the one we just discussed from *Bigger Than Life*. Here again, the female protagonist watches the man she is devoted to, perhaps at all costs, leave. In the lead-up to his exit, Erika has attempted to gain sexual mastery over Walter by touching him, sometimes cruelly. She uses her hand and mouth to stimulate him only to withdraw physically from him as he approaches orgasm. In this context, it is surprising when the scene shows him leaving with what seems suddenly like the upper hand (see Figure 5.10). The camera is positioned close to Erika's head, looking at Walter with her as he jovially says, "Don't be so serious pretty lady." He thus undermines her ped-agogical and sexual power over him by presumptuously instructing her, and by condescendingly referring to her looks. As he prepares to leave, we cannot see Erika's face [1:12:32–1:13:04].

In a Classical Hollywood melodrama, our not seeing the female protago-nist's face would be mediated by music that communicated her inner life, as when Raksin's music crescendos after Lou turns her face away from the cam-era. For another representative example, there is the way that *Now, Voyager* (1942) introduces its main character, Charlotte: the film gives a close-up of her hands rather than her face, an ironic precursor to how *The Piano Teacher* often shows just Erika's hands at the keyboard. In *Now, Voyager*, however, the delay to reveal Charlotte's face is both marked and compensated for by the *forte* cue by Max Steiner that primes us to sympathetically perceive her. We hear Charlotte's mother cruelly lamenting her very existence to a psychiatrist she has enlisted to prevent her daughter's seemingly imminent mental breakdown. The camera moves decidedly away from her mother, and up the stairs, searching for Charlotte. Much as the camera moves to and for Charlotte, the accompanying

FIGURE 5.11 Erika passively, silently watches Walter literally run away from her.

music moves us to understand the significance of her being so cruelly treated as well as preparing us for her potential beauty *even before we see her face* or can form any visual judgment of her. We might even perceive that the music's familiarly gorgeous aesthetic contours anticipate the visual transformation of Charlotte into a recognizably iconic presence, in keeping with Bette Davis's star power.

There is no such music for Erika. Instead, she silently watches Walter, seemingly powerless to interrupt him as he condescendingly speaks to her, and as he makes several athletic movements as if warming up for a sports game. For several seconds he jogs on the spot while exhaling with the sort of manic energy associated with a boxer about to fight in the ring. Then he runs out of the scene while she watches him, not speaking and barely moving, reduced to complete passivity (see Figure 5.11). In a rule-following melodrama there would surely be music to represent the agony of this moment for Erika, and to compensate for our not seeing her face. The music would elevate her experience, and thus supersede the ugly elements of the scene we just saw. Ironically, the only music we hear is the dulled sound of students practicing Bach's Brandenburg Concerto No. 4 in G Major, the anempathetically harmonious lightness of which belies the pain of the scene for Erika. As Lisa Coulthard writes, the Bach of this scene playing in the background ironically gives the "effect of a kind of lavatory Muzak" (2011c, 78) while at the same time "we can hear the Foley edits of body, skin, and mouth sounds at a disturbingly loud volume" (78). Here and elsewhere in *The Piano Teacher*, Haneke's avoidance of conventional music has everything to do with his commitment to representing reality responsibly. A woman like Erika, growing older, having failed at professional greatness, and without a family, is not recognized by the world around her—so why, we might ask, should music tell a lie of giving her power?

An Unconventional Musician-Focused Drama

Along with ironically recontextualizing the Romantic meanings of Schubert's *Winterreise,* and parodying Classical melodrama, *The Piano Teacher* challenges what we might expect from a musician-based drama. In other films focused on exemplary performers, the most disturbed characters find expressive *and empowering* solace in their music. In *Hilary and Jackie* (1998), for instance, Emily Watson plays the troubled genius Jacqueline du Pré whose greatest joy comes at the height of her musical prowess, emphasized by several scenes showcasing her breathtaking talent. In *Shine* (1996), the pianist David Helfgott is eventually overwhelmed by a mental breakdown, but his playing music provides enduring comfort and acclaim. His mind is broken but he leans expressively into the piano while playing the music that makes him whole. In *The Piano* (1993), we find an even more arresting contrast with *The Piano Teacher*. Here, the central character (Ada) is profoundly disempowered when her father forces her to marry a man she has never met. The shock of her consequent move from Scotland to colonial New Zealand is mediated by her great love of music. She plays her own compositions on the piano shipped with her. Her music is an anachronistic blend of styles that implies transcendence. In one pivotal scene, the man Ada comes to love (George Baines) takes her to the beach where her beloved piano has been abandoned by her new husband. When Ada plays the piano, her entire body seems to relax, and her face beams as she smilingly duets with her daughter. She is visually transformed by playing her own music too: the color palette of the film shifts from predominant blues to warmer, golden tones on her suddenly serene face [23:03–25:28]. Here, Ada experiences the moment of sublime transcendence: in such a scene, we witness the musician at one with the music, and able to find freedom through playing (see Figure 5.12). Such a scene prompts us to admire the musicianship, and become caught up in the experience of the music along with the performer—it is a recognizable trope of musician-based dramas that prompts us to be lifted up by Art along with the protagonist, no matter his/her circumstances. Such scenes suspend the progression of the narrative, as if everything halts out of deference to the musical talent that defies mortal limitations.

For an even more extreme example, there is the climax of a film released just a year after *The Piano Teacher: The Pianist* (2002). Here, the Jewish protagonist, Wladyslaw Szpilman (Adrian Brody), plays on command to a Gestapo officer who discovers him in hiding during the Second World War. In his autobiography, Szpilman makes it clear that the Nazi (Captain Wilm Hosenfeld) stated he did not intend to hurt him *before* he played (Szpilman 1999, 177). But the film takes artistic license by holding us in suspense about Szpilman's

FIGURE 5.12 While playing her beloved piano, Ada transports herself to another realm: this is the moment of sublime transcendence.

survival until after his forced performance. The equation between music and life is therefore absolute. Szpilman plays Chopin's Ballade No. 1 in G minor nervously and then breathtakingly well, earning the moment of sublime transcendence.[28] Hosenfeld witnesses this and is visibly moved, sitting down for the performance because he is humbled by it. He gives Szpilman time to transport him musically because he is transfixed by what he hears. Szpilman is terribly exposed, emotionally spent, and physically drained by his own playing, but the scene is still surely meant to gratify us. *The Pianist* uplifts the glorious power of Art in the most desperate of human circumstances, and expects our full surrender to this, forcing our inadvertant alignment with the Nazi who cannot help surrendering to the music's power—even against his own will.

The Piano Teacher gives us the story of a woman who feels no less trapped than Szpilman, although she is not trapped by others but by her own tortured psychology. This is compounded by the sad fact that Erika never lives the moment of sublime transcendence. The physicality of Huppert's performance underlines this: where other pianist-centered films show the musician physically embodying the music, moving up and down the keyboard with sensuous flair, sometimes by showing their fingers caressing the piano keys or their feet at the pedals as well as their whole bodies moving with the performance, Huppert's bodily movements are comparatively restrained, as if she is physically resisting a surrender to the music. Not only that, but the film's visual motif of showing her hands playing "as if amputated from the body" makes them

---

[28] In actuality, Szpilman played Chopin's Nocturne in C sharp minor (Szpilman 1999, 178).

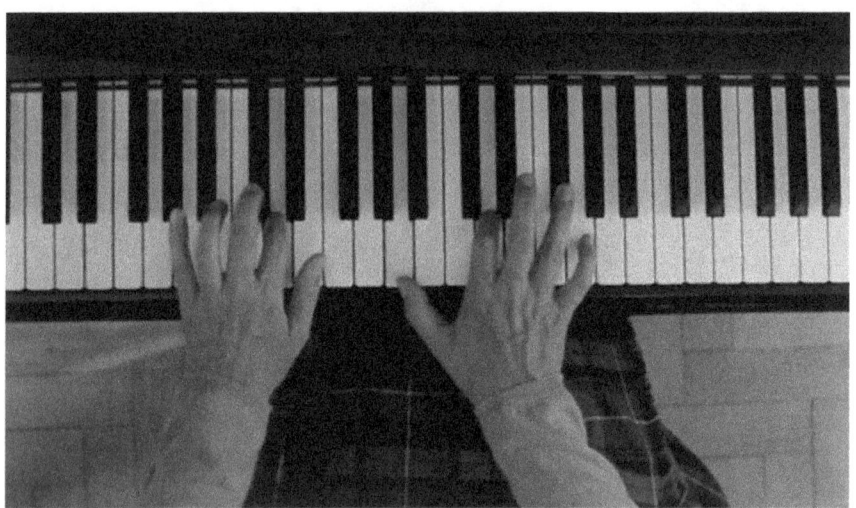

FIGURE 5.13 The first shot of Erika's hands at the piano, as if separated from the rest of her.

seem like mechanical extensions rather than conduits of feeling (Riemer 2007, 276). This means that Erika's performances never seem directly connected to her heart (see Figure 5.13). In addition, the piano often visually dominates her body, as in the early example of her standing by the window. She is not the artist in control of the music—instead, the obligation to make music overwhelms her.

Given that *The Piano Teacher* is unusually focused on a female musician, it *could* have been an empowering story for Erika. However, like Jelinek, Haneke denies us a fantasy of female triumph that would risk undermining his feminist emphasis on unending struggle. In her article on music in *The Piano*, Gorbman alludes to several celebrated films about musicians (including *Shine*), pointing out that such films tend to define the "serious musician" as "a *man* who expresses the depth of his soul through consummate knowledge, skill, and passion" (2000, 44, my emphasis). Ironically, in *The Piano Teacher*, Erika's professional musical life oppresses her to such an extent that she can find no such release. Just as she never vocally relieves herself from pain, Erika never emotionally liberates herself despite all the expressive possibilities of the music she can play. Along with the silences that stress the limits of her life, Erika's never reaching the moment of sublime transcendence means that her suffering can never be over.

Summary

The Piano Teacher fuses us with Erika's frustration by repeatedly denying us what we might expect. Obviously we cannot feel agony as she feels it, but it imposes something *like* her experience on us. As shocking as Jelinek's novel is, and as packed with attention to vile possiblities, sensorial disgust, tortured meanderings, and darkly suppressed truths as it is, there is something about perceiving the music that is not enough for Erika, being subjected to her silences and the silences around her, hearing the noises that violently define her and her hostile world, as well as seeing Erika's emotional and physical pain unmediated by a softening sound track, that makes the film impactful on a different, more physical level.

The film is an adaptation in many ways, drawing most directly from Jelinek's novel, along with combining elements of well-established film genres (including melodramas and musician-based dramas), which it knowingly invokes in order to frustrate our expectations. It adapts the meaning of Schubert's *Winterreise* songs in piecemeal and ironic terms, but without giving us the satisfaction of hearing the entire cycle or even a whole song. The snippets of songs reflect Erika's inner life, but without providing comfort: every fragment is played in a context that amplifies her alienation.

The Piano Teacher is meant to be an aurally destabilizing experience. This goes hand in hand with Haneke's critical approach to the pretentions of High Art, his commitment to representing truth, and his Brechtian insistence on creating films that prompt our aural alertness to every detail of their construction along with being affectively unique. Erika stabbing herself is the Gestic moment, the extreme concentration of all the film's energies in one unforgettably horrible act for which there is no vocal or cathartic release. Yet the silence that follows could be read as a positively definitive act of compassion: the film demands that we stay with her suffering instead of giving us the reassuring sonic escape that the character herself never enjoys.

6

Caché

THE POSTCOLONIAL RESONANCE OF SILENCES
AND SAYING "NOTHING"

Can a sound track force our confrontation with a painful postcolonial history? What silences of a film can have macrocosmic significance? When does
the complete absence of music become a crucial part of a film's political power?
What sonic patterns awaken us to the reality of broken societies in our world?
How can the smallest unit of speech, just one word ("nothing"), be an aural
motif that resonates throughout a film, and a director's work, as well as having immense political significance? When can an inaudible conversation be a
source of hope? These questions drive this postcolonial analysis of *Caché* as
it represents the legacy of France's colonial history with Algeria, demanding
that we rehear this past and the related racial inequalities that endure. We shall
explore how and why *Caché* employs extremely noticeable sonic patterns of
verbal ellipses, silences, and absent music to enforce themes of repression, guilt,
shame, denial, and loss. These themes define the lives of the central characters,
and everything we hear comes from their diegetic space, but *Caché* reverberates
far beyond them—the characters are like tuning forks for perceiving a whole
world "out of tune."

The Backstory: A Silenced History

Haneke was inspired to make *Caché* after learning about the 1961 police massacre of Algerians in a documentary titled *Drowning by Bullets/Une journée
portée disparue* (Philip Brooks and Alan Hayling, 1992). The massacre took
place toward the end of the Algerian War for Independence (1954–1962).
Maurice Papon, then head of the Parisian police, led an unprovoked attack
on thirty thousand pro-FLN (National Liberation Front/*Front de Libération
Nationale*) demonstrators that culminated in approximately two hundred of

them being "shot or thrown into the Seine."[1] Papon then worked on a govern-
mentally enforced cover-up to convince most of the French press that Algerians
had precipitated the massacre by firing on police (Kline 168).[2] Consequently,
as Haneke himself says, the massacre "wasn't mentioned for four decades"
(Crowley 2010, 267).[3] In 1999, Papon was convicted of crimes against humanity during the Vichy regime, and his trial included documents and eyewitness
accounts that *also* exposed his "active role in what is now perceived to have
been a brutal massacre of a peaceful demonstration" (Roderick 2011, 230).
Surprisingly, when Haneke saw *Drowning by Bullets* on the Franco-German
channel Arte on October 17, 2001 (Crowley 268), most French people were
still unaware of the massacre. Though Haneke is at pains to emphasize the collective guilt in *any* country, especially in his interviews about this film (Porton
2005, 50), *Caché* most explicitly resonates with this particular example of
suppressed truth.

Along with explicitly referencing the Paris massacre of October 1961,
Caché taps into the broader history of France's suppressed colonial guilt—this
extends back to the French invasion of Algeria in 1830 and the long, violent,
and complicated ensuing process of colonization until Algeria finally gained
back independence in 1962. The importance of *Caché* is also very much of the
present. As Cybelle H. McFadden writes, both France and Algeria "*have yet
to detangle the cultural ties that one hundred and thirty-two years of colonial
occupation produced*" (2009, 112, my emphasis). She cites the failure to inte-
grate "French citizens of Algerian descent, specifically children, grandchildren,
and great grandchildren of Algerian immigrants who came to work in France
during the 1960s and '70s" (112). Alex Lykidis explains that many Algerian and
other immigrants were especially encouraged to enter France "to fuel [postwar]
reconstruction and growth" from 1945 and 1970 (2010, 463). He says these
immigrants were largely "invisible" (or, we might say, "hidden") in French
society, but during the economic downturn of the 1970s immigrants suddenly
became more visible as "social problems and [perceived] threats to national
security" (457). By the 1990s, immigration was presented by the government
and its opponents as "a threat to national cohesion, national identity, and the
security of national borders" (Lykidis, 458). By extension, multiculturalism
became attached to insecurity due to a widespread perception of there being

---

[1] This is Haneke's phrase (Crowley 2010, 267). On 17 October 2001 a commemorative plaque for
the Algerians who died was placed on the Pont Saint-Michel (Roderick 2011, 230). Because accounts of
the numbers killed vary, the words on the plaque are simply "In memory of the many Algerians killed
during the bloody repression of the peaceful demonstration of 17 October 1961."

[2] This massacre is graphically represented, along with evidence of the cover-up in *Nuit noire* (Alain
Tasma, 2005), a television movie released the same year as *Caché*. For more on other films documenting
the massacre and the related cover-up, see Ranjana Khanna (2007).

[3] Penney provides a fuller account of the October 1961 massacre in relation to his psychoanalytic
reading of *Caché* (2010, 77–78).

more immigrants, though the number had remained "relatively stable since the 1970s" (Lykidis, 458). Like McFadden, Lykidis attaches the increasing unrest over immigrants to the increasing prominence of children and grandchildren of immigrants (459). *Caché* represents these widespread, historically loaded patterns of prejudice in the hostility of its main white character: Georges. Though played by an internationally revered, and charismatic French star (Daniel Auteuil), Georges is a shockingly unsympathetic character. He is particularly condemnable in his aggression toward a man named Majid, the son of Algerian immigrant workers who were killed in the massacre of October 1961.[4] Georges also unleashes aggression at Majid's son in several confrontational scenes that show how racial prejudice endures.

The entire form of *Caché* brings the history of colonial oppression into the present. The massacre of 1961, a vital part of the main characters' shared past, is connected with various levels of suppression—silenced people, silenced remembering, and silenced attempts to recover the truth. *Caché* is, in turn, a film largely structured by different forms of silence: quiet moments, pared-down sonic textures, noticeable pauses, unspoken implications, and absent music. The film is thus sonically structured to remind us of that which is underrepresented historically *and* cinematically.[5] *Caché* uses its sound track to most affectively prompt our alertness to the white privilege enjoyed by Georges in contrast with the Algerian oppression embodied by Majid. The sound track also demands we fill in what neither Georges nor Majid can say—Georges being limited by his own repression, guilt, shame, and denial; and Majid being limited by his own marginal position as well as his greater comprehension of that which exceeds speech.

Aural Patterns

Caché shares several aural patterns with *The Seventh Continent, Funny Games, Code Unknown,* and *The Piano Teacher*, including: sounds that change *on* the cut and thus deny us a sutured experience; offscreen voices that delay or withhold from us the phantasmatic possibilities of cinema, and loaded silences that demand attention. However, the overall sonic experience of *Caché* is more subtly unsettling. From the start, the film *quietly* alerts us to the sounds that lie to us, as well as those that exert transformative power over the image. Therefore,

---

[4] Majid is played by a lesser-known actor, Maurice Bénichou, who plays kindly old men showing rare compassion and moral strength in both *Time of the Wolf* and *Code Unknown*. This intertextuality primes those familiar with Haneke's work to read his character sympathetically, especially when Georges is comparatively aggressive toward him.

[5] In this way, *Caché* resonates with *The Battle of Algiers* (1966) as a renowned representation of colonial rule that subversively sides with the colonized. T. Jefferson Kline (2010) fully explores the connections between *Caché* and *The Battle of Algiers* as well as a long French literary history of representing violence against Arabs.

along with being comparatively subdued, the film requires that we be even more aurally alert.

The first sounds of *Caché* accompany the first long take of the street where Georges lives with his wife (Anne) and his son (Pierrot). The sound track seems to be entirely diegetic, as is typical of Haneke: we hear cars in the distance, a cyclist passing by, a slight breeze blowing, and the quiet calls of birds. If we listen more closely, we realize that the birdsong is out of place in the built-up residential street: it echoes, as if across wide spaces, whereas the *mise-en-scène* is filled with lines of buildings that cut across the frame. Later, the film attaches this sound to the place where Georges and Majid grew up: the film's second-to-last long take, showing Majid forcibly taken from the country home of his foster parents, features a more extended use of birdsong.[6] Thus, from the beginning, the diegetic sound both belongs *and* does not belong to the onscreen space, anticipating an entirely different location, and subtly suggesting a connection between the two. We later understand that Georges' life cannot (nor should) be separated from the past he shares with Majid: Georges' parents decided to adopt Majid, whose parents were killed in the French police massacre of October 1961, but Georges told vicious lies that forced them to send Majid away. More specifically, Georges told Majid to kill a rooster that his father "wanted dead," and then told his parents Majid decapitated the bird just to scare him.[7] The birdsong we hear at the start of *Caché* may ironically allude to this dead bird, along with being a poignant evocation of the country life that Majid lost due to Georges' actions against him.

The first shot of *Caché*, almost three minutes in real time, initially appears to be a take of unmediated reality. But this impression is disrupted when the anxious voices of the two main white characters (Georges and Anne) intrude upon the sound track: "Well?" he asks; "Nothing" she responds [2:36–2:40]. At this point, we understand that we are not watching a scene as it happens, but a recording as it is viewed by the characters within the diegesis. The opening take—which hitherto appeared to be an establishing *and* objective shot—is thus

---

[6] Elizabeth Ezra and Jane Sillers argue that the sonic connection between the opening and closing shots allows us to perceive the absence of "Majid's screams" in the former (2007b, 220). This connection also retrospectively suggests that the opening sound track is subjectively indicative of Georges' suppressed guilty memory.

[7] This parallels some unsettling birdsong in the original *Funny Games*. For instance, there is the first interchange between Anna and Peter, in which the initially quick back-and-forth of their dialogue is broken up by awkward, and increasingly hostile, pauses until his exit [10:57–16:27]. Ironically, we frequently hear birds outside during this and other conversations of the film during the day, reinforcing the family's (and initially our) illusion of being in a safe country space. In an early scene of *71 Fragments Based on a Chronology of Chance* showing a thief stealing guns (including the killer's weapon for the climactic mass shooting), there is the quiet and intermittent sound of birds chirping—the aural detail suggests a disturbing thematic clash between the beauty of nature and the violent capabilities of humankind. The wildlife comes from no visible source, and its aural presence is all the more marked for being overtly artificial [8:40–10:01]. The significance of ominously ironic birdsong is even more marked in *The White Ribbon* as it relates to the terror of the Real—we explore this further in due course.

revealed to be a subjective, and easily manipulated, construction (see Figures 6.1 and 6.2). Not long thereafter, tracking marks appear over the image of the residential street, indicating that someone is pressing fast-forward on a videotape. So begins the film's unsettling emphasis on the indeterminacy of the image and

FIGURE 6.1 The deceptive opening shot of *Caché*. The attentive viewer may notice the street sign "rue des iris" on the right, a detail that provocatively asks us to *see* more than the "nothing" perceived by Georges and Anne. This street sign is more visible in several subsequent shots within the first sequence (see Figure 6.2).

FIGURE 6.2 A later shot [3:37] within the opening sequence showing Georges having stepped out on the street in search of the culprit behind the first "terrorizing" tape delivered to his home. Here the street sign "rue des iris" seems to silently mock him with his initial inability to "see" the significance of the tape.

what it signifies. *Caché*'s opening therein echoes the intrusion of Zorn's music near the beginning of *Funny Games*, disrupting our sense of the image's stability.

The intriguing strangeness of this opening immediately establishes suspense, and has led some critics to write of *Caché* as a Hitchcockian thriller like *Rear Window* (1954) (Yacowar 2006, 229). However, *Caché* is far from being a clear-cut thriller because it incorporates familiar elements of the genre in order to upset our expectations. Where the protagonist of *Rear Window* solves a murder through spying, Haneke's film leaves the mystery unsolved: indeed, the question of who sends videotapes to Georges and Anne (the first scene showing but one of several) becomes far less absorbing than the question of why they matter. Or, as Catherine Wheatley (2007) puts it, "[i]t's not the tapes themselves that constitute a threat but their unspoken significance." The tapes wind up being a MacGuffin[8] because, as Maurice Yacowar puts it, Georges is ultimately forced to "investigate himself" and to "acknowledge his own guilt" rather than discovering the perpetrator behind them (230). Much as *Funny Games* invokes the "rules" of family-in-peril thrillers only to sonically emphasize its refusal to provide us catharsis or closure, and *The Piano Teacher* echoes Classical Hollywood melodramas only to deny us the comforting consolations of an empathetic non-diegetic score, *Caché* invokes the "rules" of a thriller only to frustrate our expectations that characters will eventually speak the whole truth. In *seeming* to be generic, *Caché* quickly establishes expectations of itself as a classic realist text: a text that will, in Catherine Belsey's words, move "inevitably towards *closure* which is also disclosure, the dissolution of enigma through the re-reestablishment of order, recognizable as a reinstatement or a development of the order which is understood to have preceded the events of the story itself" (65).[9] In the end, however, *Caché* defies such generic resolution.[10] It resists resolution through many aspects of its unconventional form: uncommonly long takes from long-shot distances that lack clear points of focus, unpredictable breaks in continuity that rupture a clear-cut sense of cause and effect, and numerous narrative ellipses that resist closure even in the final frames of the film. These are all disconcerting elements of narrative construction that recur throughout Haneke's work along with the unconventional patterns of its sound track. The unconventionality of *Caché* is set apart from Haneke's other films,

---

[8] A MacGuffin is an element of narrative that is the catalyst for its narrative development but which does not matter much in itself. Alfred Hitchcock popularized the term. An example from his cinema is the robbery committed by the character played by Janet Leigh in *Psycho* (1960): after stealing money from her workplace she stays at the Bates Motel while on the run, which in turn leads to her murder and the remainder of the plot. (Mark Lawson [2006] also refers to the videotapes in *Caché* as a MacGuffin).

[9] For a full discussion of thriller conventions invoked in (and then manipulated by) *Caché*, see Helen Macallan and Andrew Plain's article for *Senses of Cinema* (2007).

[10] The anti-generic, unanswerable questions of *Caché* are widely acknowledged: Elizabeth Ezra and Jane Sillers introduce their dossier of articles on the film for *Screen* by referring to it as a "puzzling" experience that "resists attempts to read it as a puzzle to be decoded" (2007a, 211).

however, in its *complete* absence of music. This sonic extremity is a crucial part of the film's uncompromising, and far-from-generic, postcolonial engagement with history: the film creates a sense of open-endedness that relates to the never-ending legacy of colonial harm.

Absent Music

Caché begins by denying us the music that we typically expect from an opening film sequence. The insertion of music would, of course, change and narrow the interpretive possibilities of a film that confronts a painful history and then refuses to resolve it. It is the music of countless other film openings that makes the almost-silence of Haneke's opening scenes, and the start of *Caché* in particular, "deafening."[11] When the characters break the extreme quiet (with "Well?" "Nothing."), the film immediately raises even more questions than its visual elements: questions about what the first tape signifies, what inspired its making, and what its intended effect might be (in the absence of musical accompaniment or "decoding"), even before the simple question of who sent it. From the beginning, the film thus primes us to actively decode the tape's meaning, though not necessarily as its main characters do. Georges immediately assumes Majid is behind the tape's making and delivery, and reads it as a sign of Majid's aggression. The overall film prompts us, by contrast, to consider how Georges embodies a long history of "hidden" colonial violence, and to perceive how he misreads the tape because of his own buried guilt. Thus, the quiet of the film gives way to the conceptual "noise" of our actively broader comprehension.[12] If we accept Haneke's implicit challenge to fill in the blanks presented by the initially inscrutable *Caché*—to confront, for instance, the collective past represented by Georges' guilt—the film becomes "louder" than musical punctuation would perhaps allow it to be in our own minds. Thinking back to Timothy Walsh's writing on the meaningful possibilities of absences within art, Haneke inspires our imaginative engagement by making us repeatedly perceive the absent music of *Caché*.[13]

The film obliquely references its own lack of music in a key scene between Georges and his mother. This scene occurs well into *Caché*, after the plot has

---

[11] Here is an allusion back to that moment in *The Piano Teacher* when Erika confronts a teenage pupil about his looking at porn magazines. When he refuses to speak, she exclaims that "the silence is *deafening*," thus indirectly alluding to the self-consciousness with which Haneke uses silence or relative quiet as an important expressive tool.

[12] *Caché* not only taps into the devastating past between France and Algeria. It also, as Giuseppina Mecchia writes, seems "uncannily resonant" with the infamous race riots that occurred in France in November of 2005, just a few months after the film's release. The riots occurred after two young men of North African descent electrocuted themselves on an electric fence while trying to escape from French police (Mecchia 2007, 133).

[13] We incorporate a fuller discussion of Walsh's work within the chapter on *Funny Games*.

become more intriguing and terrifying, especially through images that have been anonymously delivered to Georges at home and work. The first is a sketch depicting a child with blood streaming from its neck, while the second shows a rooster with blood at its neck. Both are visual allusions to Majid's backstory. Georges' son, Pierrot, receives a postcard at school with the same image of the child with blood streaming from its mouth. (The postcard reads, "Pour Pierrot, de la part de son papa," thus pointing to Georges' guilt, though without explanation.) In addition, Georges has received the second and third videotapes: one of his street/apartment and another of his childhood home from which Majid was forcibly taken away.

By the point Georges visits his mother, his prejudicial fear has become dangerous. A few scenes earlier, the volatility with which he responds to a near-accident with a black cyclist indicates his latent, barely contained, and unconscious racism, inevitably resonating with Majid's backstory and the broader historical context of fractured race relations within France (see Figure 6.3). When he visits his mother, Georges has also irrationally and intransigently identified Majid as *the* enemy. The scene is dominated by pregnant pauses of varying lengths, repeatedly pointing to the truths that Georges cannot bring himself to acknowledge. Juliette Binoche (the "Anne" of *Caché,* as well as *Code Unknown*) speaks of how Haneke literally writes such silences *into his scripts*: "it's often written 'pause,' 'short pause,' 'long pause,' 'after-pause' [. . .] It's like music [in that] there are quarter-notes, half-notes and rests and all that is very calculated."[14] In the scene between Georges and his mother, the first scene in which Majid is mentioned by name, the numerous pauses call attention to the subtexts of repression, guilt, shame, and denial underlying everything Georges says. It is no less revealing that his mother's face immediately falls as soon as he brings up the memory of Majid (see Figure 6.4). His mother, though obviously weakened and in bad health, is willful enough to profess having forgotten the violent and regrettable history of the child she forced away. Her decision to not adopt Majid brings up the bigger question of whether France "is willing to accept the North African Other as part of a larger European family or transcultural community" (McFadden 2009, 115–116). In refusing to remember Majid, Georges' mother stands for a nation in denial of colonial oppression and its ongoing impact, and especially for the slaughtering and the silencing of Algerian innocents.

The conversation between Georges and his mother soon changes to their day-to-day news. Out of the blue, Georges' mother tells him, "I miss not hearing the piano, ever since your Dad died" and she asks Georges whether he

---

[14] Though Binoche explains that the exact pause lengths will change in the process of filming, the changes are individually agreed upon by Haneke and his actors based on new situations that organically arise in shooting. Binoche's comments come from the documentary by Yves Montmayeur on the Sony DVD release of *Caché.*

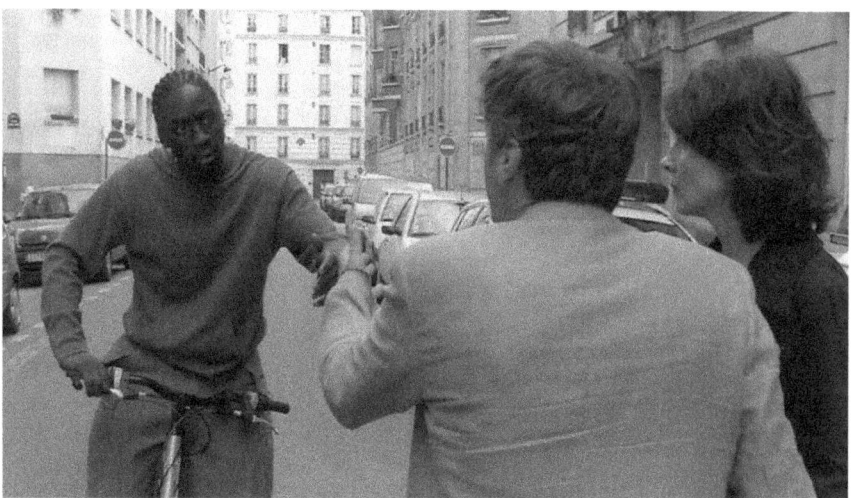

FIGURE 6.3 Georges' confrontation with an anonymous black cyclist. The positioning of the camera allows us to temporarily lose sight of Georges' face, ironically undermining his presence while he speaks.

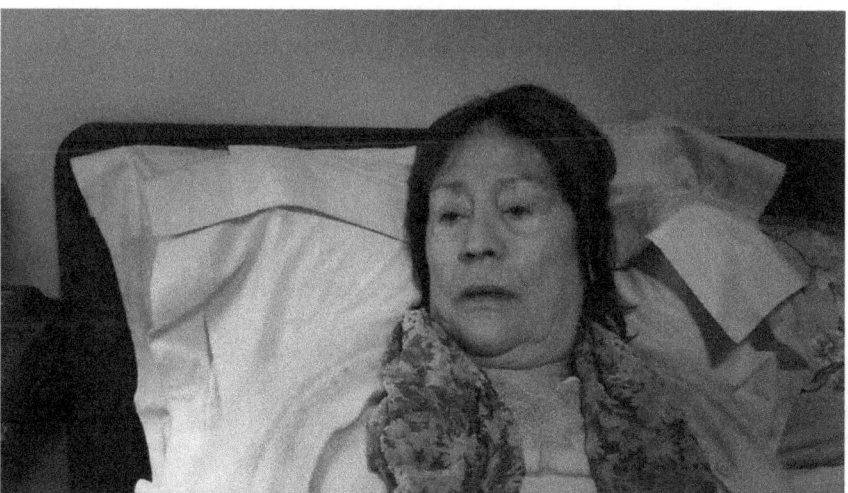

FIGURE 6.4 Georges' mother's face falls when Georges mentions Majid. "You've lost me," she says, claiming to have entirely forgotten the boy she nearly adopted.

still plays. "No," he flatly responds. Here, then, the absence of music is directly associated with actual death. At the end of the *same* conversation Georges tells his mother, "I need my bed. I'm dead." Through this closing turn of phrase, the end of Georges' making music is implicitly associated with a figurative death— a deliberate loss of consciousness that is turning away from a terrible past. Such denial is most obvious near the end of the film when, after witnessing Majid's shocking suicide, Georges takes two sleeping pills and lies down alone in the dark in a newly deafening silence.[15]

Caché calls attention to its own lack of music in that there are numerous points, in addition to the opening, at which we might consciously expect (and would typically get) some form of musical punctuation: there is no musical punctuation in the scene when Georges directly threatens Majid, nor when Majid eventually kills himself, nor when characters interact in public places where music is often heard (such as a café, a book shop, a school, a large convenience store, several residential streets), nor when individual characters (Majid, Anne, Georges) express their despairing isolation by crying in private (scenes during which we might expect a sympathetic score). The implication of this pattern is a subtly symbolic suggestion that neither society nor individuals are living "in harmony." The creatively controlled absence of music is especially noticeable during a scene where Georges' television show is being filmed. An offscreen director (another of Haneke's acousmatic voices)[16] calls out, "cut," but asks Georges and his guests to keep their seats for the credit sequence: they enact the convention of continuing to talk without being audible. This Brechtian moment robs us of conventionally affective form, reminding us that we would usually experience music to accompany the final images of such a show. In the absence of a musical buffer, the emphasis falls on the strangeness of watching Georges and his guests pretend to continue meaningful conversation, and the falsity of his friendly professional manner in contrast with his austere presence in other, more private scenes.

Rather than music reinforcing the import of what *any* character experiences or says in *Caché*, it is the silences between actions and words that stand out. The timbres of different voices—in panic, in fear, in hopelessness, in sadness, and in cold flatness—have special impact in what is often otherwise a sonic void. In the complete absence of music, all diegetic sound carries great emotive weight. Aural motifs of isolated footsteps, slamming doors, quiet nighttime sounds (solitary cars, insects, wind through leaves), echoing voices, and different kinds of weeping repeatedly communicate aloneness, alienation, and the haunting sense of individual lives existing within an unfeeling, static vacuum. There are sounds of relative privilege, such as those of Georges pouring wine and grating fresh parmesan cheese, or of Anne dishing up during a dinner party. There are sounds that further amplify the film's thematic emphasis on social inequalities, such as the monotonously unsettling, rattling sound of the

---

[15] Moments later, the quiet sound of birdsong anticipates the cut to show the flashback of Majid being forcibly taken away from Georges' family farmhouse [1:50:34]. As Murdoch Jennings writes, the sound advance "connects the two events and time periods, adding a synchronic dimension in which the present includes its own past, signifying 'the return of the repressed'" (2014, 20–21). This leads us back to the significant birdsong of the very first scene.

[16] Levin similarly mentions the pattern of acousmatic voices in the film (citing Pierrot's swimming coach who instructs him offscreen) as an important "rift between audio and visual components" (2010, 76).

van in which Majid and his son are taken into police custody after Georges wrongly accuses them of abducting Pierrot.[17] And there are isolated sounds that are truly horrific, particularly without the mediation of music: the sound of blood pumping from Majid's neck; and the sound of the decapitated rooster flailing against the ground, flapping its wings into death. The impact of so many thematically loaded diegetic sounds in *Caché* most strongly parallels *The Seventh Continent*. In both films, diegetic noises "take the place" of traditional scoring, "creating unsettling ambiences, tension and anxiety" (Macallan and Plain 2007). With *Caché* in particular, Helen Macallan and Andrew Plain argue that diegetic noises "function both as source sound and scored music. They are natural sounds behaving unnaturally." This pattern refects Haneke's overall emphasis on defamiliarizing cinematic form to renew the medium's radically political effects.

In one of the few articles focused on Haneke's use of sound, Chion argues that the absence of music in *Caché* creates the impression of "a world 'in prose,' of a dry and lucid world, in which it is forbidden to dream" (2010, 164). He says, "we can glimpse nothing that would allow us to flee from its inescapable reality, where all actions have consequences" (165). Here, Chion automatically attaches music to aesthetically pleasing dreams of escapism. Though this is not generally applicable (think of Zorn's songs in *Funny Games*, for instance), it is accurate that Haneke invokes the positive associations of music by obviously problematizing benign possibilities—much of *The Piano Teacher*, for example, relies upon our perceiving this pattern of withholding, in parallel to Erika's repressed and austere life.

Like both *The Piano Teacher* and *Funny Games, Caché* includes many noticeable "traces of other films it could have been" (Leitch 2007, 17). If *Caché* included suspenseful and/or sinister music to support Georges' reading of the videotapes, for instance, we would be cued to align ourselves with him. Equally, if compassionate and melodramatic music played when Majid was onscreen, the character would be sentimentalized and singled out, perhaps leaving us less critically cognizant of, or alert to, the far-reaching politics that make his backstory representative. The film would thus lose its Brechtian emphasis on socially motivated and historically grounded, over personal and conventionally generic, storytelling. The absence of music cues connects with other conspicuous absences within the film, especially its narrative ellipses.[18] Of course we expect certain

---

[17] After Georges has received some threatening tapes and sketches, Pierrot goes missing for a night. Georges assumes Majid's guilt without evidence and informs the police accordingly. The police then take Majid and his son into custody. Ironically, the very next morning Pierrot returns safely home, after having simply stayed the night with a school friend without thinking to inform his parents.

[18] There are numerous blatant ellipses in *Caché*: a fact almost invariably mentioned by critics and reviewers. The questions raised by these ellipses dominate the reviews of *Caché* by Paul Arthur (2005), Mark Lawson (2006), and Catherine Wheatley (2007), among others.

aspects of narrative to be left out in a thriller—but we expect such gaps to be filled in by such a narrative through its conclusion. *Caché* dupes us into believing it is a kind of familiar "whodunit" with a definable outcome including discoverable and authoritative answers, and it is especially easy for the film to disorient us because it eschews the use of music that could reassuringly suture and decode scenes, provide cohesion, aestheticize the action, and/or guide our responses.

The absence of music from the beginning of *Caché*, much like the absence of uncomplicated aural consolation in *Funny Games* and *The Piano Teacher*, generates "an anxious expectation, a palpable desire, for what is missing."[19] The noticeable absence of musical reassurance makes it an especially severe confrontation with the colonial past as it haunts the present: the quiet of the film ironically *amplifies* the disturbance it imposes on us. More positively speaking, the film interrogatively explores a history that is underrepresented in all media, and it audibly demands our involvement in that process. Early on, Anne tells Georges that the first videotape runs for "over two hours," thus making it longer than the duration of *Caché* itself: this metacinematic detail reinforces the impression of our needing to continue the process of the film by considering what its questions mean, even after it ends. It thus parallels *Code Unknown* in leading us through an open-ended effort to understand the realities of different peoples.

Georges is the example of withdrawing from the world that the film would not have us follow: in the final sequence of *Caché* he takes sleeping pills, pulls his blackout curtains closed, and climbs into bed under the covers. Crucially, though, the film does not end on Georges, but on two long takes that emphasize the presence of children in both the past and the present:[20] first, young Majid being physically forced away from his foster home, during which he screams in protest [1:50:40–1:54:01]; and second, Pierrot and his classmates quietly leaving school for the day, and Pierrot meeting Majid's son for a short, apparently affable conversation [1:54:02–1:58:05]. In the first of these long takes, we can clearly hear Majid's protests, as well as the officials scolding him to "calm down." Though we view the action from a long-shot distance, the sound track thus brings us close to everything they express (see Figure 6.5). By contrast, the final take from a similar long-shot distance does not allow us to hear anything that Pierrot and Majid's son say to each other (see Figure 6.6). Again, the absence of sound is meaningful. The film asks us to imagine what they are saying. Perhaps it even asks us what we *would have them* say. *Caché* thus ends on an invitation for us to make a new narrative line, pointing to the future.

---

[19] This is another reapplication of Walsh's words to our specific context of considering *Caché* (1992, 79).

[20] The fact that these takes are of nearly the same duration subtly but symbolically stresses the thematic importance of understanding that both the past and the present deserve equal attention, which resonates strongly from a postcolonial perspective of recognizing the lasting impact of colonialism.

FIGURE 6.5 The long shot showing Majid as a child being forcibly taken away from Georges' home by childcare authorities. Georges' parents can be seen turning away from the child's pain by re-entering their home, while Majid's shouts and screams carry across the open space.

FIGURE 6.6 The last long take, outside Pierrot's school. Pierrot and Majid's son are talking to each other inaudibly on the left-hand side.

Roy Grundmann argues that the inaudibility of the final conversation is a cop-out because it suggests a solution is possible in a "universal language" (2010a, 37). Similarly, Yacowar reads "complacency" in the final shot because, in show-ing Pierrot and Majid's son together on the school steps, it obfuscates the "count-less Arabs" who have been "denied the country's privileged education" (2006, 232). He even argues that the race riots of fall 2005 relate to this: "The newsreel footage of burning cars and looted stores seems the implicit consequence of the complacency in Haneke's last shot" (232). Loren and Metelmann perceive the last conversation as potential evidence of the boys conspiring together on the tapes, which creates "a Möbius strip, as it might be inserted metaleptically before the opening sequence" (2013, 85). On a more open-ended and positive note, Lykidis argues that the conversation between Pierrot and Majid's son "provides us with hope that the younger generation will resolve the seemingly insurmountable differences that have divided their parents" (2010, 469). Similarly, Max Silverman writes that the conversation between Pierrot and Majid's son suggests that "the colonial barriers and atavistic reflexes of previous generations may be loosening through dialogue and a new attitude to difference" (2007, 249). However we interpret the last scene, our hearing the sons' conversation would close down the story: we might hear them conspiring, or resolving to conspire, or becoming friends, or affirming their existent friendship. Any such end would shut down possibilities. Instead, *Caché* ends by inviting us to continue its own process by imagining the unheard, pushing beyond the limits of conclusion built into some of Haneke's other films.[21] The final title cards of *The Seventh Continent* close down the emotional turmoil of the film, silently and factually stating the film's basis in an actual suicide pact. *Funny Games* ends by showing us that the killers will continue: the same cycle of violence will surely repeat. *The Piano Teacher* leaves us with the horror of Erika's self-harm, a symbolic death if not a literal one, and without melodramatic catharsis. By contrast, *Caché* is more hopefully open-ended because the sons' inaudible last conversation invites us to continue creating the story and, by extension, to keep actively considering its meaningfulness. It therefore has most in common with the ending of *Code Unknown,* which focuses our attention back on the children who attempt to communicate with each other. In the final shot of *Caché*, we may therefore perceive the auteur's hold over us while the film also, paradoxically, allows for the "birth of the reader."[22] The sound track can only be completed by us, just as the legacy of colonialism *should* prompt an ongoing, unfinished, and involving conversation. This is how the politics of film form most manifestly extend to us.

A Non-Sutured Experience

Just as *Caché* replaces the scarcity of music in Haneke's other films with its complete absence, and its silences and inaudible conversations are all the "louder"

---

[21] This inaudible dialogue thus works very differently from the faux final-credit conversation of Georges and his television guests, where the absence of conventional music lays bare the artificality of Georges' professional life as graciously engaging television host. The inaudible dialogue between Majid's son and Pierrot seems to be an authentic attempt to communicate, as opposed to being forced, and its placement right *before* the final credits roll allows time for us to dwell on its greater significance.

[22] This is, of course, an allusion to the end of Roland Barthes' seminal essay, "The Death of the Author" (1977).

for that, it takes the non-suturing patterns of his other films to a polemic extreme. Where Haneke's earlier films include rare but memorable examples of diegetic music playing over several cuts (including Jennifer Rush's performance of "The Power of Love" in the scene of Evi's death in *The Seventh Continent*, the children's drumming over the final montage in *Code Unknown*, Zorn's songs while Paul stalks Georgie in *Funny Games*, or Schubert's music playing over tracking shots of Erika in *The Piano Teacher*), *Caché* features none. As Chion writes, there are no sounds that precede their corresponding images in *Caché*: "as we move from one scene to another the cut is as sudden for the ear as it is for the eye" (167). There are many points at which the sudden sonic shift *on the cut* is extremely noticeable in *Caché*, such as the cut from a quiet family dinner scene (featuring low voices, delicate sounds of utensils, and politely soft chews) to Pierrot being coached at the school swimming pool (a coach shouting commands, several boys splashing through the water, and all noises amplified by the acoustics of the large indoor space) [8:21]. There is an equally noticeable transition from Georges having coffee in a convenience store, after his having a secret confrontation with Majid, to the hubbub of Pierrot's swimming race. Georges' quiet solitariness is a brief respite after the relentless tension of the scene with Majid, but only until there is the "wake-up" shock of the cut [55:54]. The swimming race scene is filled with people cheering and clapping as the boys compete, and Anne screaming with joy when Pierrot wins. Here, the rare moment of family joy is thus compromised by an effect of aural violence. Then comes an equally sudden cut back to the relative tension of Georges' earlier conversation with Majid, now viewed by Anne and Georges from a different angle, and within a video recording [56:34]. Following the end of some dialogue we have already heard between the two men, the camera stays focused on Majid sitting alone after Georges' departure, as he slowly breaks down in tears. We hear Anne's voice say, "That's it. It runs for one hour if you want to watch how he feels." As with the first take of the film, the intrusion of her voice reframes the image, here breaking up the experience with an aural reminder of the choice to keep witnessing Majid's distress. This "break" parallels the numerous non-sutured cuts of the film. All these ruptures within the film's form parallel its thematic emphasis on lasting damage.

In a later scene, after Anne confides in her boss and friend with whom she may or may not be having an affair, and who gives her the emotionally charged physical intimacy that is lacking in her marriage (holding her hand, hugging her, and stroking her hair), the film suddenly cuts to a television *Euronews* broadcast [1:10:15]. The sudden intrusion of television news is an important motif within Haneke's oeuvre: in both *71 Fragments of a Chronology of Chance* and *Benny's Video*, television newscasters report international stories of violence and desperation with the familiarly monotonous intonations of news reportage worldwide, much like that which we hear in the radio broadcasts of *The Seventh Continent*. In *Caché*, the news stories begin with the Barbara Contini affair: after her

Italian governmental convoy was fired on by U.S. troops in Iraq, Contini called for new "rules of engagement" that would be applicable to all the occupying forces of Iraq. Then comes another story about Palestinians protesting violent attacks on their countrymen, including the image of "several bloodied bodies of Palestinians being carried past the camera" (Kline 2010, 175). The *Euronews* initially fills the screen, but then *Caché* cuts to a long shot showing Georges at a desk on the left, the television near the center of his living room, and Anne coming home on the right [1:10:58].[23] The *Euronews* keeps playing as Georges and Anne speak, the tension rising between them as they simultaneously discover Pierrot is missing (see Figures 6.7 and 6.8).[24] Anne does not even mute the television when she calls to check with one of Pierrot's friends about her son's whereabouts. Both Georges and Anne are nearly immobile in the frame while the television shows different people moving in life and being carried in death: this creates a strong compositional tension that heightens the ordinariness of Anne's tone during the phone call despite her rising concern, as well as paralleling the contrary impact of concurrent vocal lines (Georges and Anne's conversation versus the news stories). We attend to Georges and Anne "at the price of listening" to the news stories (Crowley 2010, 273). The effect might be reasonably described as polyphonic, though there is no music: like a Bach fugue, the lines of sound during this scene compete for our attention, though obviously without anything like the harmonious intricacies of such music. In addition to this, the screen image itself is fractured because our attention is divided between the main characters in the foreground and the equally-in-focus television screen in the background. Here, the non-sutured cuts of earlier sequences are thus superseded by the audiovisual brokenness within a single-take scene. This structural brokenness parallels the stories of global fractures reported by *Euronews*, the brokenness of Georges and Anne's marriage, and the brokenness of their family in Pierrot's absence. All this breakage resonates with the film's larger focus on the cross-generational divisions associated with the legacy of colonial France.

Elizabeth Ezra and Jane Sillers argue that during this scene the "conventions of bourgeois melodrama and of classical realism compel viewers to attempt to shut out news of the outside world in order to focus on the apparent domestic crisis." Further, they argue that we easily "fail to identify with (or even notice) real events" while simultaneously "identifying with Georges and Anne" even though they "are not particularly sympathetic" (2007b, 218). Such a reading fails to address the sonic strangeness of the scene as well as the centrality of

---

[23] Before Anne enters, the news stories resonate ironically with the rising agitation between Georges and her: the newscaster speaks of Contini demanding "greater openness on the subject" and the need for "the same rules of engagement."

[24] During this conversation, Georges demands to know why Anne switched off her cell phone while she was out with her boss—in other words, she was unreachable through sound, a detail that emphasizes her withdrawal from him.

FIGURE 6.7 As Anne returns home, the film does not cut to the expected close-up or medium shot to focus on her: instead, the *Euronews* remains at the center of the image.

FIGURE 6.8 Even when Anne calls her son's friend's house to begin the search for Pierrot, the television stays on: the sound of the news competes with Anne's voice, reminding us of a world beyond her apartment.

the television image that is clearly placed to prompt something more complicated than easy identification with the main characters. Though Georges and Anne are visually closer to us, the sound of the news is consistently louder. The scene forces us to perceive how *they* make the world background noise: the fact that Georges and Anne continue to speak at normal volumes while the television news blares out stories of real-life brutality is surely enough to undermine our identification with them. Haneke cues us to understand their story within a broad sociopolitical and multinational context, rather than becoming caught up in it on a purely personal level.

Hearing between the Lines

The more specific postcolonial significance of *Caché* comes to the fore about halfway through the film. Following Georges and Anne's having received several videotapes, and Georges' consequent first confrontation with Majid, Anne demands some explanation of Georges' suspicions. His speech in response to her is the verbal pivot point of the film:

> His [Majid's] parents worked for us. Dad liked them. I guess they were good workers. In October '61, the FLN called all Algerians to a demonstration in Paris. October 17, 1961. Enough said. Papon. The police massacre. They drowned about 200 Arabs in the Seine. Including Majid's parents most likely. They never came back. Dad went to Paris to look for them. They said he should be glad to be rid of a couple of jigaboos [59:37–1:00:12].

In this abbreviated speech, Georges fails to provide anything like a full explanation for the death of Majid's parents, yet he does here allude to an abundance of historical detail. The speech is filled with ellipses that signify failures to completely acknowledge a shameful history. As Georges speaks, he looks straight ahead and downward, never directly at Anne, and they barely move from their seated positions: the emphasis of the scene is on his words, without a shifting dynamic between the characters or any physical movement to detract attention away from what he says (see Figure 6.9).

FIGURE 6.9 When Georges speaks to Anne of the 1961 police massacre, he loses eye contact with her, a strong suggestion of his unacknowledged shame.

Every detail of Georges' speech reverberates with subtextual, haunting realities, even despite its succinct and elliptical form.

> His parents worked for us. Dad liked them. I guess they were good workers.

The words communicate George's relative privilege, though that is not his emphasis. He aligns himself with his father and thus with his father's upper-middle-class privilege, though not with his father's perceivable generosity. Because Georges here explains his father's attachment to Majid's parents solely in terms of their being "good workers," he unwittingly asserts his embrace of the colonial circumstances that empowered white French families at the expense of Algerians. He reveals a begrudging willingness to acknowledge anything positive about Majid's parents, and perhaps only out of deference to his father.

> In October '61, the FLN called all Algerians to a demonstration in Paris. October 17, 1961. Enough said.

As we have already explored, October 1961 is now an infamous date in French history. Yet, as noted above, the horror of this event, and the truth of its being covered up, came to light only comparatively recently. When Georges says, "enough said," he both denies and perpetuates the systematic and institutionally enforced burial of this truth. He assumes his audience's (Anne's and, by implication, our) complete knowledge by initially evading details. Ironically, he quickly follows this up with some specifics, suggesting some tacit and taciturn acknowledgment that there is more to be said.

> Papon. The police massacre. They drowned about two hundred Arabs in the Seine. Including Majid's parents most likely. They never came back.

As mentioned above, Papon became an infamous figure in French history, and the horror of the two hundred deaths covered up for so long has been broadly acknowledged. But Georges fails to acknowledge the cover-up, and still assumes Anne's (and, by extension, anyone's/our) immediate comprehension without need for fuller explanation. This parallels Georges' suppression of his own guilty part in Majid's disenfranchised life. His guess that Majid's parents were "most likely" among the victims, as opposed to his stating this certainly, may remind us of the haphazard disposal of many anonymous bodies without care for the individuals they were. Though this is not Georges' manifest intention, his own speech ironically prompts us to perceive this submerged reality. Again, his few words undermine his authority.

> Dad went to Paris to look for them. They said he should be glad to be rid of a couple of jigaboos.

Here, Georges separates his father from those with violent prejudice against Algerians. The "they" here refers to the force of mass, white, prejudiced French opinion. The word "jigaboos" is a derogatory term for any black person, and carries with it a failure to acknowledge the specific ethnicity of an Othered people.

The term invites us to understand Georges' story as representative of countless other tales of colonial violence around the world. In an interview with Richard Porton about *Caché*, Haneke says "it seems to me that, in every country, there are dark corners—dark stains where questions of collective guilt become important. [For instance,] I'm sure that in the United States there are other parallel examples of dark stains on the collective unconscious" (2005, 50). The film is more particularly, retrospectively prescient in light of the infamous November race riots in Paris during the same year of its release (2005), thus extending its resonance far beyond October 1961.[25] The film has been read in another specific, post-9/11 context with Georges as "stand-in for the US and its fear of imaginary WMDs" and "Majid representing the already-defeated Iraq, falsely-accused as a threat to the very power by which it is vanquished" (Seshadri 2007, 32).

Despite the fragmented and succinct form of Georges' speech, this close analysis reveals its implied fuller form: we can perceive the speech's troubling omissions as well as its historical and contemporary reverberations. Paul Gilroy critiques the film's "overly casual citation of the 1961 anti-Arab pogrom by Papon's police in Paris" (2007, 233), in the context of arguing that the dead in the film "are used as a mere narrative device" (McFadden 2009, 119). But to critique the film this way is to conflate Georges with Haneke, sidestepping how critically the character is represented throughout the film. And even if Georges himself seems "overly causal," he seems desperately so: indeed, his inability to even meet his wife's gaze as he gives the speech above suggests his intense discomfort borne of a desire to skip over loaded details as quickly as possible.

"Nothing"

Just as *Caché* demands that we read between its fragments (the staccato scenes, the abbreviated and elliptical speeches, and the sonically hard cuts), it expects us to read beyond the "nothing" that its characters frequently say. Moments after the above speech, Georges explains that his parents decided to adopt the orphaned Majid. Anne then asks what he did, to which he responds "Nothing. I told lies about him." Here, the word "nothing" signifies Georges' denial of the significance of his own lies that led to Majid's being forcibly taken into institutionalized care. Moments later, Georges reveals that he brought up Majid with his mother and, when Anne asks what she said, he replies, "Nothing. [pause] She's getting old. She can't remember. Or doesn't want to, I don't know. It's too unpleasant for her" [1:03:29–1:03:38]. By this point, we know that Georges'

---

[25] As noted above, the riots occurred after two young men of North African descent electrocuted themselves on an electric fence while trying to escape from French police (Mecchia 2007, 133). Tarja Laine usefully summarizes what happened, explaining that the riots escalated less because of the accident than the way it was (mis)handled by authorities (2010, 255).

mother's failure to remember Majid is hardly "nothing," and it certainly amounts to more than ordinary old age or unpleasantness. Though Georges tells his mother about finding his own dreams of Majid "odd," she insists there is "nothing odd about it. I often dream of my childhood. It comes with age" [34:25–34:33]. Here she uses "nothing" as part of a disavowal of the memory's particular significance, as well as a way to briskly calm her son. In the same scene with his mother, Georges insists that "nothing's changed" for him and his family, and when his mother still senses something is wrong ("You're all pent up. What is it?"), he replies, "Nothing, I'm fine." [32:23–32:27]. Now, "nothing" signifies deliberate deceit. Another scene shows Georges' macabre, subjectively remembered vision of the young Majid wiping blood from his mouth. After we see this as Georges does, Anne pulls him back into the present reality by asking him, "What's up? What's wrong?, Georges?," in response to which Georges assures her, "Nothing. Nothing" [13:30–13:44]. Here, "nothing" signifies his inability to address his own disturbing and warped vision, as well as his lack of honesty with Anne. When Georges reenters his home from the street after answering the doorbell, only to find yet another videotape left by his door during a dinner party, he initially lies to his guests and Anne by saying, "nothing" (as in, "there is was no one/nothing there"). Anne repeats the word "nothing?" as a question in response [28:04–28:09]. Georges simply answers, "There was nobody. There was nobody outside." Now "nothing" refers to the videotape he hides, the person behind them, and indicates Georges' increasing separation from the people around him.[26]

In later scenes of the film, the word "nothing" increasingly means its opposite: *everything*. When Pierrot's friend's mother brings him home after a night during which he seems to be missing, and Anne over-effusively thanks her, she simply says, "it's nothing." She is speaking out of embarrassment about her part in the false alarm and not wanting to be over-thanked. Her response seems inadequate because Pierrot's return is clearly *everything* to Anne. Moments later, when Anne asks Pierrot, "what's wrong?," he insists, "nothing" [1:23:22], only to soon reveal that he rebuffs his mother's affection because he believes she is having an affair. After Majid's suicide, Georges explains to Anne that Majid asked him to come over "so he could explain about the tapes. So I went." "And?," Anne animatedly asks. "And nothing," Georges responds, before then adding "He said, 'I want you to be present and cut his throat'" [1:33.29–1:33:36]. Here Georges reduces the impact of the suicide scene to the bluntness of the act, yet again using the word "nothing" to deny something of great significance.

---

[26] Kevin L. Stoehr mentions the aural motif Haneke's characters saying "Nothing" when "the truth is difficult to communicate or when an individual becomes indifferent to the need to share the truth" (2010, 477). He argues that with Georges in *Caché* it is an "almost mechanical reaction to questions about what is really going on" (477). He connects this, in turn, to Georges' willful forgetting and its political resonance.

The word "nothing" is a haunting aural motif through Haneke's films. Seldom has but one word accrued as many meanings within an auteur's work, let alone a word that literally means naught. In *Funny Games*, when Georg intervenes in Anna's first uncomfortable conversation with the killers, Paul assures him that "Nothing's going on," though we can already sense an atmosphere of menace [23:42–23:44]. In *The Seventh Continent*, Anna asks her husband, "what's wrong?" after he wakes in the night, and he assures her, "nothing" [33:34–34:03], but this comes directly after an image of the Australian shore that is retrospectively attached to the family's suicide. In a later scene at Evi's school, after the family have decided to commit suicide, her teacher stops a class because she is distracting other pupils by vigorously scratching her body. The teacher examines her body after Evi says, "it itches" and briskly responds that "it's nothing" [57:42]. Though we can see no visible sign of disturbance on Evi's skin, we must sense that the teacher's disallowance of any problem ("it's nothing") is brutal. "Nothing" is repeatedly a lie in Haneke's oeuvre. It resonates like a dissonant chord across a big-scale piece of music. It should be unsurprising, then, that it recurs most often in *Caché*, a film in which Mark Lawson (2006) suggests that *every* line is a form of deceit.

Toward the end of the film, Georges exclaims to Majid's son that he has "nothing to hide" [1:42:53–1:42:54]. "Nothing" registers ironically here because it has been consistently associated with forms of dishonesty. Indeed, the only character who seems to use the word "nothing" truthfully is Majid's son: in the same scene, he tells Georges the tapes "were nothing to do with me," and it is difficult to doubt his assured tone [1:43:31–1:43:32]. Moreover, Majid's son consistently maintains more composure when he says "nothing," demonstrating his mastery of polite French language in a way that only seems to madden Georges all the more. As Crowley explains, "mastery of French language has been, throughout the period of the French Republican Empire, a signifier of the colonized's successful assimilation," but Georges responds to Majid's son as though his speaking was "a parody of French cultivation" (2010, 275). When Georges finally, aggressively asks, "what do you want?," Majid's son simply says, "Nothing anymore. I wondered how it feels, a man's life on your conscience. That's all. Now I know." Such honesty is shocking enough to Georges that he has no response beyond a disingenuous disavowal of any problem, along with something like the sarcasm of a stereotypically moody teenager: he sulkily says, "Great, everything's okay then. Do you mind if I go now?" [1:45:46–1:46:01].[27]

The fact that only Majid's son uses the word "nothing" for its straightforward meaning sets him apart within *Caché*, subtly suggesting that he embodies

---

[27] In his being verbally "outmanoeuvred" here, Lykidis connects Georges with several of Haneke's other bourgeois main characters who "display mastery of language when speaking amongst themselves" but in "multicultural encounters, they tend to lose their ability to deceive, persuade, or intimidate others verbally" (2010, 460).

a genuine capacity for truth-telling that can potentially live beyond the film. "Nothing" is the second word spoken in *Caché*, and is all that Georges and Anne can understand by the first videotape at the outset. But the film warns us about ever assuming there is "nothing" to see or hear, even with the first representation of a quiet and well-to-do neighborhood. In that same neighborhood there is a person whose denial, dishonesty, suppression, and deceit leads to another man's suicide. And the tension between these two men resonates with the history of France and Algeria, white and minority French people, white and minority peoples the world over, colonizing and colonized countries. One image sets this all in motion when "nothing" is said: the word comes with the videotape being revealed as such, and carries along with it broad implications far beyond the image itself. Like the absent sounds and silences that shape so many of Haneke's scenes, the aural motif of "nothing" necessitates our active engagement because it always means *something*. To return to Walsh's words, "a living quality of uncertainty, of untapped and unrealized potential, resonates perceptually around and within the work" (1992, 70). "Nothing" is often negatively spoken in Haneke's cinema, but he uses it optimistically with regard to us. His use of "nothing" assumes our potential willingness to hear and to understand more than his characters do.

Majid's Suicide

Caché culminates in the death of Majid, a scene that implicitly asks us to consider all the other Algerian deaths that have *not* been represented. Everything within the scene seems precisely "scored," in keeping with Macallan and Plain's arguments. The sound effects of the scene, subtle though they are, warrant as full attention as the absence of music and dialogue. The scene begins very quietly, with Georges' walking up the corridor to Majid's apartment [1:27:51]. Georges then holds the door buzzer down longer than necessary, aggressively breaking the quiet [1:27:59–1:28:01].[28] In terms of the film's narrative rhythm, it matters that this scene occurs three-quarters of the way through, thus being the precisely timed climax of the action in a Classical Hollywood sense (though it is far from Classically handled in the following scenes that deny us narrative closure).[29] When Majid answers the door and invites Georges in, his tone is as quiet as Georges' tone is demanding. Majid quietly and politely speaks to Georges ("Thanks for coming, come in," "sit down") while Georges questions

---

[28] Georges' aggression with the buzzer communicates his sense of entitlement, especially because it echoes the police demanding entry to Majid's apartment in an earlier scene where they wrongly assume his holding Pierrot hostage (having followed Georges' tip).

[29] For more on the typical timing of different Classical Hollywood narrative components, specifically in relation to *Jerry Maguire* (1996), see Bordwell's *The Way Hollywood Tells It* (2006, 64).

him accusingly ("what's this all about?," "what do you want?"). Less than a minute passes before Majid says, "I called you because I wanted you to be present" and then promptly slits his own throat. Majid's last line is strongly suggestive: perhaps he wants Georges to be fully with him, rather than locked in a past that they share. By extension, the film asks us to consider what Majid's death means in our own present, a point that chimes with the ongoing racial tensions in France, as well as the relatively recent general awareness of what happened in October 1961. Equally, the sound track forces us to be present in the moment of Majid's death itself, not only because it catches us off guard, but also because it sonically imposes the disturbing details of that death on us. Majid's killing motion seems rehearsed but still awkward, especially as we hear and see him fumbling in his pocket for the knife. Every sound is uncomfortably amplified: the blade cutting his flesh, the splatter of blood on the wall, a kitchen chair squeaking slightly as he bumps against it on falling to the floor. For an extended time, the sound track focuses attention on Majid's last gurgling and bleeding out, and Georges' breathing, except for some quiet traffic outside. Georges quietly moves away from the body, out of the frame, and then slowly back toward the door, coughing with discomfort as he gets closer to the body [1.28.51–1.29.53]. Because Majid's body is in the way of the door, Georges cannot make a quick escape: instead, his exit is hesitant and drawn out (see Figure 6.10). The sudden action of Majid's suicide is thus followed by the slowness of Georges' first response. This one representation of a death and its aftermath resonates immeasurably with the countless other Algerian lives lost in the long-standing fight for Independence from France, and the slowness of the nation to acknowledge many related tragedies. Overall, the scene of Majid's

FIGURE 6.10 After Majid kills himself, his body blocks Georges' exit, symbolically emphasizing the deliberation involved in Georges' choosing to "step past" his death.

death is another Brechtian experience, one that asks us to cognitively inter-pret every detail even as it has a devastatingly affective impact. The scene ends with a hard cut to the outside of the movie theatre, and traffic rushing past the camera at high speed and volume [1:29:53]: the brutality of this cut forces us to perceive a world rushing past, oblivious to the brutality behind closed doors and the hidden truths that need attention. It is a powerful echo of the traffic we have already heard in *Code Unknown* and *The Piano Teacher*, as well as the car racing in *Funny Games*.

Chion rightly notes that Majid's apartment, if naturalistically portrayed, would include noises "from the courtyard, from the staircase, from neigh-boring televisions," whereas Georges' "bourgeois apartment would be calm, soundproofed."[30] Instead, "every space in the film enjoys the same silence, and this silence, far from being comforting, evokes a sense of danger, of a possi-ble disruption" (2010, 165). Though Chion therefore implies that every sound constitutes an equivalent sense of warning, the sounds of Majid's death are the most excruciatingly extended in *Caché*. Majid's knife stroke prompts audi-ences to make their own sounds too: critics often mention the "collective gasp in every movie theatre" where *Caché* was first screened, in response to this action (Seshadri 2007, 46).[31] Ricardo Domizio's argument that the film renders Majid's suicide "with the same detachment and studied banality as the open-ing scene" (2011, 246), and Gilroy's assertion that Majid's suicide is "an exclu-sively aesthetic event, devoid of all meaning," (2007, 234) are therefore most misleading.[32]

Summary

Like Haneke's other films, *Caché* features confrontational sonic strategies—especially non-sutured scenes, meaningful silences, and absent music. Like *The Seventh Continent*, the film stresses a hostile diegetic space through amplified sound effects, though its overall impact is comparatively subtle and quiet. Echoing *Code Unknown, Caché*'s sound track stresses extreme social and

---

[30] Georges' home is in the quaint but pricey Cité florale quarter (79) whereas Majid lives in a "run-down housing project" (HLM—*habitation à loyer modéré*) (Penney 2010, 80).

[31] Similarly, Wheatley (2007) mentions the "collective gasp" of the Cannes audience in response to this moment. Sterritt makes a parallel point for *Funny Games*: "every time I've seen it, viewers have audibly gasped when Anne shoots the intruder" (2007, 256).

[32] Gilroy even goes so far as to accuse Haneke of providing his audience with a sadistically reac-tionary form of relief in Majid's death: we can "derive a deep if guilty pleasure from it precisely because that horrible death can represent the flowering of [our] own investment in the idea that Europe's immi-grants should be induced to disappear by any means possible" (2007, 234). Such a reading connects with those many other scholarly works we have already cited that tend to demonize Haneke and assume his detachment from the trauma to which he subjects his audiences.

cultural divisions. Like *Funny Games, Caché* represents Haneke's subversive manipulation of genre, but its aural surprises take us even further from the generic. Like *The Piano Teacher, Caché* features many moments of aural brokenness: where the earlier film's sound track thus parallels the divided subjectivity of its protagonist, the aural brokenness of *Caché* stands for broken men, families, and nations.

All of Haneke's films show humanity under threat: *The Seventh Continent* explores the noisy threat of consumer-driven culture; *Code Unknown* presents the cost of failing to hear different (or Other) people; *Funny Games* wants us to rehear the life-changing impact of violence; *The Piano Teacher* makes us understand that no art, even the most beautiful music, can save an oppressed woman; and *Caché* confronts the devastating impact of the silenced colonial history between France and Algeria. Wheatley argues that "socio-political readings need not be dwelled upon" because *Caché* is not about revealing "something about society" but "about the spectator's relationship to the screen" (2009, 156). Haneke himself, however, extends the meaning of *Caché* beyond metacinematic ingenuity, describing the film "like a Russian doll with dolls inside dolls inside dolls. The same story can be seen on different levels, can represent different levels: the personal level, the family level, the social level, the political level" (Badt, 2005). To ignore these interconnected possibilities is to not hear the film.

7

The White Ribbon

HEARING SYMBOLIC OPPRESSION AND
THE REAL IN REBELLION

How can a sound track relay psychoanalytic ideas and conflicts? What sonic patterns communicate Lacan's concept of the Symbolic: that is, the Law of the Father enforced by language and social strictures? What sonic details can possibly convey the "unrepresentable" Real: that is, the Lacanian concept of what lies beyond signification, the unmappable terrain of always-present but always-elusive threat? How can a sound track amplify tensions between the Symbolic and the Real as realms of order versus disorder, social control versus uncontainable threat, the knowable world versus the terror of the unknown?[1] Moreover, how can a sound track communicate these abstract Lacanian concepts with affective power?[2]

This chapter is a psychoanalytic response to *The White Ribbon: A German Children's Story*, Haneke's most haunting film. The story is grounded in a fully realized depiction of the past, but its form demands our active involvement in such a way that nothing seems "safely" distant. The Symbolic realm of the film is

---

[1] For fuller definitions of these fundamental Lacanian concepts (the Symbolic and the Real), and some extended application of them to two sound tracks (*Bigger Than Life* [1956] and *Shutter Island* [2010]), see Walker (245–323).

[2] Though *The White Ribbon* is ripe for psychoanalysis, this is not to be confused with psychological realism. Haneke is famously anti–psychological dramas, or what Coulthard calls "psychologisation—motives, clear causal explanations, character desire and insight are all intensely restricted. Instead we are shown actions and effects, and are left to fill in the gaps in between" (2011b, 185). Similarly, Grundmann writes that in Haneke's work, "a focus on psychology is substituted by an exterior portrait of the consequences and effects of characters' decisions and actions" (2010b, 591). Or, as Zolkos argues, it "is not simply that the plot is psychologically enigmatic or overdetermined, but that it precludes the spectator's identification relation to the film's characters" (Zolkos 2015, 208). The sound track of *The White Ribbon* resonates strongly with Lacanian concepts, but understanding this requires our *active* comprehension of the characters as they exist within a broadscale context, as opposed to functioning as individuals with whom we might identify.

sonically defined by sounds of cruelty, death, patriarchal speech, and controlled music. This restrictive environment is a breeding ground for all forms of violence. The sound track foregrounds every violent act, often making us hear what the film does not show, and thus folding us into its own action by requiring our imaginative effort to "complete" the picture. The film thus creates a sense of the dangerous Real as it emanates from within the toxic Symbolic realm, yet which is always bigger than we can grasp. We always know we have never perceived the awful "whole," which has far-reaching implications beyond the characters' world and time. When it comes to the Real, Slavoj Žižek explains that "no matter what we say about it, it continues to expand." He likens the Real to the radioactive rays of the Chernobyl disaster in that they "are thoroughly unrepresentable, no image is adequate to them" (1991, 36). Listening hard to *The White Ribbon* means always sensing the elusiveness of the Real along with feeling its devastating impact.

A "Song Cycle" of Pain, a Strangely Dispassionate Voiceover

The White Ribbon is ambitiously structured: it has more than a hundred scenes set in Eichwald, a fictional "rural, north German Protestant village" (Williams 2010, 48). The story takes place during the months leading up to the outbreak of World War One.[3] The locale seems small and provincial, but the numerous elliptical glimpses into village life evoke expansive disturbance, which culminates in the film's final scenes anticipating global disaster. The scenes work like the songs within a song cycle that cumulatively convey an overwhelming theme:[4] virtually everything that happens in *The White Ribbon* relates to the fear of, fallout from, or repression of, violence. The most distressing violence includes unsolved crimes against children: the Baron's son (Sigi) is kidnapped, stripped, beaten, and left for dead; and the disabled Midwife's son (Karli) is almost blinded in the film's most brutal offscreen attack. Children commit other acts of violence as revenge against their abusive fathers: the Pastor's eldest daughter (Klara) crucifies her father's pet parakeet, and one of the Steward's sons (Georg), leaves a window open to chill his baby brother to death. The film's relentless emphasis on such dreadful actions makes one sonic element especially strange: an

---

[3] Though Haneke is hesitant to identify a definite point of origin, he says the genesis of the story began with his seeing a documentary about "[Adolf] Eichmann and his trial in Israel. Despite Eichmann's notoriety as "one of the key architects of the Holocaust" (Blumenthal-Barby 2014, 95), Haneke was shocked to hear German people defending him in the documentary as "a dutiful civil servant" (Grundmann 2010b, 596). Martin Blumenthal-Barby connects the fictional name "Eichwald" with both Eichmann's name and the Nazi concentration camp Buchenwald (2014, 95). This coinage alerts us to the aural deliberation with which Haneke evokes a past that is both familiar and newly conceived. (For more on the infamy of Eichmann in relation to *The White Ribbon*, see Waldron 2013, 148–149, 154.)

[4] For more on how a song cycle can cumulatively convey meaning, see the analysis of Schubert's *Winterreise* as it approaches the theme of unrequited love from numerous angles (within the chapter on *The Piano Teacher*).

avuncular-sounding old man provides a voiceover narration. He is the village Schoolteacher, pictured onscreen as a young man and now looking back on the film's events as an attempt to understand "what happened in this country." [5] In the final sequence, the Schoolteacher initiates a resolution that might end all the violence: he tells the Pastor that he strongly suspects the older children (including some of the Pastor's own family) have committed the village's unsolved crimes. However, the narrative denies us a satisfying denouement: the Pastor responds by threatening the Schoolteacher with denunciation and takes no further action.

Given the lack of justice for those innocents who suffer most in *The White Ribbon*, the Schoolteacher's voiceover is surprisingly dispassionate. Along with relaying his emotional and temporal distance from every action of the village, his words evoke the Real that is too terrible for words. His first narration begins as follows:

> I don't know if the story I want to tell you is entirely true. Some of it I know only through hearsay. After so many years, a lot of it is still obscure, and many questions remain unanswered. But I think I must tell of the strange events that occurred in our village. [1:40–2:05]

Given Haneke's tendency toward writing extremely lean scripts with little repetition, the narrator's emphasis on the unreliability of his narration is marked. Within just a few seconds, the English subtitles include five different ways through which he expresses the contingency of truth: "don't know," "hearsay," "obscure," "unanswered," and "strange." Over the last sentence of his opening voiceover the film fades in, showing a field with wintry trees as well as evergreens, and a cloud-filled sky, along with the rising sound of many birds. The birdsong echoes the opening of *Caché,* but the birds' visual absence is more immediately obvious with the countryside setting.

Birdsong soon becomes an ironically important aural motif in *The White Ribbon*, a sound of life that contrasts with dire and "unnatural" onscreen action.[6] In the film's opening, during which we witness the village Doctor's near-fatal accident on horseback, birdsong suggests the massivity of nature that is impervious to human suffering. A tripwire has been placed between two trees on the Doctor's route home: his horse trips over it mid-gallop, throwing him from the saddle. It is but one of several violent acts for which no perpetrators are identified or punished. The birdsong is dimly perceptible as the scene

---

[5] In *The White Ribbon*, characters are often named by their profession rather than by their given names, so we follow that pattern here.

[6] We see two birds onscreen in later scenes: the parakeet (Peepsie) belonging to the Pastor, and the orphaned bird that his son Gustav gives him. Gustav's gift is a rare gesture of compassion after Klara, his sister, kills Peepsie in retaliation against their father's tyrannical control. These onscreen birds represent the "caged" existence of the Pastor's children (the restrictions of the Symbolic), in contrast with the free birds outside that exceed his control and which we never see (representing the expansiveness of the Real as it exists in nature).

fades in [2:00], but soon becomes very noticeable as the accident is about to happen [2:09]. Along with implying the Real as it exceeds what humankind can control, there is something oddly playful about the birdsong: it jars with the ostensible subject of the first scene, the Doctor's grave injury.

The Schoolteacher's narration is oddly perfunctory during this scene too: it simply describes what we see and therefore seems unnecessary. We see the Doctor falling from his horse just as the narrator says, "Entering the garden, his horse tripped on a wire strung between two trees." Haneke thus provides us with an unusually straightforward audiovisual match. But a gap soon opens up between what the narrator/Schoolteacher says and what we see. He tells us that the Doctor's daughter, Anna, "saw the accident from a window, informed their neighbor who informed the estate's steward, so that the agonizing Doctor could be transported to the district hospital over 30 kilometers away." This bland narration does nothing to address the pain of the scene: the horse writhing and grunting on the ground, the daughter's horrified face, the evident agony of her father, and the discomfort of her reaching to touch him as he shouts and recoils from her (see Figures 7.1 and 7.2). Later we learn that Anna is being sexually abused by her father, so the awkwardness of their initial physical interaction takes on retrospectively excruciating significance.

The daughter is in black, as if in mourning for her father already. The dress is an extremely high-cut, constrictive piece of clothing.[7] It is more than a piece of the period detail: the physical containment of her body alludes to her father's wrongful control of her person. Because the levels of pain within the scene (for the horse, and the daughter, as well as the Doctor) are not described by the narrator, the film underlines the limits of his speech. In addition, we cannot help being aware that the narrator did not witness the scene (nor many others of the film) directly. The inadequacy of the voiceover is even more noticeable because Haneke avoids such narration in his other films, as part of his general resistance to any pleonastic utterance.[8] This invites us to read far beyond what the voiceover says to question why it exists in the first place. The terror of the unknowable, uncontainable, and uncontrollable Real is thus suggested within the film's very opening in several prominent ways—through the narrator's phrases expressing profound uncertainty, the ironic birdsong as it represents the insuppressible power of nature, and the tonal strangeness and incompleteness of the voiceover in relation to what we see. From the outset, the sound track primes us to fear more than can be spoken or heard.

---

[7] The Pastor's wife wears a similar, black, chin-high dress with a cameo at the neck. Given she shares the name "Anna" with the Doctor's daughter, they are thus audiovisually connected, like generations of a similar self.

[8] For more on defining pleonastic sound tracks, see Walker (2015, 24). Haneke does incorporate some lean voiceover for his television adaptation of Franz Kafka's *The Castle* (1997), and *The Seventh Continent* features letters read in voiceover. In both these other cases, however, the voiceover often provides us with more information than we can see before us.

FIGURE 7.1 The Doctor's horse writhes in agony.

FIGURE 7.2 The Doctor recoils from his daughter Anna when she rushes to touch him after the accident. His flinching response suggests something more than pain from the accident—his counterintuitive inability to respond to her genuine and instinctive care.

In most psychoanalytic responses to a film, we approach the Real only after the Symbolic order is established. The typical analysis begins by establishing the "rules" of the Symbolic world before exploring how a film reaches beyond what can be rule-bound.[9] In short, we read a shift from what we know

---

[9] For a good representative example, see Juliet Flower MacCannell's (1994) analysis of the two films of *Cape Fear* (the 1962 original and the 1991 adaptation) as they critically represent the Symbolic order and allude to the terror of the Real beyond it.

to what is beyond signification. However, *The White Ribbon* begins by sonically implying the terror of the Real so strongly that this is where we must also begin. The film's opening does not simply set up narrative expectations based on suspense and the desire for cause-and-effect clarity (answering the question of who planted the wire, for example). The film's meaning immediately exceeds anything we can feel safely sure about. By visual analogy, it is as if we saw the skull *before* the men of Hans Holbein's *The Ambassadors* (1533). Lacan uses this painting to describe the Real, and there is a logical order of perception in his summary of the painting's impact: we see the men and their signifiers of wealth and power *before* our changing viewpoint makes the skull manifest. With this new vantage point, we then comprehend the Real (Lacan 1998 [1977], 72; McGowan 2003, 29; Walker 2015, 254). By contrast, *The White Ribbon* reverses this order because the Real makes its presence felt right away, even if we cannot immediately identify it as such.

The film's opening also breaks from standard expectations that a voiceover will provide some reliable grounding—denying us a sense of intimacy with a single character (as in the first person narration of *Never Let Me Go* [2010], for example), *and* withholding a reassuringly authoritative third-person perspective (as in the omniscient narration of *The Age of Innocence* [1994], for example). Indeed, the voiceover of *The White Ribbon* seems immediately intent on frustrating us more than explaining *to* us. Throughout the film, the voiceover remains peculiar, whether through redundancy or incompleteness. The redundancy comes with the Schoolteacher's narration matching what we see. The incompleteness is in his often skipping over the surface of distressing incidents, and his own admission of having a questionable memory. His narration is further hampered by his being focused on his own desires—sometimes endearingly, and sometimes unconscionably so. He enjoys redirecting the unpleasantness of narrating other villagers' lives to himself and his courtship of a young nanny named Eva.

Occasionally, the perfunctory tone of the Schoolteacher's voiceover is more cruelly incommensurate with the onscreen action, creating the most pointed structural discordance. For example, with minimal vocal modulation he moves on from describing the Doctor's accident to the death of the farmer Felder's wife after a tragic "work accident." Mrs. Felder died from falling through some rotten floorboards at the Baron's sawmill. When the Schoolteacher narrates that the Steward sent her there for "easier work" because an arm injury left her unable to complete harvesting chores, the awful implication is that her impaired physical ability made her dispensable. There is a palpable tension between this nasty subtext and his impassive delivery.

The Schoolteacher's narration directly after Mrs. Felder's funeral scene is even more strangely dispassionate. Felder continues working for the Baron although his eldest son, Max, believes his mother's death was planned. The farmer is powerless to investigate her death because he cannot risk losing

FIGURE 7.3 The extreme long-shot view of Mr. Felder's funeral procession.

employment while providing for his large family. Because the film emphasizes Felder's powerlessness within the socioeconomic realities of the Symbolic order, his death points to the enduring inequalities that have tragic consequences. In grief for his wife, Felder hangs himself. His body is discovered by one of his younger (unnamed) sons, in a scene of heartbreaking quiet.[10] We later witness Felder's funeral procession in an extreme long shot, a viewpoint that allows for our emotional distance, and which therefore feels counterintuitive [1:24:08–1:25:42]. The stark wintry terrain is a poignant and lasting reminder of Felder's grief-stricken withdrawal from everyone, including his own children (see Figure 7.3). We see a horse-drawn cart pull the coffin across snow, followed by just a few villagers. We then observe Max entering the scene and shaking hands with mourners, though he is silently snubbed by one of them. The absence of much sound in this scene beyond footsteps on snow, and the inaudibility of any dialogue in particular, points to an unspeakable level of incomprehension, irresolution, and the film's refusal to assure us of anything. After the cut at the end of this funeral scene to another shot of the village in winter, and empty of human life, the Schoolteacher's voiceover is unmistakably, jarringly frivolous: "The year ended with fine weather" [1:25:45–1:25:47]. This mismatch between his aural lightness and what we have just witnessed is more than ironic, playful, or simply odd.[11] The mismatch suggests the narrator's

---

[10] Felder's middle son's silence is offset by his noisy younger siblings playing outside and the quietly efficient sounds of his elder sister cooking inside. The entire scene lacks decipherable speech, making his silence even more movingly "eloquent" [1:17:57–1:19:28].

[11] It has become a cliché to incorporate ironically light music with scenes of horror, but the impact of this mismatch between narrative tragedy and *voiceover* is more than a familiar kind of audiovisual tension. For more on ironic mismatches between music and horror, see Ireland (2012).

willful obliviousness to the social significance of Felder's death. This is surely meant to discomfort us: though *he* may be disengaged, Haneke wants more from *us*.

The Schoolteacher's voiceover narration *never* seems much engaged with the characters who are visibly in pain. Ironically, the Schoolteacher and the subject of his adoration, Eva, are frequently mentioned by reviewers as providing solace within the malevolent context of the village. For Jonathan Romney (2009), he embodies an unusual "degree of lightness, even hope." For Grundmann, he is the film's "moral center" (2010b, 594). For A. O. Scott (2009), the Schoolteacher is "by far the most benign—if also the most ineffectual—authority figure," and an "obvious surrogate" for Haneke as "an intellectual whose pursuit of the truth is enabled by his inability to change anything."[12] John Orr simply calls him "semi-naïve" (2011, 261).[13] Yet the Schoolteacher's inadequate storytelling, simplistic and lacking in awareness as it is, surely points to something far more sinister than these critics suggest, even if that something lies beyond what he can possibly embody. The film prompts us to rehear his words after their first utterance, or at least positions us to question his avuncular voice and affable onscreen presence. This brings us back to Lacan's conceptualization of the Real in relation to Holbein's *The Ambassadors* ([1997] 1998, 85–90). If we take the painting at face value, it is a fairly nonthreatening, almost jolly image of two men. But if we adjust our view to perceive the painting from a different angle, and the large skull is manifest in the foreground, everything within the painting becomes troubled, including the round-faced men who look blankly out at us. This applies to the Schoolteacher's voiceover. He takes everything at face value, and the obvious inadequacies of his speech ironically amplify the terror that exceeds any solace he can provide.

The difference between what the Schoolteacher narrates and what we see is most marked in the film's final scene. *The White Ribbon* ends with his voiceover anticipating change after Germany's declaration of the First World War, and then his brief description of what happened to him after the film's diegetic action. As he speaks retrospectively, we see him as a younger man onscreen, conducting the children's choir in church. After silently counting them in to begin the hymn, he stands to sing while they face outwards instead of towards him (see Figure 7.4). So, he begins the music only to become subordinate to sounds over which he no longer has control.

---

[12] However, Scott (2009) goes on to accuse Haneke of being aligned with the Pastor as an "emblem of blindness and hypocrisy," as part of his larger criticism that Haneke is sadistic toward his audience. This is another of those misleading correlations between the director and his most frightening characters that we first explored in the introduction.

[13] Coulthard is among the few to complicate this view on the Schoolteacher—she argues that his problematic unreliability "casts a slight shadow on the courtship" (2011b, 187). Similarly, Landwehr writes that "naiveté in the face of violence serves as no excuse for an adult's obliviousness to evil surrounding him" (2011, 128).

FIGURE 7.4 Though the Schoolteacher conducts the choir to begin, he quickly becomes just another singer as the children face outward and away from him.

Just before the singing begins, this is what the Schoolteacher says:

> The solemn service next Sunday was attended by the whole village. There was a feeling of expectation and departure in the air. Everything was going to change. Eva's father, in view of the approaching war, had taken his daughter back home and, at her behest, had come to Eichwald, where his future son-in-law lived and worked, to look over it. The prospect of soon calling this beloved creature my wife also made this a day of celebration for me. The Pastor never mentioned our conversation again and apparently never went through with his threat to denounce me. I was called up at the start of 1917. After the war, as my father had died meanwhile, I sold his house in Vasendorf, and with the money opened a tailor's shop in town. I never saw any of the villagers again. [2:18:48–2:20:01]

This final voiceover raises many questions. First, the fact that the whole village attends church belies the many social and familial fractures we witness within it. This raises the question of how everyone could be suddenly united in an apprehension of fearful change. Given the anticipation of war, the Schoolteacher's reference to his "day of celebration" is tasteless at best, which makes us further question his ability to be self-aware or socially conscious. We might also reasonably wonder why the Pastor never took any action based on the Schoolteacher's accusations. This reduces the Pastor to "the same level of collective responsibility and guilt as his parishioners" (Williams 2010, 50), which leads to a broader question of what else will be repressed within the village at its population's peril. In addition, we might ask how the Schoolteacher has survived. As James S. Williams writes, "What actions [. . .] were committed by the narrator to ensure his own survival through two world wars up to the indeterminate present moment of his narration? On this specific point [. . .] he remains glaringly silent" (2010, 48). His complete disengagement from village life after 1913 raises the overarching question of why he has chosen to recount his memories of it at all.

After the Pastor begins the choir's singing and sits down at the church balcony, various other villagers make their way down the aisle, like a strange form of wedding party. The Pastor makes a last, visually prominent entrance down the middle. He slowly walks up the aisle alone as the image darkens and he then sits down before the complete shift to black. This raises a question of who will lead the service before the image fades away and the voices dwindle into silence. Since the camera is positioned at the front of the church, we are implicitly placed at the front, as if about to lead the ceremony: the film might be asking what *we* are about to say. When the villagers fade with the scene before us, the film visually evokes ghostly presences from a nightmare. The slowly controlled annihilation of the final image into blackness surely reminds us of the deliberation with which millions of lives were soon to be wiped out from 1914 to 1918. We might ask ourselves whether everyone before us will die, or who will survive. In this light, Williams calls the final scene "a photographic elegy for the soon-to-be-slaughtered" (50).[14] All these unspoken questions amount to a confrontation with what we cannot know, a triumph of the unrepresented over the manifest, the shadow of the Real presiding over the Symbolic.

As with all Haneke's films, music is used sparingly throughout *The White Ribbon*, but the sound track reaches an "apposite climax" in this final scene when the children sing Martin Luther's Protestant hymn "A Mighty Fortress Is Our God" (Grundmann 2010b, 593) [2:19:50–2:20:42]. Roy Grundmann contextualizes the hymn in relation to the German Protestant practice of secularizing divine law "though a series of paternal stand-ins (emperor, pastor, paterfamilias) who seemed to embody and enforce authority." He connects these stand-ins with the sanctification of family and nation as institutions of "unquestionable importance and divine standing," and the perception of rebellion against them as "treason" (593).[15] *The White Ribbon* communicates the Symbolic realm in these terms with overwhelming clarity but, in the end, the terror of the Real still looms largest through the voices of the

---

[14] We might see everyone in the church this way, though the children's aurally dominant singing pointedly reminds us of their aggressive potentialities too: we perceive "the strength they draw from raising their voices in public" (Stewart 2010, 47).

[15] Haneke says the hymn is personally important to him because he was raised Protestant and learned it by heart. He alludes to the "general meaning" of the hymn being about God "as a fortress against evil and Satan," but stresses that the hymn gains a "second meaning in relation to the outbreak of war. Evil is now understood as the enemy of the nation [. . .]. The last scene, which takes place in the church, shows four young lads walking to the from with little bouquets in their lapels. These are the first enlistees" (Grundmann, 2010b, 604). Haneke thus implicitly connects the hymn with the anticipation of young lives lost despite its ostensible emphasis on the protective presence of God, further ironizing its meaning.

children.[16] Their voices take over the sound track just as they stand on a balcony over the congregation. Every line of the hymn resonates ironically, pointing to what awfulness lies beyond the children's singing: after all, we have reason to suspect that least some of them have committed acts of extreme and damnable cruelty. Moreover, by the time the children's singing fades away, the screen has turned symbolically black: they have sung us into a lasting darkness.

Though we only hear a fragment of the hymn in the film's last scene, it recalls the whole—much in the way that the piece of Berg's Violin Concerto in *The Seventh Continent*, and the song extracts from Schubert's *Winterreise* in *The Piano Teacher*, recall entire works. In *The White Ribbon*, we hear the entire first verse before the voices fade along with dissolving final image:

> Ein' feste Burg ist unser Gott,
> Ein' gute Wehr' und Waffen;
> Er hilft uns frei aus aller Noth,
> Die uns jetzt hat betroffen.
> Der alt' böse Feind,
> Mit Ernst er's jetzt meint,
> Groß' Macht und viel List
> Sein' grausam' Rüstung ist,
> Auf Erd' ist nicht sein's gleichen.[17]

> [A mighty fortress is our God,
> a good defense and armory,
> he helps us get free from every difficulty
> that befalls us.
> The ancient wicked foe,
> grim is his intent,
> great might and much deceit
> are his ruthless weapons,
> on earth he has no equal.][18]

The *entire* hymn ultimately stresses that God reigns over the devil: He triumphs with but "one word," and the kingdom of heaven thus "remains ours." However, taken on its own, the first verse of "A Mighty Fortress Is Our God" dwells on the *need* for God because there is no earthly force strong enough to

---

[16] A. O. Scott (2009) argues that "Taken alone, the film's final image might conjure a mood of gentle, pastoral nostalgia.... The camera sits inside an austerely beautiful village church that is illuminated by winter morning sunlight, its pews filling with congregants whose dark clothes and weathered faced bespeak hardy old virtues of work, faith and family." His analysis here *only* works if we completely ignore the ironies of the hymn, as well as the sinister implications of the fading final image.

[17] The hymn lyrics are here quoted from, and provided in full by, Harry Plantinga for *The Hymn Society* (2007).

[18] This translation of the hymn is quoted from the San Francisco Bach Choir website (2013).

defeat the devil. The absence of the rest of the well-known hymn after the first verse in *The White Ribbon* matters—the film therefore denies us verbal *and* musical reassurances. Where the overall last scene points to many unanswerable questions, the verse expresses certainty about humankind's susceptibility to evil. The final credits in silence, another norm for Haneke, give interpretive space to comprehend the scale of destruction to come. And perhaps more than any of his other credit sequences, this silence prompts us to perceive the power of the Real that always exceeds signification.

The Symbolic versus the Real

The White Ribbon presents us with a profound tension between that which is clearly represented and that which is implied. In some respects, the visual messages of *The White Ribbon* are unusually lucid. Williams mentions the "pellucid monochrome" of Haneke's *mise-en-scène*, and the dazzling crispness of Christian Berger's "immaculately crafted, crisp cinematography" in homage to the "sharp," confrontational portraiture of the German photographer August Sander (2010, 48). The overall visual impact of *The White Ribbon* creates an ironic impression of supreme clarity, and an exacting approach that belies the many ellipses and aural cues about what awfulness cannot be fully seen and/ or known. Throughout *The White Ribbon*, this stylistic emphasis on a tension between the known and the unknown reflects an ultimate conflict between the Symbolic and the Real: where the Symbolic is manifestly cruel, the Real is unspeakably painful.

As Lacan defines it, the Symbolic realm is ultimately and historically presided over by "the Father."[19] *The White Ribbon* reveals deep ruptures within the Symbolic because it discourages us from accepting the words of those patriarchs who dominate many scenes. Even the film's very title is part of this pattern. "The White Ribbon" refers to how the Pastor punishes his two eldest children (Klara and Martin) for being late home from school. After pronouncing he has "purified" them with a cane, he commands their mother tie white ribbons on their arms as reminders of "innocence and purity": we cannot help feeling the wrongfulness of his words along with the children, even as he speaks of himself being authorized by God.[20] The white ribbons are visually paralleled by the white bandage worn by Karli after he is attacked in a later scene. The

---

[19] Lacan writes about the Symbolic Order that is ruled by the language-based "Law" of the Father as follows: "It is in the *name of the father* that we must recognize the support of the symbolic function which, from the dawn of history, has identified his person with the figure of the law" (*Écrits*, 66, original emphasis).

[20] The white ribbons are incorporated as a reflection of Haneke's extensive research on actual education methods in Europe during the early part of the twentieth century (Grundmann, 2010, 604).

attack is by unidentified children rebelling against their elders, as evidenced by the note from Exodus that they leave by Karli's body: "For I the Lord your God am a jealous God, visiting the inequity of the fathers upon the children unto the third and fourth generation."[21] The note signifies rebellion against the Symbolic order that is ruled by characters like the Pastor who wield violent authority, destroying the "innocence and purity" that he claims to protect.[22]

Karli is the only visibly disabled character in the film, and his having Down syndrome makes the attack on his face particularly nasty: this violence is the most disturbing demonstration of where the Symbolic order leads its children. Though we do not see his attack onscreen, the scene of his being medically treated is the most harrowing of *The White Ribbon*. The Doctor places a white bandage over Karli's bleeding and bruised eye sockets, firmly enough that it hurts him (see Figure 7.5). The bandage is to help Karli heal, but it represents an all-too-flimsy and frightening effort to cover pain. Karli slowly raises his voice to scream: the most searing sound of the film. We hear his agony while the film stays on a close-up of the Doctor applying the bandage and saying "everything will be fine again." We view the Doctor from a low angle, not quite from Karli's point of view, but close enough to align us with him visually (see Figure 7.6). Through most of this scene, the Doctor looks down at Karli and speaks calmly, but as he moves away from the bed Karli's cries rise [1:49:40–1:50:46].[23] Then comes the most shockingly moving image of the entire film: a close-up to show Karli's hand gripping the Doctor's hand while his cries crescendo (see Figure 7.7). "I have to go now Karli, don't worry," the Doctor says, pulling away despite Karli's loud resistance. At this point, we do not see the hands separate: instead, the film cuts to show the Doctor's body shift away from Karli, walking past his mother to the door. We lose sight of Karli entirely, but we keep feeling the pain of his offscreen cries.

Haneke argues that offscreen voices tend to reveal truth more clearly than those associated with onscreen presences. Synchronizing sound and image allows for the deceptive illusion of audiovisual unity to happen easily, masking the construction of a film and therein compensating for the actors' deficiencies in representing reality. In the absence of audiovisual unity, a voice cannot gain power from the image but must be believable in its own right. Haneke explains this as follows: "off camera you hear every wrong tone. On camera you don't. The actor's presence covers it up. Off camera, you notice immediately if the emotion is wrong. That's why, even when I was still working in theater, I'd often sit like this during a rehearsal [he bows his head, eyes closed]

---

[21] For the full quotation in context, see Zolkos (2015, 221n8).

[22] Stewart ironically suggests that the white ribbons possibly anticipate "the black arm bands of the Hitler Youth as compensatory badges of domination" (2010, 42).

[23] Williams wonders whether Karli is attempting to name his attackers (2010, 52), though his cries seem to be in direct response to the Doctor's action.

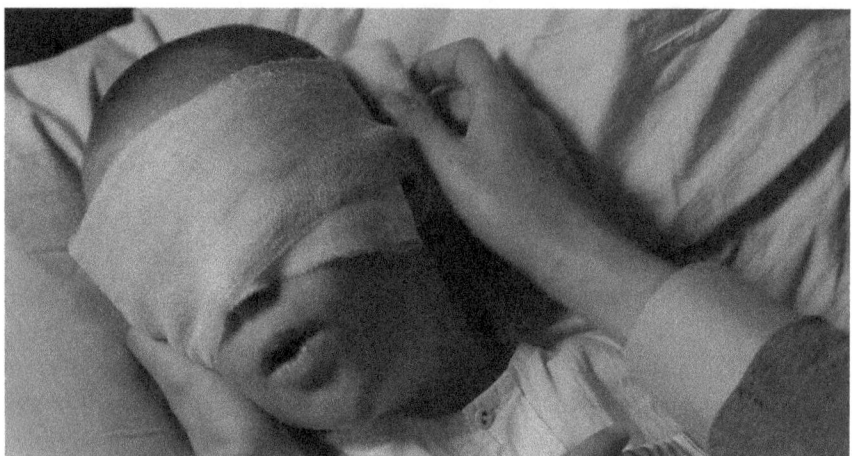

FIGURE 7.5 At first, Karli murmurs in pain as the Doctor applies the white bandage. But his murmurs soon become cries of agony, making him aurally dominant.

FIGURE 7.6 Karli's screaming offscreen makes the Doctor's relatively expressionless response look brutal.

and one of the actors would complain 'You're not even looking at me!' But I'd say, 'I see you better this way.'"[24] Karli makes the most frighteningly truthful sounds of *The White Ribbon* in that they "speak" of suffering that exceeds words or images. He becomes the tragic embodiment of the Real, something far beyond what can be fully acknowledged or understood by the Doctor (even though he is triply powerful within the Symbolic order as man, father, and

---

[24] This quotation comes from an interview with Haneke on the Criterion Blu-ray edition of *Code Unknown* (2015).

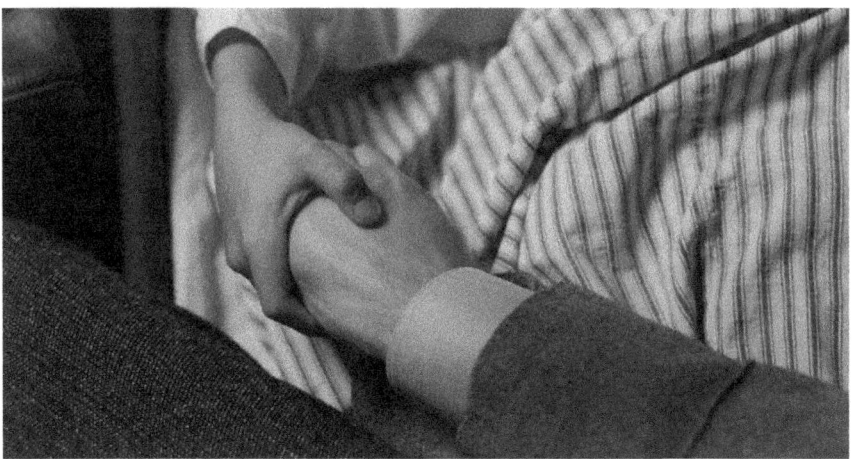

FIGURE 7.7   Karli grabs the Doctor's hand in a moving close-up.

qualified professional).[25] Though Karli's white bandage reminds us of the white ribbons worn by the Pastor's children most specifically, his cries resonate with the suffering of *many* children in the village. The film's audiovisual emphasis on Karli's agony is a haunting rebuke of the entire Symbolic realm that has engendered a newly toxic generation (including his attackers).

Because Karli expresses a sonically extreme truth, it makes sense that the film's central thematic statement is attached to him via the note from Exodus. As Williams says, the message about sins of the father being passed on "has been taken literally to grotesque ends. As we attempt to read the note in close-up, we hear it being read aloud verbatim." Here, the pleonastic form, or the double statement of sight and sound, serves for emphasis like a suddenly clanging chord in suspension. Williams mentions the "remarkable aberration" that "the voice is not the narrator's. Although we assume it to belong to one of the unidentified villagers who have found the boy, the speaker remains unseen" (2010, 54). The acousmatic quality of this voice gives it uncanny power. It is the closest we come to Haneke speaking directly through the film. Haneke himself says that his "basic idea was to tell the story of a group of kids who make an absolute of the ideals that are hammered into them by their parents and educators. They turn inhuman by appointing themselves as judges of those who do not live by what they preach" (Horwath 2009, 26). He calls the quotation from

---

[25] Karli's cries while the Doctor leaves are even more poignant given that he may be the Doctor's illegitimate son, although this is implied rather than voiced certainly within the film. We guess this possibility having witnessed the unpleasant affair between the Doctor and Karli's mother, the Midwife, and because the Schoolteacher mentions it as a piece of village gossip in his voiceover toward the film's end. More disturbingly, the Schoolteacher tells us that "some claimed" Karli was disabled because his mother "tried to abort him so their relationship wouldn't be found out."

Exodus "horrific" because "it's what Father taught. For [the children] it legitimizes the torturing of the weakest person in town" (Horwath, 30). The biblical fragment is a partial explanation of the offscreen terror Karli has experienced at these children's hands. Its being read by a disembodied presence evokes the traumatic Real that is always in excess of representation.

The Dread of "Nothing"

The White Ribbon further amplifies the terror of the Real through its emphasis on silences, pauses, muted sounds and paradoxical references to "nothing." As is typical of Haneke's oeuvre, most conversations are heavy with the quiet between words, but *The White Ribbon* takes this to a polemic extreme. The film builds an incremental atmosphere of fear, danger, and malevolence through its numerous interstices marked by absent sound and lowered dynamics.[26] Characters frequently speak in a near-whisper, refusing to use the full capacities of their voices, as if they fear what they might say if they gave themselves free rein. Heavy pauses and marked silences build a dreadful sense of ambiguous meaning and indeterminate direction in most scenes. The word "nothing" chimes in scene after scene like a composer's chordal signature. As we have already explored, particularly in relation to *Caché*, "nothing" is a defining and loaded aural form of punctuation across Haneke's films. So much so that it has the immediate memorability and impact of something like Stravinksy's Petrushka chord (two major triads placed a tritone apart from each other, creating dissonance through the blend). Like the Petrushka chord, "nothing" in a Haneke film creates an immediately recognizable dissonance because it usually means something far from that, and often the opposite. If the word "nothing" is one triad, "everything" is the triad simultaneously implied by it. And both reverberate for us at the same time—for when one character professes "nothing" as absolute negation, denial, absence, or a noncommittal state of mind, the contesting logic of the film around their word is just as loud, if not louder, telling us that this same "nothing" is a lie.[27]

In *The White Ribbon*, we first hear the word "nothing" when a policeman questions the Midwife about the Doctor's accident. With marked incredulity, he

---

[26] The reference to interstices here might lead the reader to suppose that this film is modernist in the way of T. S. Eliot's *The Waste Land*—but where the poem is made of fragments that implicitly prompt us to piece together a whole with the aid of the poet's own explanatory notes, *The White Ribbon* resists our assuming that it can be assimilated into one digestible structure as a whole made of parts. Instead, the film is designed to provoke an unending dialogue, largely through what the characters do not say. Haneke figuratively describes the importance of what is unsaid in aurally physical terms: "what is named by its name is artistically dead, has stopped *breathing*, and can only be recycled in *discussion*" (Grundmann 2010b, 605, my emphasis).

[27] A purist would hold that the "Petrushka chord" is specifically a C major triad and F-sharp major triad—but, as Steven Jacks (2013) explains, the term can be more liberally applied to any combination of two major triads that create dissonance.

observes that the wire was wrapped around two trees and vanished. Then he asks her, "But you saw nothing?," clearly meaning, "you *must* have seen something of significance" [12:25]. The word "nothing" has parallel impact in a much later scene when the Doctor visits the Steward's family. We know that the Steward's baby has nearly died during the night after Georg left the window open near his crib. However, the unknowing Steward insists that his children heard "nothing" though the doctor looks doubtful [1:06:31]. "Nothing" rarely means a sweet something: when Eva wonders why the Schoolteacher mentions where she comes from (Treglitz), his response of "nothing" means he is bashfully disavowing his keen interest in her [18:41]; and when he asks her, "you miss nothing?" [1:42:08] after she has taken a job elsewhere, she sweetly brushes against his hand, understanding that his "nothing" refers to himself and their relationship. These are striking exceptions to the rule by which "nothing" means a terrible something.[28]

Many other nothings echo through the film with darkly ironic force. The Baron angrily says his wife noticed "nothing" when their son Sigi disappeared before being attacked [42:10]. Later, he taunts the villagers by saying he hopes "nothing like that happens to any of your children." The film cuts to show various silent members of the congregation who passively absorb his words, clearly perceiving his subtextual malice [45:53]. The word becomes most painfully loaded in a partial conversation between the Midwife and the Doctor, after we have witnessed his using her for professional assistance, domestic duties, and sexual satisfaction [1:04:09–1:04:29]. With tears on the tips of her eyelids, she observes that he did not miss her when he was hospitalized. "What's that supposed to mean?" he asks impatiently, with muffled aggression. "Nothing. I just said it because it's true," she responds with an embarrassed shrug. The Doctor sardonically quips, "Nothing like a nice dose of self-loathing, is there?" "What?" she asks, in a moment of real incomprehension. "Nothing. Forget it," he answers, retreating from the relative innocence of her question. Here the signature chord of "nothing" is thus sounded several times in twenty seconds. In this particular scene, it is connected to the Midwife's hurt as well as the Doctor's cruelty in their affair. In other, later scenes, "nothing" points to children's guilt. The Schoolteacher believes that Klara and Martin know the culprits of the unsolved crimes within the village, but tells their mother and then their father they know "nothing" just minutes before he backtracks by telling the Pastor they might be culpable and therefore know *everything* [2:11:24; 2:13:22].[29]

---

[28] Equally, there are few pauses that are positive like the long pauses of sweet awkwardness shared by the Schoolteacher and Eva in the scene of their first meeting [18:06–21:15]. Far more representative are the many painful pauses during the Pastor's speech to Martin about the dangers of masturbation [58:33–1:02:32].

[29] The "nothing" motif connects *White Ribbon* with Haneke's two-part television series *Lemmings* (1979), which similarly focuses on a toxic and implosive society where children feel trapped and rebellious in response to being oppressed, and where diabolical violence is associated with children while being passed on from one generation to the next. As in *White Ribbon*, the word "nothing" is repeatedly, and obsessively, used by characters hiding lies, secrets, or hurtful truths.

The dialogue of *The White Ribbon* also features a pattern whereby one character asks a series of questions in quick succession without receiving complete answers to any of them. For example, after the Schoolteacher witnesses Martin nearly attempt a suicidal leap from the bridge to the river, he asks all of the following: "Are you insane?," "You want to break your neck?," "What's wrong?," "Have you gone mad?," "Do you know how high this is?," "Didn't you hear me shout to you?," "Well?", "*Well?*", "You saw me and wanted to impress me, is that it?," "So why?," What are you saying?," "Who doesn't want you to die?," "Why would God want you to die?," "Promise me you won't do it again, yes?," "You don't trust me?" [15:53–17:05]. Although Martin vocalizes his intent to discover whether or not God wants him dead, his other responses here are minimal, except for the end of the scene where he shouts in protestation after the Schoolteacher threatens to speak to his father, the Pastor ("Please, don't tell him, sir!"). We can guess what lies behind Martin's quiet while the teacher questions him: the oppression he feels from his father that has led him to this self-destructive point, and a fear about himself that he cannot vocally acknowledge. But these are unacceptable and unspeakable things within the film's Symbolic order.

The Midwife asks the Doctor a very different series of questions with escalating intensity, revealing and probing the depths of his abusiveness toward her and his daughter: "Why do you despise me?," "For helping to raise the boy?," For watching you finger your daughter and saying nothing?" [1:22:57–1:23:07]. The Doctor's response is to slap her so hard on the cheek her body shudders with the impact. Refusing to capitulate in pain, she continues: "For helping you to deceive yourself?," "For listening to you claim how you loved Julie, when everyone knew you treated her as badly as me?," "For loving you, when I know you can't stand being loved?" [1:23:11–1:23:29]. After the first of these questions, the Doctor moves out of the frame, away from the Midwife, subtextually suggestive of her voicing the truth that he wants to sidestep. As the Midwife finishes the third question, the film cuts to show him move brusquely towards his desk saying, "That's it. Now get up. I have work to do." His clipped, monosyllabic response could be the end of the scene, but the Midwife prolongs it by becoming more desperately assertive. She provides the answers he will not give: declaring that he "can't afford" to get rid of her, that he does not know what he says, and that he is dragging her down to see what happens. When he remains unmoved, she becomes cruel, saying, "I have two retarded kids: Karli and you. You're the most troublesome one" [1:23:59–1:24:03]. She asserts this standing next to the Doctor's desk, assuming a power we know she does not have in the Symbolic order. He witheringly glances up to voice the cruelest question of the film: "My God, why don't you just *die*?" [1:24:06–1:24:07]. Here, the series of questions thus leads us to a murderous wish. The bluntness of the doctor's final, rhetorical question is shocking because he overtly states his feeling when so much of the dialogue in *The White Ribbon* suppresses feeling or relies on subtext, as in the numerous "nothings" that mean somethings.

The cumulative impact of the film's numerous "nothings" and questions is to keep pushing toward an answer that never comes, except in the form of the cruelest fact of death. And the unknown terrain of death is the ultimate nightmare of the Real. This is poignantly represented in a scene focusing on the Doctor's children [21:16–23:57]. While their father is still critically ill in hospital, Anna confirms the reality of mortality to her much younger brother, Rudolph ("Rudi") (see Figure 7.8). Though the scene brings the relief of a candid question/answer exchange between siblings, the brutality involved in Anna telling Rudi the truth makes this straightforwardness hard to hear. In under three minutes, Rudi newly understands that Felder's wife has died, that his mother has died rather than gone "on a trip," that everyone dies, that Anna will die, his father will die, that he will die, and that there is nothing he can do to prevent death. The word "dead" is spoken by Rudi and Anna six times in this scene, and the word "die" three times, in addition to which Anna uses euphemisms for death ("when you don't live anymore," "when you stop living"), along with multiple allusions to nearing death ("very old," "very ill," "badly hurt," "so bad that your body can't take it anymore"). The scene ends with an important stinger after the relatively quiet conversation: in response to everything Anna tells him, Rudi swipes his soup bowl onto the floor so it smashes. It is a small form of aurally marked rebellion, but one that "we hear in ear-splitting intensity" (Williams 2010, 52).

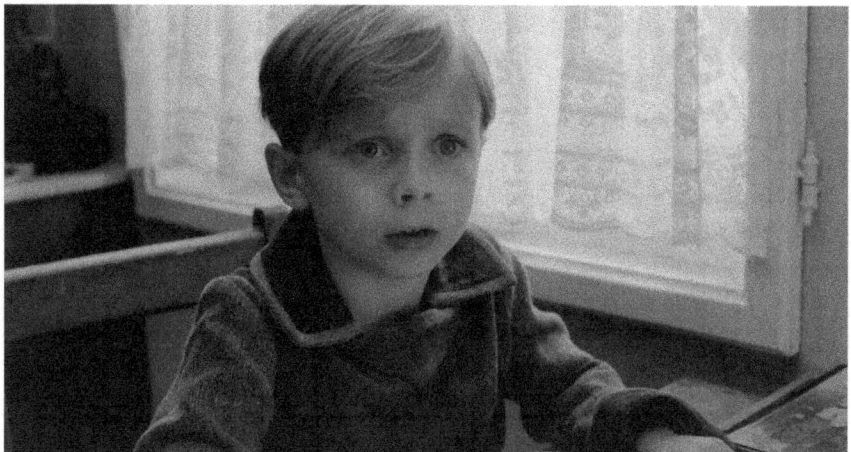

FIGURE 7.8 Rudi struggles to absorb the truth of death as his sister tells it, the dim light on his beautiful face suggestive of his innocence fading away.

Nature and the Dominant Real

Death is present throughout *The White Ribbon*, which is underlined by an aural motif of flies buzzing. Though they are usually unseen or visually indistinct, their noise is sometimes unnervingly strong within the relatively thin sonic texture.[30] Flies buzz as Felder approaches his wife laid in state [13:37–15:09], and in a later scene showing one of her children confronting her dead body [27:46–29:28]. Outside the Doctor's home, there is the ironic dissonance of birds tweeting (representing life) *along with* flies buzzing [for example, from 56:28–58:32]. Shortly after the Doctor's return from hospital, he looks his daughter up and down, asks her age, and observes that she looks "so like" her mother. When she turns and smilingly whispers "Papa" in response, the sound of flies becomes prominent—it is a grim harbinger of the cruelty we later learn he enacts on her body, and the death-in-life of her lost innocence. Like the birdsong, these buzzing flies "speak" beyond anything that can be encapsulated in words. We hear their noise at the most intense moments of grief and suppression. Together, these creatures of life and death allude to a world beyond the limits of the frame, yet again gesturing to the formidable power of the Real.

So, the Real of *The White Ribbon* is in several sonic patterns: the signature chord of "nothing," the numerous silences and pauses, the open-ended questions, the verbal emphasis on death, and the aural motifs of invisible birds chirping and flies buzzing. Yet perhaps the most fearful evocation of the Real comes with the scene where Georg attempts to drown Sigi [1:50:46–1:52:39]. In yet another scene featuring ironic birdsong, Georg shares a conspiratorial look with his younger brother Ferdinand before grabbing Sigi and forcibly pushing the little boy into the lake. Sigi, the privileged Baron's son, has been innocently playing his clear-sounding whistle in an immaculate sailor suit (see Figure 7.9). The two older boys, sons of the Steward (servant to the Baron), are dressed in simpler, everyday clothes, Ferdinand tapping a stick while Georg unsuccessfully attempts to make a scratchy musical sound from the whistle he has roughly carved. The emphasis upon class distinctions and relative wealth, both of which largely define the Symbolic order, could not be more audiovisually clear. The moment when Georg suddenly pushes Sigi into the water is difficult to watch because it is *so quiet*. In saying nothing but acting with such deliberate violence, Georg embodies the threat of unstoppable aggression that is often inaudible but *always* present in *The White Ribbon*. Georg shows no sign of compassionate regret, simply standing by as Ferdinand rescues Sigi. This

---

[30] The sound of flies is prominent enough that James Williams incorrectly notes them as the "sole markers of nature" (2010, 52), despite other sounds of birds and wind. That said, the film does sonically stress enclosed environments, as evoked by critics' descriptions of its "stifling universe" (Romney, 2009), its "prison-like community with its oppressive atmosphere" (Blumenthal-Barby 2014, 96), and its characters' "claustrophobic social vacuum" (Wortel 2011, 5).

FIGURE 7.9 Sigi nonchalantly plays his clear-sounding whistle, lying back in his immaculate sailor suit: an audiovisual representation of the child oblivious to his own relative privilege.

is the worst violence we witness onscreen. And though the action is before us, Georg's strange behavior implies much more awfulness "behind the scenes," as if he comes from a place beyond what *The White Ribbon* can bear to show or ever encapsulate.

By attacking Sigi, Georg prompts his father's fury. Georg defies the Steward's reaction by playing the whistle he stole from Sigi at high pitch [1:55:27–1:55:43]. His rebellious musical "scream" is punished most savagely: the Steward quickly reaches for his cane and beats Georg offscreen while his mother begs him to stop for fear he will kill their son [1:55:45–1:55:51]. This is a representative scene of cruelty that is sonically expressed while being visually repressed (the inverse of the near-drowning scene where the danger is shown onscreen while the sonic elements are subdued). The Steward's violence against Georg is an embodiment of the Symbolic order that is founded on extreme repression and hypocrisy. It reflects the village's cyclic hostility too: the son's violence, beget from being violently raised, is punished with more of the father's violence. Ironically, the extremity of the Symbolic is what gives rise to a Real that will always be bigger and more frightening than what the village patriarchs can possibly control or be sure about.

Critically Representing the Symbolic

The sound track of *The White Ribbon* consistently stresses the repressiveness of the Symbolic order, especially through the voices of violent men. Where children are usually silently, quietly, and indirectly resistant to figures of authority, patriarchs *speak*. Mothers and wives are mostly silent in the presence of patriarchs as well. However, because most of the children are named, as opposed to their unnamed oppressors, we are more encouraged to view them as individuals. This personalized emphasis on victims over aggressors is representative of Haneke's commitment to social change, as well as being another implicit rebuke of the film's Symbolic order. The film is even more overtly critical of Eichwald's patriarchal society through showing fathers committing indefensible acts of violence. The scene in which Martin is caned by his father, the Pastor, is another crucial example. The Pastor's violence upholds hypocrisy (he speaks of religious devotion while inspiring hate), male privilege (the children and their mother, his wife, follow his orders), and repression (the violence happens within a private domestic space).

Martin is caned behind a closed door. There is no visual movement or stimulus for us to focus on, thus leaving us little option but to focus on the boy's screams, which become progressively more pained [27:22–27:32]. We have time to imagine the scene behind that door: the Pastor's forceful whips through the air, the still silence of the other children and their mother, the new marks on Martin's body (see Figure 7.10).[31] Recalling Haneke's argument that offscreen voices can be heard better, the authentic agony of Martin's cries is undeniable and unmissable. Such a scene inverts the audiovisual logic of Mother Courage's silent scream because we are hearing the action without seeing it. This makes us mindful of the cinematic construction, along with appealing to our hearts and imaginations. The sounds of offscreen violence prompt us to dwell on the agony endorsed by the Symbolic order and the unthinkable trauma that children like Martin experience. This leads us back to the Real in a circular way: the violence of village life creates a backlash as toxic as poisonous gas. And in the end, it will spread far beyond Eichwald.

The White Ribbon uses many other sounds to stress the dangers of unchecked tyranny within the Symbolic order. While the Real buzzes through *The White Ribbon* like invisible flies around a dead body, and we can never quite pin it down, the Symbolic order is straightforwardly perceivable, just as its impact is more concrete: the specific social, patriarchal context for every vignette of the film is explicitly represented. Fathers dominate numerous scenes, while their absence dominates the others: when children are left to their own devices in the village, their speech and action either revolves around the rules of the Symbolic or their attempts to break that order. The repression of the Symbolic order is in the motif of children being hit (whether slapped or caned), the staid familiarity of scored music played by the Schoolteacher and sung by

---

[31] The deliberation with which the film removes what we might see in this scene is even clearer if we consult the screenplay that describes what happens behind closed doors, including the "faces of the other brothers and sisters" (some turning away, some starting "to cry with pity and fear"), and a close-up on the Pastor showing he "is breathless" with "beads of sweat on his forehead." (This quotation comes from Haneke's script as translated into English for *The Screenplay Database* [n.date, 19].)

FIGURE 7.10 The long take of the closed door gives us little visual detail to focus upon: we are prompted to imagine the scene of violence we hear but cannot see.

the children's church choir, the sounds of doors closing, characters' crying in the dark, children making noiseless footsteps around adults or while adults sleep, the Pastor's quotations from scriptures, and many characters' silent submission to patriarchal authority.[32] The repressive power of the Symbolic order is additionally obvious through a visual motif of characters averting their eyes from each other as they speak, suggestive of how often they have to speak in counterintuitive or uncomfortable ways in accordance with social expectation or against themselves. Ironically, the status quo is shown to be intensely vulnerable, for in the end it is subject to imminent turmoil on a global scale. This resonates with how Haneke describes the First World War as a turning point because "God, King, and Country lost their authority," and the "untouchable position" of the "divine" count or landowner was lost (Grabner 2010, 25). In other words, *The White Ribbon* is set during a transitional moment in which Haneke perceives the undoing of established patriarchal norms: this could sound reactionary were it not for the fact that *The White Ribbon* shows this turmoil as stemming from, and as a form of rebellion against, the violence that is bred *within* the Symbolic order.

A collective desire to rebel against the Symbolic is audibly marked in many ways too. There is rebellion in Georg's playing Sigi's whistle so hard that it catches his father's most violent attention [1:55:27–1:55:43], the whipping sounds of Max's scythe as he beheads the Baron's cabbages in revenge for his mother's

---

[32] As Haneke explains to Grundmann, the Schoolteacher plays Bach's "Sicilienne" and before that a piano piece called "Liedchen" by Robert Schumann—the Schumann is an "easy exercise" whereas the "Sicilienne" is "a particularly intimate piece, which he plays to console [Eva]" (2010, 604).

death [32:58–33:14],[33] and Karli's cries in protest against the Doctor bandaging his eyes [1:49:51–1:50:46]. The Pastor's eldest son, Martin, also resists the Symbolic when he makes a lot of "noise" from his bed. He has been physically constrained by his father's instruction, his arms tied down by his side to prevent him from masturbating. When he views a fire from his bedroom window he begins shouting, waking his mother and siblings in his father's absence as he begs to be untied [1:14:55–1:16:09]. His mother scolds him and insists that the fire is "*nothing*" [1:16:31, my emphasis], though the film cuts directly after this scene to show the uncontrolled flames climbing [1:17:35]. The sound of the fire is comparatively loud as the flames reach beyond the frame. Unidentified men shout and run around, attempting to stop the damage with a single hose. The clash between the fire's power and the mother's disavowal of danger matters. She denies the emergency to the point of supervising one of her young children tying Martin back down in bed again so that he is not only constrained, but *incapacitated*, while the fire continues raging in proximity to their home (see Figure 7.11). No reason for nor culprit behind the fire is identified here or subsequently. It represents the uncontained toxic power of the Real, while Martin's mother embodies a hegemonic accordance with her husband and his authority within the Symbolic order, even against the natural instincts and safety of her children. The scale of the fire anticipates how the children will rebel in devastating ways. It foreshadows the breathtakingly rapid rise of National Socialism when the children will come of age, alluding to the huge number of bodies that will rise in smoke.[34]

The Pastor's daughter, Klara, provides us with the strongest aural example of onscreen resistance to the Symbolic [1:29:07–1:33:02]. At the beginning of her standout scene, the village children are behaving in an uncharacteristically unguarded and innocent way: in a rare moment of relaxation, Klara eats an apple as other children noisily flood out, back in, and around the schoolroom. As soon as she sees the Pastor approaching with the Schoolteacher, Klara hurries in and tells the others to "watch out, he's coming! Be quiet! For God's sake,

---

[33] Max beheads a crop of the Baron's cabbages during a festival presided over by the Baron's family. The sounds of the scythe and Max's breathing are noticeably louder than the string-led village festival music offscreen, an amplification of his strong physical statement against the existing Symbolic order.

[34] Though *The White Ribbon* is directly focused on the lead-up to World War One, it encourages us to perceive "premonitions of National Socialism" from the beginning (Williams 2010, 48). There is a more particular critical consensus that the film shows how "social pathology marks the path to National Socialism" (Stewart, 2010, 40). Stewart argues that the attack on Karli particularly represents "the incubation of Nazi barbarity in childhood trauma," anticipating the "arbitrary scapegoating," and the "racial cleansing and eugenics" of Hitler's regime (45). If we "do the math," as A. O. Scott (2009) bluntly puts it, "it's 1914. In 20 or 30 years, what do you suppose these children will be up to?" This consensus aside, Jonathan Romney (2009) argues that it is "reductive" to read the film as "an explanatory account of the origins of Nazism" because "hindsight might allow us to feel superior to these people who can't see the twentieth century coming." Haneke himself resists reducing the film to one national history because the film is dealing with a "broader theme" of any dangerously extreme ideology that grows out of pain and hopelessness (Grundmann 2010b, 595–596).

FIGURE 7.11 The fire rages while children like Martin are literally constrained by their elders. The fire symbolizes the unstoppable destruction engendered by that tyranny.

FIGURE 7.12 Though the Pastor is in the foreground, filling a third of the frame, Klara is the focal point of the shot, much as his voice dominates the sound track but her silence is "louder."

be quiet. Quiet!" The Schoolteacher scolds some of the unruly children for staying at school when Divinity Class is about to begin, and then hastily leaves, thus deferring to the Pastor before his exit. The Pastor then frog-marches Klara by her ear to the back of the room, and does not speak right away, as if her conduct is unspeakably reprehensible. Then he makes her face the back wall in shame (see Figure 7.12).

Following a heavy pause, the Pastor sternly commands, "Let us pray." After leading the children in the Lord's Prayer, he tells them to sit while Klara remains standing. The long shot of the class through the entire prayer

FIGURE 7.13 The Pastor's speech is interrupted by Klara's fall: his immediately closed lips signify that she has robbed him of aural control.

is unbroken, suggestive of the film itself being held captive by his leading voice. The Pastor then chastises the children by mentioning their upcoming Confirmation, and claiming that "for months I've tried to being God's word closer to you and make responsible human beings out of you. Who do I face today? Yelling monkeys." He speaks of his own sadness because his "own daughter plays the leading role in this pitiful display," despite his attempt to help her "avoid sin, selfishness, envy, indecency, lies and sloth." As his speech builds in intensity, he raises his voice with the following: "At the start of the year, I naively believed that she was now mature enough not to need the ribbon anymore, that she'd become responsible enough, as the daughter of the spiritual leader of—." Suddenly, as the Pastor's speech breaks off we hear the noise of Klara falling offscreen [1:32:59], and the film cuts to show that she is no longer standing. The other children turn their heads to see her. Perhaps they perceive that Klara has made a sound of protest without speaking. One boy rises to move towards her before the cut. The order over which the Pastor presides is thus both visually and aurally broken. Klara's worldless fall trumps his speech of mounting condemnation, robbing him of an oratory climax that would give him the satisfaction of reasserted aural control (see Figure 7.13). It is an unforgettable act of defiance.

(Towards a) Summary

In popular reviews about *The White Ribbon*, there is scant consideration of its aural impact, excepting some references to narrative rhythm: Keith Phipps

(2009), for example, describes the film as "deliberately paced," and Gary Thompson (2010) says the "story is achingly slow to unfold." Most reviewers miss the subtleties and affective power of its sound track, and many have critiqued it by making assumptions of the director's misanthropy. Steven Rea (2010) argues that Haneke's "doom-laden view of humanity—awful creatures, easily swayed to do dastardly things—oozes with contempt. Contempt for his subjects in their not-so-sleepy little town, but contempt for his audience too." Similarly, David Edelstein (2009) argues that before Haneke even shot the film his "contempt for humanity had congealed into dogma." He argues that *The White Ribbon* is testimony to Haneke's "basic sadistic impulse [having] never evolved." We thus return to the patterns that we first explored in the introduction whereby critics connect the awfulness of what characters do in Haneke's films with the director's assumed moral deficiencies. In another, even more extreme review, Kyle Smith (2009) writes that "Your admiration of Haneke's work is likely to depend on whether or not you gaze upon the heart of man and see sewage." What reviewers like Edelstein, Rea, and Smith fail to understand is how much faith Haneke places in his audiences to not only experience the traumas of his work but to make sense of how and why they happen. Moreover, they miss the critical role of sound in these processes.

The White Ribbon is filled with silences that Haneke surely expects us to fill. Each lack of sound is a gaping wound that can be healed only by our making some sense of it—over and over again, the film quietly demands that we consider why something is not or cannot be said, and why an utterance or noise demands quiet for contemplation. The film presents us with aural extremes that demand our active comprehension too: the birdsong that connotes life, the flies' buzzing that connotes death, and all the dangerous "nothings" in between that hurt a child, an adult, a family, a village, and a nation. The film disallows us comfort with its music and voiceover narration, but there is still faith in its clarity of purpose. *The White Ribbon* makes us aurally alert to the agony within a Symbolic realm that gives rise to an unstoppable Real with devastating and historically documented impact.

8

Amour

THE SCREAMS OF LIFE ANSWERED WITH LOVE

How can a sound track fully communicate love when characters never say "I love you"? What nuances of speech, dialogue, and silence honor the value of lasting love without melodrama? Why does it matter when a film stresses a woman's voice, even after her capacity for speaking breaks down? How is it possible to give a female protagonist's grief sonic precedence without resorting to any aural clichés of portraying femaleness, suffering, or pathos? Can a film self-consciously position us as perceivers of sonic newness, while also drawing us in to an intimate experience of sonic authenticity? What makes a quiet film the emotional highpoint of a director's career? These are the driving questions behind this return to auteurist analysis with *Amour*.

This chapter is a final challenge to those critics to perceive Haneke's work as overly austere and morally questionable. In the introduction, we surveyed many vitriolic scholarly responses to Haneke's work that misleadingly claim his inhumanity. No Haneke film has excited more extreme responses than *Amour*, despite its being his most understated work, and critics *always* mention the auteur in their assessments of it. *Amour* certainly echoes the aural patterns of his other films, but it also incorporates sonic surprises that only register as such in relation to the Haneke intertext. In other words, the principle of *interamplification* is in full effect here: knowing the director's aural tendencies allows us to hear what *Amour* does better.[1] The action takes place almost entirely indoors, and every tiny sound is perceivably significant within that confined space. In this way, it is Haneke's most subtly startling creation. The storyline is relatively

---

[1] See the final section (or "coda") of Walker's *Understanding Sound Tracks through Film Theory* for more on this principle of interamplification, especially with regard to the feature *Gravity* (2013) and its accompanying short *Aningaaq* (2013). *Aningaaq* is a significant development of one character who is heard but not seen in just one scene of *Gravity*, and it therefore gives a new visual context to everything he says, thus prompting us to return to the scene where we only hear his voice with fresh ears. In this way, the two films "interamplify" each other (Walker 2015, 413–415).

straightforward: an elderly woman (Anne) suffers a series of strokes that leave her increasingly debilitated until her husband (Georges) euthanizes her and then prepares himself for death. Though Anne's suffering and death are agonizingly drawn out, what makes *Amour* most moving is its surprising tenderness. It is an unforgettably affective appeal to our imaginations and hearts.

In contrast with *Amour*, Haneke's earlier films are referred to as "confrontational" (Debruge 2012), "clinical and dispassionate" (Warren 2013), "astringent—some have said merciless" (Nehme 2012), and "darkly pessimistic" (Quart 2016). *Amour* is described as comparatively "gentle" (Prentice 2013), "poignantly acted, uncommonly tender" (Debruge), and as surprisingly centered on the "portrayal of a warm and loving relationship" (O'Neill 2012). Critics argue that it represents a sea change in Haneke's directorial personality: Amy Taubin (2012) calls *Amour* "the most finely wrought work by this usually heavy-handed director" because it "honors the characters and the actors who portray them, rather than reducing them to pawns in his game"; Peter Debruge sees his "Austrian austerity" being replaced by a "possible mellowing"; and Ann Hornaday (2013) argues for Haneke's change from being "a notoriously gimlet-eyed filmmaker [who favors] austere style and facile pessimism" to one making "a genuine step toward humanism." Francine Prose (2013) simply calls the film "Haneke with a heart." Yet again, critics often assume equivalency between the content of Haneke's films and the director's personality.

Amour has its extreme detractors too. Iain Bamforth (2013) maintains that Haneke "is unsparing, clinical even, in his depiction of the indignities and humiliations of old age." Jim Vanden Bosch (2013) accuses the film of "feeling-*less*ness, especially on the part of Georges." Richard Brody provides the most damning critique, saying: "what comes through is that Haneke likes filming a killing, takes a smirkingly ghoulish look at the act, and takes unconscious pleasure in the unconscionable." So, despite *Amour* having won the Palme d'Or at Cannes, an unusually high-profile accolade given Haneke's having received the same honor for *The White Ribbon*, we come full circle to the familiarly caustic assumptions of the director's malevolence. Yet *Amour* offers us much more than a ghoulishly excruciating experience: it is Haneke's most compassionate representation of characters living through pain. And because it is unlike his other films in revolving around a love that outdoes violence and death, it is all the more powerful for that. Ultimately, we will find that *Amour* presents us with the greatest kindnesses of Haneke's sonic universe.

Echoing Haneke's Other Films

Amour shares many arresting aural patterns with Haneke's other films: ordinary domestic sounds are symbolically loaded; characters are largely defined in terms of sounds rather than images; the closely miked sounds of the characters gives us a sense of sonic intimacy with them even when the camera is relatively far away; and sounds often suggest that which is offscreen or beyond that which the cinematic frame can encapsulate, both literally and figuratively speaking. The aural deliberation of *Amour*, the sense of every sound being precisely orchestrated, is manifest enough that its sound track is more often mentioned in critical responses than the sound tracks for Haneke's other films. Scholars most frequently notice its tempo. Kevin Bongioroni (2016, 32) says the "pace is slow—agonizingly so," and Steven Goodrick refers to the "measured and nuanced tempo" of the film (2012, 1027). Philip A. Ringstrom writes that "The scene [where Georges prepares himself to die], like so many in the film, goes on at silent length so has to draw us into a sense of the real time he awaits before he passes out" (2014, 161).[2] The film allows us time between *sounds* as well as images, and this reinforces its distinctively Hanekean gravitas along with providing ample opportunity for contemplation (Warren 2013). Hilary and Steven Rose (2012) argue that "the silences, and the slow pace compel the viewer into profound self-reflection." This claim could apply to many scenes throughout Haneke's work.

Amour works like a virtual anthology of Haneke's sonic patterns, but it takes these patterns in newly poignant directions. The most obvious echoing of the earlier films is in using the names Georges and Anne. However, where the earlier films reuse these names to stress the representative, rather than psychology-unique, nature of the characters, here the names are more about stressing the universality of the story. Hillman sees the film as "a compressed ageing of humanity" and "Western civilization" (2015, 224), because it explores the challenges of many populations living longer (222).[3] *Amour* is more specifically connected to *The Piano Teacher* through the presence of Isabelle Huppert in several scenes, but where the earlier film revolves around her character's isolation and self-destructive desires, *Amour* makes her an unsympathetic character of unwitting cruelty. She plays Eva, the self-absorbed only child of Georges

---

[2] Bongioroni also notes the impressions of real time through the film as part of her argument that *Amour* outdoes the impressions of authenticity in the Neorealist classic *Bicycle Thieves* (1948, 31). Unlike De Sica's film, which incorporates various dramatic devices such as Antonio running into the thief, and the near-drowning of a boy who resembles his own son, Bongioroni notes that "*Amour* makes few concessions to cinematic or narrative conventions, in this sense representing a somewhat purer form of Neorealist ethos" (2016, 30). We might add that where *Bicycle Thieves* features a sympathetically coercive, non-diegetic, violin-led score by Alessandro Cicognini, *Amour* is aurally restrained, only using music that comes from the characters' diegetic world and not at all as their situation becomes most desperate.

[3] For more on the increasing number of films representing a universally aging population, see Drukarczyk et al. (2014). In connection with this, part of *Amour*'s poignancy is that the octogenarian protagonists are played by two actors most celebrated for roles they played in their youth: Jean-Louis Trintignant for *A Man and a Woman* (*Un homme et une femme*, 1966) and Emmanuelle Riva for *Hiroshima Mon Amour* (1959). For sustained analysis of the star power and intertextual importance of casting Trintignant and Riva, see Royer (2015).

and Anne, who demands to know what her father will do with her debilitated mother. She insensitively tells Georges she remembers the "reassuring" sound of them making love when she was a child.[4] She also tells him of her husband's affair, and her own attempted suicide, with an icily unmoving face. What she says about her own life suggests she is a world away from the necessarily quieter, slower, and more difficult reality of Anne's approaching death. Her bitter vocal outbursts about her mother's condition seem self-indulgent in relation to the selfless role her father assumes as primary caregiver.

Eva and her mother embody the sonic extremes that so often define Haneke's characters. The daughter's incapacity to engage with or understand her mother's pain is obvious in their different ways of speaking in one particular scene [1:08:24–1:10:28]. While Anne lies motionlessly silent in bed, Eva prattles at a near-breathless pace about financial investments, being worried about the stock her husband lost in the financial collapse, and being "addicted" to house ads as prices boom after her return from Scandinavia. Anne then attempts to speak back to Eva with a labored, stuttering effort on every word, and breathy gasps after each syllable: "I've . . . grandmother . . . woman with house . . . not . . . after . . . money." The scene continues like this for two more painful minutes before a sudden cut shows Eva having left the room without staying to interpret her mother's fragmented speech. She impatiently interrupts a conversation between her father and husband to say Anne has become "unrecognizable" through "speaking gibberish." Her description seems callous given the passionate effort Anne makes to communicate with her. The disparateness of their voices underlines this callousness, and what has broken between them as well: Anne's slow, quiet, breathily faltering speech followed by Eva's suddenly louder, abrasive, staccato exclamations.

Like all Haneke's other films, *Amour* also uses music sparingly and pointedly. At Haneke's insistence, music is consistently cut off through the film: the original title was "When the Music Stops" (Higgins 2016, 87).[5] The first example is an abrupt end to the opening concert music, after Anne and Georges return home and discover an intruder's attempted break-in. This is another familiar Hanekean element used surprisingly. Recall how the classical cues at the start of *Funny Games* are frighteningly broken off, with the music of John Zorn cutting into any aural sense of familiarity and safety even as the family continue to smile. The parallel pattern of cutting off music in *Amour* registers differently, partly because Haneke invites an utterly new kind of relationship

---

[4] Eva's comment on remembering the sound of her parents making love is punctuated by a cut to show two men installing a new bed with mechanized lever controls, audiovisually suggesting there will be no more "making love" for Anne, thus underlining Eva's insensitivity [20:51].

[5] As Higgins (2016, 86) explains, Haneke considered using the title " 'Les Vieux,' after a 1963 recording by Jacques Brel. The film nevertheless incorporates "narrative elements from the song" because "Brel describes an old couple who have abandoned their music ('their pianos are closed') and who rarely venture out ('their world has shrunk')."

with the main characters. Both Georges and Anne are devoted to the music we hear in *Amour* with an emphasis on its memorial significance, rather than its being ironically incorporated as a thin veneer for the brutality beneath the surface of "civilization" (as we hear in both *Funny Games* and *The Piano Teacher*). Opera is critically attached to the privileges of the family in *Funny Games*, and classical music is heard and/or played by the sadomasochistic protagonist of *The Piano Teacher*, both films therefore ironizing the status of such revered compositions.[6] In *Amour*, by contrast, the uplifting possibilities of canonized music are upheld in relation to what Georges and Anne share, and how Anne has professionally defined herself as a pianist. These possibilities are connected with what they both lose through her illness, as well as the transportive beauty that unites them. Those moments when the music suddenly stops sympathetically underline all this.

Another familiar Hanekean device is the emphasis on "jarringly intrusive" noises (Higgins 84).[7] Lynn A. Higgins mentions that many ambient noises are closely miked within *Amour*, even when the image is from a comparative distance: "where a more naturalistic approach would call for more muted sound representation [. . .] ambient noises are recorded with crisp precision from extremely close up [. . .]: plastic wrapping being removed from a mattress, water flowing from a faucet, the ringing of a telephone, a toilet flushing, a razor's buzz, doors opening and closing, a vacuum cleaner's hum, tape being ripped off a spool." She also refers to how Georges' nightmare, a subconscious reaction to his wife's rapid deterioration, is sonically "rendered realistically" (2016, 84). This particular scene includes a ringing doorbell and dripping water from a flooded hallway, Anne's muffled voice calling out behind a closed door ("what's going on?," "who is it?"), and Georges' splashing through the flood before a disembodied hand reaches around his face to smother him. He is then suddenly "awakened by his own scream" (Higgins, 84) [54:49–56:40]. After a complete blackout with the scream, a visual punctuation for Georges' aural distress, the film cuts to show him in bed waking up next to Anne. Consider how this both echoes and changes a dominant pattern of human voices under threat in Haneke's other work, as in *The Seventh Continent*. Where the earlier film ends with the television static, and Georges' dead, isolated silence after the worst trauma of the film, here the trauma of a nightmare ends with another Georges' *scream* in the presence of the woman who loves him. Moreover, as Georges wakes we see Anne immediately reach out to him in a gesture of concern, tenderness, and reassurance, even despite her comparatively limited physical agility.

---

[6] As noted in the chapter on *Funny Games*, we use "classical" music in the loosely colloquial sense of referring to canonized and so-called serious music (as opposed to "Classical" music dated from 1730 to 1820). For more on this distinction, see Walker (2015, 423).

[7] Higgins connects Haneke's amplification of everyday life noises with the French New Wave filmmakers and thus, by implication, their radical break from mainstream Hollywood norms of representation (2016, 84).

"Calm down," she says, having just woken with a start to his loud distress. Her reflexive response of touching him conveys years of being physically in tune with his movements and sounds. Although *Amour* is about the "nightmare" of living with a loved one's terminal illness, it is essentially more interested in waking us to the significance of unending love and connection. Anne's hand to Georges' shoulder is the unforgettably compassionate connection between characters that we are denied over and over again in Haneke's cinema. This makes it both strange and uncommonly precious (see Figure 8.1).

Amour thus consistently sets itself apart from Haneke's other films even as it recalls them. The very first moment of *Amour* prompts us to understand this with the highest level of aural alertness: firemen force open two heavy doors, with a hard cut from the opening credits in silence [0:51]. By interrupting the silence this way, the film immediately echoes the numerous non-sutured moments of Haneke's other films. But the audiovisual emphasis on opening up heavy doors has a deeper figurative meaning too: just as the film recalls what we have heard in Haneke's oeuvre many times before, *Amour* opens up a new level of intensity. The title alone knowingly takes us into unchartered territory: "*Amour*" registers ironically in relation to Haneke's pre-established reputation, though we learn through the film that it is "in fact sincere and unpretentious" (Grønstad 2013, 187). Moreover, in contrast with Haneke's other work, the violence of *Amour* is subdued: the film confronts us with what is difficult to hear, but the end of a life (Georges euthanizing Anne) is relatively quiet, emphasizing the physical and emotional agony of what he decides to do with uncompromised restraint. Indeed, the entire experience of *Amour* is understated in comparison with most of Haneke's other films. But it is only by having the other films in mind that

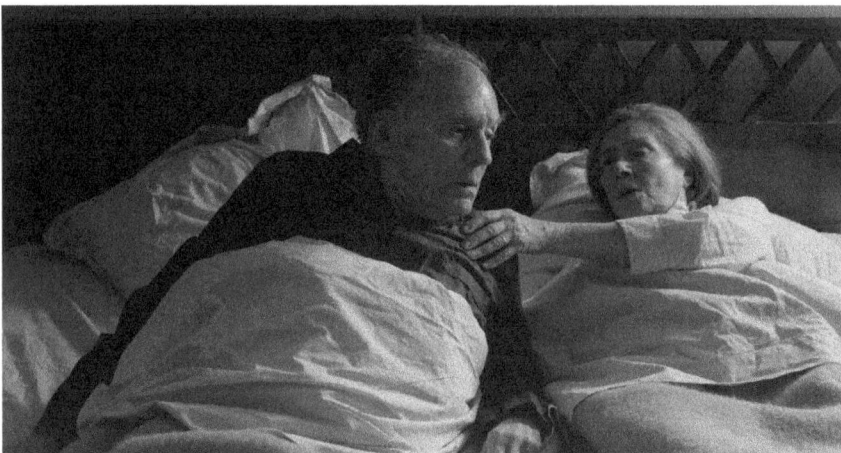

FIGURE 8.1 Anne's reflexive response to Georges' distress, and her urging him to "calm down," is one way of saying, "I love you." Though neither of them ever says it, such moments make their love manifest.

we can fully appreciate its gentleness and its most subtle dynamics. From *The Seventh Continent*, to *Funny Games*, to *Caché*, to *The White Ribbon*, to *Amour,* Haneke's sound tracks have become exponentially quieter, as if the auteur's controlling hand has slowly turned the volume down. So, *Amour* does not simply play out what we might already attached to "a Haneke film," but becomes part of a process whereby Haneke's films talk to each other.

A Non-Generic Love Story

Despite incorporating many familiar Hanekean sonic strategies, *Amour* is further set apart from his other films in that its violence is inextricable from love. This makes it hard to classify generically. The film has frequently been described as a horror. Farran Smith Nehme (2012), for example, refers to the sound of the running tap in the scene of Anne's first stroke as a sonic reminder of Hitchcock's most infamously terrifying work: "Death is toying with [the characters], quietly announcing its presence via the most dread-inducing running water since Janet Leigh turned on the taps in *Psycho*." For Andrea Gogröf (2015), Georges and Anne embody a "monstrous dimension" in many respects, including how they bear "the fatal and brutal mark of illness and age."[8] The film therefore echoes many others that "portray old age as a threat" (Bosch 2015, 1). Francine Prose (2013) gives the most sensationalist response: "Michael Haneke's *Amour* is the ultimate horror film. With its portrayal of the shocks, the cruelties and indignities to which old age and disease subject a happily married Parisian couple, it's far scarier and more disturbing than Hitchcock's *Psycho*, Kubrick's *The Shining*, or Polanski's *Rosemary's Baby*." Such movies make fascinating comparisons with *Amour* because they *sound* completely different. Notwithstanding its sometimes eerie use of silence and Anne's offscreen voice, the film's use of music is never fearful. Works by Schubert are most memorably included for all their artistic beauty, in relation to Anne's former, aurally defined life. Georges experiences a flashback of her playing Schubert at the piano before she became ill, in complete control of the sounds she makes [1:14:52–1:15:41]: this is not an ironically inserted highbrow cue (as in *Funny Games*), nor is it disturbingly incorporated (as in *The Piano Teacher*). It is music at the heart of a precious and sacred memory. Compare such music with Bernard Herrmann's shrieking violins for the shower scene in *Psycho* (1960), or the terrifying modernist music

---

[8] Such a reading resonates with how films typically represent "old age as a horror story," and the "ongoing pathologization of changes associated with age." Despite the upsurge in cinematic representations of elderly characters, older women are most often "presented as exaggeratedly maternal or monstrous," and their living with illness is shown as "considerably more terrifying than the seemingly expected end of life" (Chivers 2011, xviii, 148, xvii, 139). By contrast, we explore how Anne is much more than a grotesque or stereotypical female victim of old age, especially through the film's nuanced emphasis on the significance of every sound she makes.

in *The Shining* (1980),[9] or the haunting subjectivity of Krzysztof Komeda's score for *Rosemary's Baby* (1968).

Two recent anthologies about horror movie sound tracks allow for some more instructive aural contrasts with *Amour*. Where *Amour* incorporates music sparingly, the horror film often features music "for triggering feelings of horror, fear, and rage" (Lerner 2010, viii). Neil Lerner identifies specifically familiar techniques for horror like "repetitive drones, clashing dissonances, and stingers (those assaultive blasts that coincide with shock or revelation)," experimental harmony and instrumentation, and any kind of music that "makes us feel threatened and uncomfortable" (ix).[10] Philip Hayward's introduction to a similarly eclectic collection of essays on horror sound tracks begins by stressing the decisive role of music in creating horrific impact, dwelling on a key example of John Carpenter's original score for *Halloween* (1978), which features eerily synthesized sounds, frequent stingers, and a main theme with the unsettlingly irregular time signature of 5/4 (2009, 1–2). Arguably, then, those critics who critically refer to *Amour* as horror confuse and/or conflate the genre with the adjective "horrific": the film certainly contains disturbing semantic elements (Georges' nightmare, Anne's deteriorating body, and the threat of death), but its genre classification is still complicated.[11] The film lacks scenes of sonically heightened violence. Moreover, it avoids the frequent stingers that are *most* common in horror, let alone Haneke's other cinema (such as the gunshot in *Funny Games*, or the smashed soup bowl in *The White Ribbon*). In addition, everything we hear in *Amour* falls within a narrative context that "*domesticates* and *tames* the scariest, and most common, fears of old age by confronting them directly" (Fileva 2014, 181, my emphasis).

Actively listening to *Amour* means experiencing the private space of woman's physical deterioration, a world away from the generic aural "shocks" of horror. This has an important moral dimension given Haneke's personal commitment to representing a slow death with authentic patience. In addition, the

---

[9] Throughout *The Shining*, music is used for its most troubling connotations, even with ironically lighter, more popularly playful choices like the old jazz song ("Midnight, the Stars, and You") over the final photograph that establishes Jack's ghostly presence in the past.

[10] It is not that well-known, canonical music, such as the piano music of Schubert, cannot be "horrific." For a supporting example, see Robin Wood's essay on Schubert's musical interpretation of monstrous threat in Goethe's 1782 poem "Der Erlkönig" ("The Elf King"), which deals with the death of an enchanted child (an example also mentioned by Lerner 2010, ix). It is beyond the scope of this book to fully explore the sonic semantics of horror movies. Suffice to say that the music of *Amour* is not there primarily for horrific effects. Though the relative quiet of the film paradoxically amplifies its rawness, the candid representation of its characters' pain has more in common with Neorealism than horror. Haneke *has* previously and self-consciously used music for horrific effects, as in *Funny Games*, but this does not apply to *Amour*.

[11] *Amour* has more in common with Ingmar Bergman's *Wild Strawberries* (*Smultronstället*, 1957), as a ponderously paced tale of approaching death, than Hitchcock's *Psycho*. That said, it is more evenhanded than Bergman's film in representing both male and female voices as significant, and connecting music with both male and female subjectivity.

film differs from his others in that it most directly "gives voice" to a painful part of his own history. Peter Conrad (2012) explains the autobiographical basis as follows: "At the age of 92, crippled by rheumatism, [Haneke's] aunt overdosed on sleeping pills. Haneke found her in time, and rushed her to the hospital. She had previously begged him to help her die; he pointed out that since he was her heir, he might have ended up in prison. A year after her first attempt, she swallowed more pills and put herself out of her misery." Along with this painful personal inspiration for the film's narrative, Haneke had the main characters' apartment modeled on his parents' one in Vienna, "Georges' stories are based on Haneke's own," and "Georges' deprecating report of a funeral is based on Haneke's father's funeral" (Gogröf 2015). *Amour* is thus the most clear-cut example we have of the director speaking directly through his film. This helps explain why some critics find it comparatively intimate (Gullette 2014; Gleiberman 2012).

So, *Amour* is a break from Hanekean norms as well as being a far-from-generic experience. More specifically, *Amour* attempts to carve out *new* cinematic terrain by focusing on and honoring old love. Where films all over the world often represent what Peters calls "the Hollywood trope of a passionate love joining two hearts as one," *Amour* is focused on "love's duration." For Amir Cohen-Shalev and Esther-Lee Marcus, the film is thus "a pioneering, experimental cinematic examination of the rarely explored territory of long-lasting love" (2015, 64). They explain the ageist negativity attached to the term "old love" as "worn out and without potential for change" (64). They argue there is therefore no adequate word or phrase for the film's "rarely explored territory of long-lasting love, love that carries two people across several decades" (65).

Amour could feel like an experience of familiar terrain even though it focuses on "old love." The narrative trajectory—an old woman slowly approaching death in her husband's presence—*might* have been the excuse for a sentimental weepie designed to prompt our uncontrollably strong responses.[12] The film itself vocally addresses this when Georges tells Anne a story about a movie that he found emotionally disabling [32:20–34:44]. He describes it in terms of being a heritage film melodrama: "A schmaltzy romance between a nobleman and a commoner's daughter who can't marry and so, through generosity of spirit, renounce each other." But such was the extreme affective impact of the movie that he cannot recall its specific subject matter: "Actually, I'm not sure of the story anymore. I remember being overcome with emotion." He even recounts crying in front of a man who asked him about it afterwards: "the emotions and tears welled up again . . . even stronger than during the film perhaps. I couldn't stop crying." By this narrative point, half of Anne's body is paralyzed from

---

[12] For a celebrated article about the kinds of involuntarily emotional and physical responses prompted by melodramas or so-called weepies, in ironic parallel to those involuntary responses prompted by horrors and porn, see Williams ([1991], 2012).

her first stroke. As Georges speaks to her, he cuts up a meal for her to easily eat with one hand. His brief description of the gut-wrenching film offsets the understated care with which he takes care of Anne's meal. Georges recounting his memory is also an act of self-disclosure that moves her: "You're a monster sometimes," she teases him, "but very kind." Her response expresses loving intimacy without either of them needing to explore the nature of Georges' experience further, and the word "monster" is so far from what Georges is that it underlines the film's difference from other, more horrific *and* sentimentally blindsiding films.

Like *Funny Games* and *Caché, Amour* contains traces of many other films it might have been.[13] Georges' anecdote reveals that Haneke self-consciously sets *Amour* apart from more familiarly impactful kinds of cinematic experience. Whereas Georges' response to the "schmaltzy romance" was so overwhelming that its content became forgettable to him, *Amour* prompts us to absorb its unconventional details without requiring that we become engulfed by them. Despite its poignant subject matter, the film allows us some self-conscious distance from its content: a more sadistic director, as some critics would have us believe Haneke is, would have surely wrung out the affective impact of Anne and Georges' grief. The detail of Georges neatly cutting Anne's food while he tells her about his memory might remind us of what we more typically "consume" in a film about a main character stricken with illness: scenes of despair, longing, anger, and grief that heighten the character's experience of confronting death through poetic speeches or, at the very least, stirring non-diegetic music that relays their interior life.[14] As Isabelle Huppert says, the film avoids "sentimentalism," but we should not confuse restraint with lack of feeling in *Amour*.[15]

Amour focuses on the daily reality of managing an illness that commonly afflicts the aged—but the commonality of this experience is rarely portrayed

---

[13] Here, we allude to Leitch's phrase, as first cited in the chapter on *Funny Games*. Though Leitch wites of such traces with regard to adaptations of novels to film that are necessarily selective interpretations, the idea is more generally applicable (2007, 17).

[14] For a risibly extreme example, recall the deathbed scene of *Immortal Beloved* (1994), a biopic about Beethoven (Gary Oldman) that begins by showing him on his deathbed, breathing heavily during a thunderous storm as the opening of the Fifth Symphony plays non-diegetically [1:05–1:17]. For a more subtly poignant example, recall the deathbed scene of *Howard's End* (1992). We see Vanessa Redgrave's character scrawling her signature to bequeath the home she loves to her dearest female companion, an honorable act of charity and largesse punctuated by Richard Robbins's comparatively delicate, impressionistic piano cue [42:31–42:50], a strong yet softening musical contrast with the hard, echoing noises of the hospital where she dies.

[15] This quotation from Huppert comes from Montmayeur's documentary, in relation to which we see Haneke directing her to sob with her back to camera, physically showing her how to fight the release of her feelings. The documentary shows his "replacing" Huppert's stifled, guttural sobs with steady, rhythmic sobbing, a fascinating and representative example of the entire film's aurally emotive exactitude.

with such aural candor. While "horror" tends to connote fantastical threat, *Amour* is interested in what happens when ordinary people are subjected to the unexceptional realities of growing old. Many scenes deal with the plausibly physicality of Anne's condition through slightly amplified sounds. Instead of representing her imminent death through any overt or Romantic stylization, *Amour* prompts us to perceive everyday details of her and her husband's increasingly difficult life. For instance, after her only stay in hospital, we hear every detail of Georges helping Anne from her wheelchair into an armchair: their little breaths of effort, their clothes touching, their short steps, the slight squeak of their shoes moving awkwardly with and around each other, and the sound of her weight resting into the chair [24:01–24:36]. Much later, as we see Georges feed Anne mashed food following her stroke, we hear the struggle of every mouthful, every breath, every swallow or partial swallow, each gulp of water, each dribble and slight cough, along with Georges gently urging her to keep going [1:16:41–1:19:23]. The absence of music to soften these and several similar scenes of the film places further emphasis on the reality of her deteriorating body as well as her increasing dependency on Georges. But the absence of music is not always disturbing and withholding, as it is in *Caché*. As distressing as the isolated sound effects of these scenes are, they communicate that Georges and Anne are struggling *together* and that *Amour* is a new kind of story about love. The overlapping sounds of their mutual physical suffering align them with the Georges and Anne of *Funny Games*, but their struggle is against an undeniably natural process rather than one against other, cruel people. Again, the aural connections ironically serve to emphasize the differences, and to make the experience of hearing *Amour* all the more surprisingly moving.

Ritualized Listening

Generic film experiences are often referred to as ritualized forms of entertainment because they repeat formulas that audiences recognize and participate in *en masse*.[16] Though *Amour* is not ritualistic in either generic *or* Hanekean terms, the film does frequently focus attention on the ritual of listening to music. This is the subject of the first post-title scene, preparing us for an experience that will demand our self-conscious receptiveness to hearing something new. The capacity to be aurally alert, as opposed to passively listening, is thematically central to *Amour* from the outset. After the pre-credit scene, showing firemen breaking into the apartment (and soon discovering Anne's body after Georges laid it in state), the film focuses on an audience readying themselves for a classical concert. The setting is the grand Théâtre des Champs-Elysées. Audience members

---

[16] For more on understanding genre films as ritualized, see Altman ([1984] 2012).

FIGURE 8.2 The camera positioning us to face the audience rather than the stage is counterintuitive, rather like our seeing someone face the wall instead of the doors in an elevator. Here, the film primes us to be unusually active perceivers from the first moment we see (even without our being necessarily conscious of) the main characters seated near the center.

find their seats, murmur to each other, look at their programs, and fiddle with their belongings. We cannot hear any of their individual voices through the first long take; the emphasis is on a collective experience over and above singling anyone out. The film's central couple is in the audience, but this is only retrospectively obvious, for they are not set apart by the camera or illuminated more than the other people. They are simply part of the group that slowly settles, soon quiets on the lights dimming, and collectively erupts in applause as the pianist takes his seat. They are part of an audience, in other words, that behaves exactly as we would expect at such an occasion. As the pianist begins, the film does not cut to show him, thus maintaining focus on the passive receptiveness of the audience [2:14–4:10]. Brecht was famously critical of concert hall music that has "purely culinary ambitions" because it could reduce the audience to "an enervating, because unproductive, act of enjoyment" (1964, 89). Here, by positioning us to self-consciously observe the concert audience, *Amour* primes us to respond more actively than they do (see Figure 8.2).[17]

The concert begins with Schubert's Impromptu No. 1 in C minor, Op. 90. It starts with an extended, strongly resounding (pedaled) *forte* chord including notes in the extreme lower and upper register, and then a surprisingly tender theme emerges. The musical impression is of sudden darkness giving way to lightness, preempting the narrative action of *Amour*—the shock of Anne's first sudden stroke that leads to the representation of enduring love. Next, the

---

[17] By demanding our active comprehension, as opposed to encouraging our passive absorption, *Amour* brings us full circle to the arguments of the introduction about Haneke's Brechtian approach.

film shows a montage of Anne and Georges congratulating the pianist back-stage after the concert, taking a tram home, and returning to their apartment [4:10–4:59]. Again, we do not hear the characters' voices. Even the sounds of the tram are subdued, with only quiet squeaking and clicking in the mix. What Anne and Georges say to each other here is unimportant because the film is more interested in showing their companionship and movements together.

It is rare for Haneke to use a montage with music that is not consist-ently attached to the diegetic space—usually, music comes from an identifi-able source within a given scene, and ends on the cut from that established source (for instance, the Muzak of the grocery store in *The Seventh Continent*). Alternatively, *Amour* features a montage that *sutures* the cuts from concert hall, to tram, to apartment [4:10–4:59]. This would be unexceptional in innumer-able other films but, in the context of Haneke's productions that repeatedly foreground brokenness, any music that provides continuity stands out. Here, the use of music to create the suturing effect of formal seamlessness parallels the union of Anne and Georges. For Higgins, the music is "analogous to a point-of-view shot in the visual realm, [because] this sequence installs a 'point-of-audition' that persists throughout the sequence, as the concert's afterglow infuses the characters' bodies and gestures, while the music's pacing determines that of the shots" (2016, 85). Such a response suggests a touching equivalency between the intact bodies of both main characters (*before* Anne's stroke) and the body of the film.[18]

Quiet Power and Different "Nothings"

Just as our experiences of Haneke's other films lead us to perceive the opening montage of *Amour* as exceptional, they prepare us to perceive its quiet compas-sion more strongly. Even the most distressing scene in which Georges euthanizes Anne is relatively subdued. Right before this, Georges calms Anne with his story of having a miserable time at a school camp and the consolatory arrange-ment he made with his mother. After his being forced to attend the camp, they agreed that if he was having a good time he would send her a postcard with a

---

[18] This sequence provides us with the most calming audiovisual "harmony" in Haneke's work to date. There are few instances of suturing music in Haneke's other films. The most often noticed example is an infamous, darkly humorous montage from *The Piano Teacher*, showing Erika rehears-ing Schubert's Piano Trio in B flat major, Op. 100, and then her walking alone through a mall to a sex shop to view a porn video [22:18–25:03]. When the montage cuts from the rehearsal trio, the Schubert continues as underscoring but "abruptly stops" when she enters a private viewing booth (Palmer 2011, 187). The music is "interrupted by the sound of [her] inserting tokens" into the pornographic video machine (Tweraser 2011, 201), which undercuts our enjoyment of the music along with reinforcing the film's unorthodox use of classical music in connection with Erika's disturbed psychology. The sense of cohesion and aesthetic beauty built into Schubert's music is thus ironized in *The Piano Teacher*, whereas it is incorporated with moving simplicity in *Amour*.

picture of flowers on it, and if he was having a bad time he would send a picture of stars. After having to eat rice pudding, which he loathed, and developing diphtheria, which entailed his being quarantined in hospital, Georges sent her a postcard covered in stars. Over the course of Georges' telling this story, Anne slowly stops speaking, and she regresses to the peacefulness of an infantile state in his care. Right after the story is over, with this peace established, Georges slowly reaches for the pillow and suffocates her. When Georges slowly moves the pillow over Anne's face, the sound of her struggle is muffled: a generic horror or melodrama would, of course, include the sounds of a greater physical and emotional struggle. Though Anne's legs rise up and shake uncontrollably and disturbingly under the bedclothes, the action is more like a forceful embrace than a fight. The smothering itself lasts long enough that the initial shock gives way to our being suspended in the moment of her death [1:49:09–1:49:50]. From the moment Georges enters Anne's room to the end of the scene there are no tears, just as the scene is not designed to be tear-jerking [1:44:28–1:50:30]. The slow pacing allows for our extended contemplation of the shocking action *and* its amazing kindness.

At first, there seems to be no connection between Georges' last story for Anne and his euthanizing her. However, consider that Georges' story is about honoring a private contract, and one that does not require words (the picture on a postcard). Parallel to this, Georges' action is making good on an unspoken contract: in an earlier scene, Anne tells him he must promise she will not go back to hospital, though he fails to reply immediately. In euthanizing Anne, Georges is finally providing the answer she requested from him. The long duration of the scene gives us time to remember the unspoken contract, and to perceive Georges' tenderness as well as his forcefulness in honoring Anne's wishes. Later, in the film's final sequence, after Georges makes his own choice to die and is mysteriously reunited with Anne, their final quiet exit is more like the natural phenomenon of stars "disappearing" in daylight than the trauma we have explored in Haneke's other films.

Just as the quiet of *Amour* moves away from the menace we cannot escape in the rest of Haneke's work, the word "nothing" is handled differently. Shortly before the scene in which Anne has a stroke, there is a short nighttime interlude. In the near-blackness, the sound of her soft breathing is perceptible before Georges asks, "what's wrong?" and Anne answers, "nothing." [7:06–7:10]. A cut to the breakfast scene is punctuated by an egg timer going off, a sound that retrospectively punctuates the word "nothing" [7:14]. Given that Anne has her first stroke in this next scene, we soon deduce that her "nothing" was a lie. That said, where "nothing" is primarily associated with another Georges' deliberate deceit, suppression, denial, anger, and guilt in *Caché*, and various characters' deceitfulness and hurt in *The White Ribbon*, Anne's saying the word represents a more understandable inclination to dismiss a disturbing physical sign. It may be an attempt to protect her husband too. "Nothing" is said far fewer times in *Amour* than in *Caché* or *The White Ribbon*, but the word inevitably rever-berates with the earlier films, thus inviting comparisons. After her first stroke, Anne insists she is fine, that "there's nothing wrong" [14:27], and that there is no need to call a doctor, to which Georges insists, "we can't pretend nothing happened" [14:36]. Unlike the protagonist of *Caché, Amour's* Georges immedi-ately recognizes the significance of a "nothing" and takes action. He also uses "nothing" to protect Eva from the truth, and Anne from Eva's intrusive pres-ence. He uses the word defensively after Eva scolds him for not answering the door quickly enough for her ("nothing, I was in the toilet"), though we see he needed a few moments to calm himself after her thoughtlessly unexpected arri-val. He then denies Eva access to Anne's room because her condition is much worse ("Nothing's going on here, I just want to avoid unnecessary drama"). So, in this scene, "nothing" is attached to his collecting himself and being practical in the face of Anne's undeniable decline [1:32:46–1:40:15]. In an earlier scene, when Georges begrudgingly anticipates attending a friend Pierre's funeral, Anne teasingly asks what he would say if no one attended his own, to which Georges playfully responds "nothing, probably" [36:47–36:48]. Here, "nothing" is the simplest articulation of truth, so obvious as to bring levity to the scene.

Elsewhere, "nothing" is even a signifier of love between Georges and Anne. When Anne asks Georges to promise her that she will never go back to hospital, and he is stunned into responding, "what can I say?," Anne responds, "nothing. Say nothing. Okay?" Here, "nothing" is immediately connected to their ulti-mate unspoken contract [25:34–25:42]. After Georges recounts Pierre's funeral, Anne anticipates her condition worsening and not wanting to "inflict" that on Georges and herself, in response to which he insists, "you inflict nothing on me" [42:46–42.47]. Anne tells him he need not "lie," but since Georges uses the word "nothing" with great deliberation elsewhere (unlike so many of Haneke's other characters), the film encourages us to believe him. At the very least, this "noth-ing" is a kindness. So, this one word that chimes through Haneke's films gathers new meanings in *Amour*. Only in *Amour* does it consistently affirm truthfulness, love, courtesy, and/or protection. *Amour's* uses of "nothing" resonate with the Zen concept of "Mu" as an absence that is positive: like the gaps within a floral arrangement that allow us to see the flowers, "nothing" is a necessary, benign, and beautiful element of the film's form.[19]

Georges and Anne: Hearing the Feminist Aural Logic

Along with containing new "nothings," the relationship between Georges and Anne is redemptive from a feminist perspective. Georges' particular attention to every sound Anne makes is especially significant: even as a female protagonist,

---

[19] For more on the concept of Mu, specifically in relation to Ozu's cinema, see Schrader (1972, 27).

she has uncommon aural primacy. Although all Haneke's main characters are much defined by aural detail, Anne in *Amour* is an extreme case. Indeed, Anne's identity is much more defined by aural details than images. Rather than being limited to how she appears as an eighty-something-year-old woman, we come to know Anne best through the sounds she chooses, and is able, to make. The first sign of Anne's stroke is her strange silence. Georges and she are having a routine breakfast when he suddenly becomes aware she is not responding. After attempting to make her speak, he runs a washcloth under the cold water tap and wipes her face. He leaves the room to get help, having left the tap running, and suddenly hears it stop [11:42]. When he then calls out to Anne, she gives him no initial response, but after he walks back to the kitchen she asks, "What are you doing?" [12:20]. In this scene, Anne makes no sound for about four minutes [8:19–12:20], aside from switching off the tap offscreen, but we later learn she had a stroke during this time. Yet again in Haneke's cinema, something big happens in a silence. It is rare that films foreground a woman's lack and loss of speech: far more often, women are simply or submissively silent. In *Amour*, by contrast, we feel the absence of the female voice. That the silence of a female protagonist is the most threatening sonic aspect of the film is its most loaded feminist statement.

Along with the power of Anne's silences, there is the unnerving impact of her changing voice. Reviewers frequently mention the affective struggles in Emmanuelle Riva's vocal delivery: as Kroenert (2013) writes, Anne "labors excruciatingly over every syllable she speaks" and she "howls in pain as she is showered" while Georges suffers a "quiet, living grief." After mentioning Riva's "famous, carefully articulated diction," Higgins writes of her own distress when Anne's voice is increasingly hard to understand (2016, 88). Similarly, Ruth Franklin (2013) stresses how Riva's "gentle, cultured voice is reduced to an agonized stammer that Georges patiently deciphers."[20] For Franklin, she thus becomes an "object for [Georges] to maintain" (45). Luke Davies (2013) perceives Anne's trajectory in equally devastating terms: "We see the human spirit becoming animal. We see the animal becoming vegetable. Once Anne stops talking, there seems only anger in her eyes."

The perception of Anne being objectified or reduced to an animalistic presence is debatable, for even after Anne's speech is all broken up into isolated words, she still has a complex and central sonic place in the film. Moira Weigel (2013) writes of Anne's repetition of the word "mal" as the most "notable

---

[20] Riva's sonic presence in *Hiroshima Mon Amour*, the film that inspired Haneke to cast her (as he mentions in Montmayeur's "making of" featurette for *Amour* [2012]), offers us a strong sonic comparison with *Amour*. In this earlier, career-defining film, her speech consistently dominates the sound track while she recounts memories of her lost love. Riva uses the full range of her voice, from impassioned shouting to delicate whispers, and the richness of her aural performance always gestures to that which is bigger than what the film's images reveal.

refrain" of her speech. After her severe second stroke, she repeatedly says "mal!" (subtitled as "hurts!") while a nurse showers and scrubs her down [1:20:01–1:20:46]. The nurse speaks brusquely to Anne about the process of cleaning her ("is the temperature okay?," "I'm going to tip you forward," "Don't be scared, I'm here," "Very good"), and Georges looks on silently and helplessly. Anne's only vocal response is "mal!," but the nurse's rhythm of washing her is uninterrupted. Georges, visibly pained beyond words, leaves the room and the scene cuts to show him interviewing the nurse while Anne continues to groan "mal!" in the next room. As the nurse leaves, she assures Georges that the word is only a "reflex." Georges sees her to the door and returns to Anne lying in bed, taking her hand and stroking it as her groans of "mal!" slowly stop [1:20:46–1:22:30]. As soon as he tells Anne that he needs to hire another nurse and asks her opinion, she says "mal" repeatedly again, quietly but clearly [1:22:59–1:23:11]. So, the word that Anne moans on and off for over three minutes *does* seem to have some intentionality behind it. Further, the simple fact that the word never sounds quite the same when she groans it reminds us that there are many contours to her experience. "Mal!" is like a note played a hundred different ways on the piano—Riva uses her voice as an instrument of inexhaustible expressivity.

Though "mal!" is subtitled in English as "hurts!," Weigel explains that "a more colloquial translation would be "pain." Dima mentions the possible translation of "mal!" as "evil," which she interprets as "the sound of death approaching" (2015, 171). Similarly, Milosz Paul Rosinski writes that "Anne's death is present within her, and echoes with her voice screaming 'mal, mal, mal'" (2015, 193). However we interpret "mal!," it matters that just one word spoken by a central female character prompts so much speculation. For Weigel (2013), Anne's repeated cry "captures the difference between *Amour* and Haneke's earlier work. Rather than calling us coldly and cruelly to witness crimes, it compels us to participate in an act of mourning. [The story] hurts, and it admits this."[21] The possibility of the word being interpreted in three ways supports this argument because "mal!" demands our active interpretation. This reflects the film's unconventionally minimalist approach—Riva never chews the scenery, but her repeated word echoes around the apartment with unfixable power. Her performance of Anne's vocal deterioration has distinctive status too: for Eelco F. M. Wijdicks, a Professor of Neurology, "there is no better representation" of a stroke victim on film (2013).

---

[21] The hurt of the film has inspired some reviewers' unusually personal responses. Writing for *The New Yorker*, Hannah Goldfield (2013) writes that *Amour* "depressed me to the point that my chest felt tight, that fat tears streamed down my face as I struggled to keep my shoulders from heaving too noticeably. It depressed me to the point that I seriously contemplated escaping to the bathroom to have it out and collect myself, and considered leaving the theatre altogether." Eventually, the film prompted her to relive cherished memories of witnessing the love between her own grandparents. Rose and Rose explain that they were moved enough by the film to write letters like those that "Anne, in her need and desire for death, might well have written" (2012, 1219).

In another scene of *Amour*, Riva's vocal performance is hauntingly "eloquent" despite her lost ability to speak clearly for herself. In Georges' absence, we hear another nurse roughly brushing Anne's hair while she groans in protest [1:25:44–1:26:05]. We can hear the brush's teeth pulling against each strand of Anne's hair as the nurse insists "you want to look your very best . . . so everybody can admire you." The nurse's emphasis on how Anne looks, in contrast with Georges' many attempts to hear her, is important from a feminist perspective. As the nurse holds up a mirror close to Anne's face, saying "isn't she beautiful?," she forces Anne to contemplate an image that no longer represents who she is. The nurse seems dimly aware of Anne's divided self, but only to the extent that she says, "isn't she beautiful?" (rather than "aren't *you* beautiful?"). This moment recalls countless other moments on film where the woman's presence has been reduced to an image of beauty. In this respect, *Amour* contains the traces of yet more films that it refuses to be.

The shock of Anne's losing her ability to speak more than single words, and the disturbance of her inarticulate noises, is compounded by the film's emphasis on the music she can no longer play. The aforementioned flashback of her playing Schubert is a bittersweet representation of her life before dying. She plays the Impromptu No. 3 in G-flat major, Op. 90. The piece features strong undulating harmonic lines, and a clear melody rising above them. Given there is little melody in *Amour* (let alone Haneke's entire oeuvre), with the exception of Schubert's Impromptu No. 1 in C minor, Op. 90 near the beginning, this piece gives us some exceptional beauty. The emotional accessibility of the piece is a significant contrast with some of the film's other music, particularly the technically demanding Beethoven Bagatelle No. 2, Op. 126, played by Anne's former student, Alexandre Tharaud (a real-life concert pianist), on her request [50:50–51:09]. His performance is small by comparison; he plays more out of obligation than pleasure. Anne plays Schubert with much greater gusto, and the film cuts to show Georges transfixed as he listens to her. But for Georges' appearance being consistent with the rest of the film, the scene leads us to believe we are witnessing an actual flashback. Then Georges turns off the stereo behind him, as if waking from a dream. The music suddenly stops.[22]

In the moment that Georges stops the CD, our definition of the music changes: it shifts from being what Claudia Gorbman calls "metadiegetic music" (that is, "music that is narrated or imagined by a particular character within a film") to being diegetic music.[23] This shift in how we understand and "place"

---

[22] It is surely important that Anne is not a young woman in this flashback. The scene emphasizes that Georges wishes to re-see exactly who his wife was in her old age and in their old love, not as some youthful or idealized image from the past. Parallel to this, in the final sequence his wish is granted: Anne appears and speaks as she did just before she had the first stroke.

[23] Dima explains that Claudia Gorbman coined this term with "a nod to structuralist Gérard Genette," though this paraphrase of her definition is a direct quotation from Jeff Smith (Dima 2015, 17; Smith 2009, 22). For more on defining "metadiegetic music," see Gorbman (1987, 22–23).

the music is important for showing the fluidity in Georges' mind between past and present. This music thus contributes an expansive sense of space and time, in contrast with the implosive restrictedness of the film's *mise-en-scène*. [24] We are drawn into alignment with Georges' aural memory as it relays love, loss, dread, retreat, regression, resignation, and renewed shock.[25] The click of the "off" switch hurts—it is yet another ordinary sound within Haneke's oeuvre that is surprisingly weighted with meaning. We now realize the sight of Anne was more elusive than the more tangible impression of an objective filmic flashback. That such a tiny sound can make such a devastating reality clear feels cruelly counterintuitive. The literal source of the sound is behind Georges (suggestive of the past), not before him (in the present or future). So, the *mise-en-scène* underlines the time he has lost with Anne. Because the film is structured to make us believe we temporarily see a flashback, it momentarily folds us into his shock at losing Anne as she was. This is even more painful because the immediately preceding scene shows Anne looking desperately incapacitated, and weakly groaning, while a nurse demonstrates putting a diaper on her body for Georges [1:14.00–1:14:51]. When the film cuts directly from this demonstration to Anne playing at the piano, we are forced to confront the extreme change in her audiovisual presence, along with Georges.

Amour emphasizes Anne's loss in many other significant sonically marked moments. For instance, the sound track juxtaposes her former pupil Alexandre's playing the Bagatelle for Anne and Georges with the sound of Anne's new mechanized wheelchair [51:09–51.10]. Directly after the one time we see Georges play the piano before he suddenly stops [51:44–52:16], and his sitting in slumped silence as Anne calls out from the next room in disappointment, the film cuts to show a housekeeper vacuuming noisily around the instrument [52:28] (see Figure 8.3). The sounds of the machine clash with the notes we might imagine both Georges and Anne having made before she fell ill [52:28–53:01]. After Georges begins playing a CD sent by Alexandre to Anne, the same piece they heard in the first scene of *Amour* [59.13], Anne asks him to stop the disc within less than a minute [59:52–59.53]. They then sit in silence for a while before a cut [1:00:26]. The quiet after the music highlights what Anne can no longer bear to hear, as well as the musical sounds she can no longer make. We know it is painful for her to perceive these things, and we surely feel that pain along with her (Hillman 2015, 226).

---

[24] Hillman notes the "highly restricted *mise-en-scène*," along with close-ups and the static camera that communicate confinement within Georges and Anne's apartment (2015, 224–225). Ringstrom, in turn, finds a pattern of sonic withdrawal to match the confined interiors of the apartment: after Anne becomes debilitated, Georges and Anne "do not answer their phone, nor listen to their voice messages, cutting themselves off not only from Eva, but from Anne's protégé performer Alexandre and countless others" (2014, 159).

[25] Even if, as Dima (2015, 172) says, the music was actually "always diegetic," we are not aware of this right away so its relationship to the onscreen action still changes for us.

FIGURE 8.3 A housekeeper circles the piano with the noisy vacuum cleaner. The keys are out of the frame, signifying that musical sounds have been "replaced" by a machine.

After her second stroke, Anne has not only lost the capacity to make music: her speech is irreparably broken. "Mother . . . for concert . . . Mother . . . for concert . . . no dress," she earnestly says to Georges, stammering over each word with great effort [1:19:24–1:19:45]. The isolated words are full of connotative possibility, evoking regression ("Mother"), musical memory ("for concert"), and physical vulnerability ("no dress"). Georges reassuringly repeats her words without being able to give them more sense. That he later gives Anne "melodic intonation therapy" is significant in itself too (Wijdicks 2013): he wants to hear her voice, and he recognizes its significance in terms of her identity remaining intact. A touching scene shows Anne struggling "over syllables from the song 'Sur le pont d'Avignon'." Georges and Anne work together to speak the lyrics, drawing out their "'musicality' despite her pathetically impaired articulation" (Hillman 2015, 226) [1:24:36–1:25:42]. We see the effort on Anne's half-paralyzed face working through each song syllable, even slightly smiling as she says "danse" and "tous." For Hillman, this scene shows that music remains a "pillar of joy," even after what Anne has suffered. It also stresses Georges' effort to keep his wife speaking. It is easy to think of films where people struggle to understand the speech of men: a good representative example is Robert De Niro's character after suffering a stroke and having speech therapy in *Flawless* (1999), or the deteriorating speech of Eddie Redmayne in the Stephen Hawking biopic *The Theory of Everything* (2014). It is comparatively rare that a film prompts us to dwell upon *every syllable* of a woman's speech. *Amour* expects us to hang on every sound from Anne's lips, just as Georges does.[26]

---

[26] Though Trintignant undoubtedly has more lines than Riva, the fact of that every one of Riva's words matters resonates against mainstream American trends: a recent statistical study of two thousand Hollywood scripts reveals that men dominate dialogue, and older women rarely have many lines.

Anne's Death, and Her Enduring Voice

Eventually, Anne is vocally reduced to ambiguous noises in Georges' presence, and music drops out of the film entirely. Georges kills her by covering her mouth, an act that visually emphasizes the voice she completely loses in death. The disturbing and sudden manner with which Georges euthanizes Anne is a contentious choice. For Gogröf (2015), Georges' committing euthanasia is "monstrous" even as it is "a form of Liebestod." For Prose, the act is "murder" along with being an "ultimate expression of love." More troublingly, Higgins reads Anne's death by suffocation as "the silencing of the individuality of her pneuma or spirit," though she sees poetic logic in the way Georges kills Anne by covering her mouth (2016, 91). Similarly, for Dima, Georges' suffocating Anne symbolically "takes away her voice" (2015, 176). And when Georges "buries his own face in the pillow" after smothering Anne with it, he creates "a macabre mirror image with his wife: one is on the side of death, the other on the side of life, but they are both dying, they are both deprived of oxygen" (175).

Because Georges makes Anne voiceless in death while killing her as an act of love, Dima connects love with death, and death with silence. This is a neat formulation but it does not capture the originality of *Amour*. Consider that the idea of death being equated with silence is hundreds of years old (remember Hamlet's last line: "The rest is silence"). By contrast, if we instead recall the original Brechtian silent scream, Anne's death scene unleashes the productive interpretive possibility of the Gestus. When Georges presses his face into the pillow, he is stifling a scream along with being visually and physically connected with his wife. This is a moment of suppression and release, union in motion and division in death, actual quiet and imagined sound, voiceless faces but most eloquent bodies. By equating silence with death, Dima sidesteps the productive life of silence in Haneke's oeuvre as well as the simpler fact of the film not ending there. Georges' euthanizing Anne is followed by the *return* of her voice.

We can also better understand Georges' choice to euthanize Anne in the context of the story he tells her about attending his friend Pierre's funeral [41:15–42:31]. As Georges tells it, the funeral became the story of a man's life reduced to offensive and inappropriate sounds of speech, objects, and music. The aural disappointments of the ritual were as follows: a religious speech that failed ("the priest was an idiot"), an unmoving eulogy ("a former co-worker [. . .] made a cringingly pathetic speech"), poorly chosen music on inferior equipment ("his old secretary brought along a mini-tape player and put on 'Yesterday' by The Beatles"), and inappropriate reactions ("Pierre's

---

Actresses over forty-one have about 23 percent of dialogue, whereas actors over forty-one have about 44 percent of dialogue in the collection of scripts studied. Overall, women have more dialogue than men in only 22 percent of the films. For more information on this study, visit the site for *A Polygraph Joint*, by Hannah Anderson and Matt Daniels (http://polygraph.cool/films/).

grandchildren [. . .] began giggling when the music began"). The funeral ended with the unintentional comedy and the rhythmic awkwardness of the urn being put on a small electric trolley that "crawled on for an eternity until it reached the small hold they'd dug. A lot of people cracked up. It must have been awful for Jeanne [Pierre's wife]." In response to all this, Anne says, "there's no reason to go on living." So, the film places significant stress on Anne's need to leave life before she loses all aural control.[27] This makes her return of her voice in the final sequence all the more moving as the film's *unexpected* climax.

The euthanasia scene is often referred to as climactic (Hillman 2015, 182; Conrad 2012), but this only makes sense if we interpret the narrative trajectory as generically familiar. The setup certainly leads us to expect the revelation of how Anne dies in the finale, but *Amour* does not adhere to a familiar plot line any more than a regular tempo. Though the euthanasia scene is the obvious climax that the film has us wait for, her reappearance is a new peak that we cannot anticipate. Given the drawn-out pacing of the entire film, her reappearance could even be understood as an extension of the climax (see Figure 8.4). When Anne speaks again, she stands for the possibilities of worlds beyond the earthly and explicable. The final emphasis is on what Anne embodies that Georges cannot fully understand, though he must lovingly follow her into that new realm. The scholarly tendency to dwell on the euthanasia scene reflects a sensationalist approach that goes hand in hand with comparing the film to horror. Conversely, for Cohen-Shalev and Marcus, the film's important emphasis on "late love" connects with Anne's final appearance as an "apparition" that symbolizes the

FIGURE 8.4 Anne's reappearance within the domestic space makes a mundane activity mesmerizing.

---

[27] Directly before Georges' report on the funeral, he finds Anne on the floor by a window, probably having attempted suicide in his absence. This further suggests that she is ready for the death he gives her.

"preservation of hermetic coupledom." They see the last scene as "expressing the idea that runs throughout the film, that what matters is the profound love, the old love of Anne and Georges" (2015, 77).

In the film's final sequence, Anne first announces her reentrance after death through sound [2:00:52]: Georges hears her washing dishes offscreen and finds her cleaning up in the kitchen. Her action recalls the scene of her stroke (with the water running), an earlier scene of Georges cleaning the dishes himself after she is incapacitated, and the scene where Georges washes flowers for her body to be laid in state. She has, in short, suddenly inverted the carer-patient dynamic between them. "I'm almost done," she tells him casually, without breaking the rhythm of her washing up, "Put your shoes on if you want." Georges looks shocked but voicelessly follows her direction, putting on his shoes while she does the remaining dishes and lets the water out. As he then watches Anne prepare to leave from the hallway, we can hear her brushing her hair offscreen—the noise is very quiet but clearly perceivable within the sound mix, an important echo and corrective to the earlier scene of a nurse harshly brushing her hair. The sound signifies Anne reclaiming her own body and image. Then, after reentering the hallway and simply thanking Georges when he helps her with her coat, Anne finally asks, "you're not taking a coat?" Through her last words in *Amour*, Anne reasserts her ability to care for Georges, as well as her own presence. She makes ordinary words sound incredible.

Critical reactions to Anne's appearance in the final sequence are just as various as the responses to Georges' euthanizing her: for Grundmann (2012), she is a ghost, a magic realist presence, and an embodiment of Georges' separation from reality; for Gullette (2014), she is a manifestation of Georges' "unconscious prayer" for forgiveness; and for Hillman, Anne represents Georges' "inner life that refuses to be silenced, despite aging" (Hillman 2015, 227).[28] The problem with all such readings is that they misleadingly privilege Georges' subjectivity whereas the film itself is more even-handed. Though we certainly hear Anne's re-entry from Georges' point of audition, the film has prompted us to hear loss and frustration along with *her*: the music is always cut off much like her body is broken, and the film scenes break off elliptically much like her speech becomes increasingly fragmented. Indeed, the whole form of the film could be understood as an extension of what she physically experiences and sonically expresses: the opening, sutured concert/post-concert sequence parallels the fluid control she has over her pre-stroke voice and movement, and there is nothing like it after her first stroke.[29] When she speaks again near the end, it is as if the film takes on a new life and form too.

---

[28] Haneke himself loosely refers to their final togetherness in terms of "the spiritual realm" (Malomfălean).

[29] The structure of *The Piano Teacher*, featuring repeatedly cut-off music, also parallels the broken inner life of its female protagonist. However, where the impact of such parallelism in *The Piano*

When Georges finds Anne at the kitchen sink, calmly engaged in her everyday activity, we view her with astonishment along with him. This echoes the films of Ingmar Bergman that present otherworldly possibilities without explaining them. We might consider, for instance, how *Fanny and Alexander*'s father (Oscar) first appears to them after his death, announcing his offscreen presence with a few notes at the harpsichord and then silently looking up at them when they reach his doorway [1:18:37–1:19:38]. Oscar's sudden appearance is punctuated by the eerie sound of non-diegetic wind, aurally suggesting his mysterious, spectral significance. By contrast, in *Amour*, Anne is more simply *there*, without any more immediate aural punctuation than the tap running and the quiet noises of her cleaning dishes. Yet again, Haneke amplifies the expressive significance of ordinary domestic sounds, but this time the sounds change in meaning: where before the tap running was associated with Anne's stroke, now the sounds of washing up are about restoring her peaceful domestic union with Georges. This restoration cannot be explained, and it is the only surprise of its kind in Haneke's films to date.

Summary

Amour plays out a common experience—most of us will experience health problems in old age that eventually lead to our death. But this is presented in far-from-familiar cinematic terms. *Amour*'s sound track is surprising as it both resonates with and differentiates itself from Haneke's other films, as well as being far from generic. An auteurist approach allows us to fully perceive its subtleties. This entails our understanding that every sound effect and detail of speech is precisely scored and conducted by Haneke, like music.

Despite *Amour*'s emphasis on love and compassion, Haneke is still much associated with those negatives that are repeatedly, and simplistically, attached to the name of Bertolt Brecht: coldness, alienation, and detachment. Erick Neher's summary of *Amour* for *The Hudson Review* is a good representative example of the misunderstandings that endure: "The film, like all of Haneke's work, rigorously avoids sentimentality, creating a classic Brechtian distanciation between spectator and screen and demanding objectivity in the act of observation." Later, he argues that "the careful pace of *Amour* opens up room for a more cerebral interaction with the film, an engaged detachment that is the quintessence of Brecht's strategy of alienation" (2013). Leaving aside the troublesome dichotomy between sentimentality and objectivity here

---

Teacher makes us feel the agony of Erika's subjectivity with shocking, metacinematic self-consciousness, *Amour* allows for a greater intimacy with the female lead that always transcends ingenious cinematic form—the overall sound track of the latter film is more about facilitating compassion than imposing disturbance on us.

(the implication being that there is no alternative to such extremes), as well as the problematic use of the term "alienation" in connection with Brecht, this is a profound underestimation of the film's potential impact. *Amour*'s sound track movingly demands our involvement, and provokes a response that *oscillates* between detachment and engagement, much like Mother Courage's silent scream.[30]

In Yves Montmayeur's documentary about the making of *Amour*, Riva says, "Life lets out a scream. You have to find that scream. Within, I mean." Here, she is talking about the difficulty of playing Anne, which Trintignant says often left her unable to speak for a few hours. Riva is also stressing the impact, along with the necessity, of experiencing life's actual pain. She speaks figuratively, with emphasis on the power of what we cannot hear but still feel. This resonates with every sonic absence in Haneke's work. *Amour* is an intensely intertextual experience because it invites us to make such connections with his other films, and it almost immediately positions us as self-conscious perceivers by focusing on a concert audience in the post-title scene. That said, it simultaneously prompts us to hear as Georges and Anne do, to feel the pain in her altered speech and those moments where the music stops.

For Dima, the end of *Amour* leaves us "only nothingness and silence" (177). However, if we consider that the word "nothing" is fertile ground for meaning, and the silences of Haneke's work are always loaded invitations for further reflection, the ending of *Amour* is fuller than it first appears. *Amour* relies upon our ability to "complete" its fragments of sound, and to perceive its sonic absences as much more than nothingness. Actively listening to *Amour* means perceiving love even when it is not spoken, hearing full song lyrics even when only syllables are decipherable, holding on to music even after it is cut, and attending to every sound from a woman along with the man who has loved her for decades. It is Haneke's most moving demand for patience, and it rewards us with the audiovisual possibility of absolute restoration. Whether Anne reenters the narrative as magic realist device, or as spectral presence, or as embodiment of forgiveness or fantasy, the return of her voice offscreen reminds us to think beyond the mind's eye. Her ordinary speaking from the kitchen is an extraordinary appeal to our imaginations and hearts, and we must hear this before we can see it.

---

[30] Ironically, in the very same article Neher argues the film is emotional because it is not conventionally manipulative. However, he makes this point as if emotive intent is an aftershock rather than an integral part of its design.

WORKS CITED

Adorno, Theodor W. 1998. *Beethoven: The Philosophy of Music: Fragments and Texts*. Edited by Rolf Tiedemann. Translated by Edmund Jephcott. Stanford, CA: Stanford University Press. Originally published as *Beethoven: Philosophie der Musik: Fragmente und Texte*. Herausgegeben von Rolf Tiedemann (Frankfurt am Main: Suhrkamp, 1992).

Adorno, Theodor W. 2006. *Philosophy of New Music*. Translated, edited, and with an introduction by Robert Hullot-Kentor. Minneapolis: University of Minnesota Press. Originally published as *Philosophie der neuen Musik* (Tübingen: J. C. B. Mohr [Paul Siebeck], 1949).

Allain, Paul, and Jen Harvie. 2006. *The Routledge Companion to Theatre and Performance*. New York: Routledge.

Altman, Rick. (1984) 2012. "A Semantic/Syntactic Approach to Film Genre." In *Film Genre Reader IV*, edited by Barry Keith Grant, 27–41. Austin: University of Texas Press. Originally published in *Cinema Journal* 23(3): 6–18.

Amour. 2012. Directed by Michael Haneke, Performed by Jean-Louis Trintignant, Emmanuelle Riva, Isabelle Huppert, Alexandre Tharaud. Culver City, CA: Sony Pictures Home Entertainment, Inc., 2013. Blu-ray.

Anderson, Griffin. 1995. "Alban Berg, Violin Concerto (1935), from the cover notes for CD SMK 68331 (ADD): Pinchas Zukerman, Violin, London Symphony Orchestra, Pierre Boulez." Translated by Wolfgang Stähr. Accessed October 28, 2014. http://theory.music.temple.edu/~aleck/Courses/theory.IV/Notes/Classnotes.Berg.Concerto.pdf.

Anderson, Hannah, and Matt Daniels. 2016. "Film Dialogue from 2,000 screenplays, Broken Down by Gender and Age." *A Polygraph Joint*. Accessed December 6, 2016. http://polygraph.cool/films/.

Arthur, Paul. 2005. "Endgame." *Film Comment* 41(6). Accessed June 12, 2009. http://filmlinc.com/fcm/ND05/hidden.htm.

Ashcroft, Bill, Gareth Griffiths, and Helen Triffin, eds. 2006. *The Post-Colonial Studies Reader*. 2nd ed. London: Routledge.

Badt, Karin Luisa. 2005. "Family Is Hell and So Is the World: Talking to Michael Haneke at Cannes 2005." *Bright Lights Film Journal*, November 1. Accessed November 23, 2016. http://brightlightsfilm.com/family-hell-world-talking-michael-haneke-cannes-2005/#.WDW6kTKZNE4.

Bamforth, Iain. 2013. "Amour." *British Journal of General Practice* (*BJGP*), June 1. Accessed October 1, 2016. http://bjgp.org/content/63/611/323.

Barthes, Roland. 1977. *Image/Music/Text*. Edited and translated by Stephen Heath. Glasgow: Omnia Books, Ltd.

The Battle of Algiers. 1966. Directed by Gillo Pontecorvo. Performed by Brahim Haggiag, Jean Martin, Saadi Yacef, Samia Kerbash. New York: The Criterion Collection, 2004. DVD.

Bazin, André. 2005. "Behind the Décor." In *What Is Cinema?*, Vol. 1, edited and translated by Hugh Gray, 102–107. Berkeley: University of California Press.

Belsey, Catherine. 2002. *Critical Practice*. 2nd ed. New York: Routledge.

Benny's Video. 1992. Directed by Michael Haneke. Performed by Arno Frisch, Angela Winkler, Ulrich Mühe, Ingrid Stassner. New York: Kino International Corp. 2006. DVD.

Bleasdale, John. 2011. "Haneke, Bitte?" *Electric Sheep*, January 13. Accessed January 2, 2017. http://www.electricsheepmagazine.co.uk/features/2011/01/13/haneke-bitte/.

Blumenthal-Barby, Martin. 2014. "The Surveillant Gaze: Michael Haneke's *The White Ribbon*." *October* 147: 95–116.

Bongioroni, Kevin. 2016. "Michael Haneke's *Amour* in the Light of Italian Neorealism." *Pacific Coast Philology* 51(1): 23–41.

Bordwell, David. 2006. *The Way Hollywood Tells It*. Berkeley: University of California Press.

Bosch, Jim Vanden. 2013. "Amour Killing?" *The Gerontologist* 53(3). Accessed November 15, 2016. http://gerontologist.oxfordjournals.org/content/53/3/518.full

Bosch, Jim Vanden. 2015. "Filming Successful Aging." *The Gerontologist* 55(1): 169–170. Accessed November 15, 2016. https://www.ncbi.nlm.nih.gov/pmc/articles/PMC4986597/.

Bostridge, Ian. 2015. *Schubert's Winter Journey: Anatomy of an Obsession*. New York: Alfred A. Knopf.

Brecht, Bertolt. 1964. *Brecht on Theatre: The Development of an Aesthetic*. Edited and translated by John Willett. New York: Hill and Wang.

Brecht, Bertolt. 1980. *Mother Courage and Her Children*. Translated by John Willett. Edited and translated by John Willett and Ralph Manheim. New York: Arcade Publishing.

Brinkema, Eugenie. 2010. "How to Do Things with Violences." In *A Companion to Michael Haneke*, edited by Roy Grundmann, 354–370. Malden, MA: Wiley-Blackwell.

Brody, Richard. 2013. "Michael Haneke's Sterile *Amour*." *The New Yorker*, January 4. Accessed December 1, 2016. http://www.newyorker.com/culture/richard-brody/michael-hanekes-sterile-amour.

Brown, Julie. 2005. "Haneke's *La Pianiste* (2001): Parody and the Limits of Film Music Satire." *Tonspuren: Musik im Film: Fallstudien 1994–2001*. Edited by Andreas Dorshel, 163–190. Vienna: Universal Edition.

Brown, Nicholas Alexander. 2015. "Concerts from the Library of Congress: Ian Bostridge and Julius Drake, *Winterreise* by Franz Schubert" (program notes). Washington, DC: The Library of Congress/The Gertrude Clarke Whittall Foundation). Accessed November 16, 2016. https://blogs.loc.gov/music/files/2015/02/Bostridge-Drake-Program.02.07.2015.FINAL_.rev_.02.19.2015.pdf.

Brown, Rich. 2015. "To the Memory of an Angel, Part III." *Good Music Speaks*, May 14. Accessed January 11, 2017. https://goodmusicspeaks.com/tag/violin-concerto/.

Brunette, Peter. 2010. *Michael Haneke*. Urbana: University of Illinois Press.

Caché (Hidden). 2005. Directed by Michael Haneke. Performed by Daniel Auteuil, Juliette Binoche, Maurice Benichou, Annie Girardot. Culver City, CA: Sony Pictures Home Entertainment, 2006. DVD.

Chandler, Adam. 2015. "Le Pen Will Be Mightier." *The Atlantic*, December 14. Accessed October 27, 2016. http://www.theatlantic.com/international/archive/2015/12/marine-le-pen-front-national-france/420348/.

Chion, Michel. 1994. *Audio-Vision: Sound on Screen*. Edited and translated by Claudia Gorbman. New York: Columbia University Press. Originally published as *L'Audio-Vision* (Paris: Editions Nathan, 1990).

Chion, Michel. 1999. *The Voice in Cinema*. Edited and translated by Claudia Gorbman. New York: Columbia University Press. Originally published as *La Voix au cinéma* (Paris: *Cahiers du cinéma* [Editions de l'Etoile], 1982).

Chion, Michel. 2010. "Without Music." Translated by T. Jefferson Kline. In *A Companion to Michael Haneke*, edited by Roy Grundmann, 161–167. Malden, MA: Wiley-Blackwell.

Chivers, Sally. 2011. *The Silvering Screen: Old Age and Disability in Cinema*. Toronto: University of Toronto Press.

Chivers, Sally. 2015. "Empty Husks, Disability, Care, Death, and *Amour*." In *Therapy and Emotions in Film and Television: The Pulse of Our Times*, edited by Claudia Wassmann, 72–88. Houndmills, Basingstoke, Hampshire: Palgrave Macmillan.

Chua, Daniel K. L. 2006. "Drifting: The Dialectics of Adorno's *Philosophy of New Music*." In *Apparitions: New Perspectives on Adorno and Twentieth-Century Music*, edited by Berthold Hoekner, 1–17. New York; London: Routledge.

Churman, Sloan. 2011. "20 Years Old and Hearing Myself for the First Time!" *YouTube.com*, September 25. Accessed March 19, 2017. https://www.youtube.com/watch?v=LsOo3jzkhYA.

Cieutat, Michel. 2010. "Interview with Michael Haneke: The Fragmentation of the Look (2000)." In *Michael Haneke*, edited by Peter Brunette, 139–147. Urbana: University of Illinois Press.

Clover, Carol J. 1992. *Men, Women, and Chain Saws: Gender in the Modern Horror Film*. Princeton, NJ: Princeton University Press.

Code Unknown (*Code Inconnu: Récit incomplet de divers voyages*). 2000. Directed by Michael Haneke, Performed by Juliette Binoche, Thierry Neuvic, Sepp Bierbichler, Arsinée Khanjian. New York: The Criterion Collection, 2015. Blu-ray.

Cohen-Shalev, Amir, and Esther-Lee Marcus. 2015. "'Equally Mixed': Artistic Representations of Old Love." *International Journal of Ageing and Later Life* 10(2): 61–83. Accessed November 1, 2016. http://www.ep.liu.se/ej/ijal/2016/v10/i2//15-281/ijal15-281.pdf.

Conrad, Peter. 2012. "Michael Haneke: There's No Easy Way to Say This." *The Observer*, November 3. Accessed November 1, 2016. https://www.theguardian.com/film/2012/nov/04/michael-haneke-amour-director-interview.

Coulthard, Lisa. 2011a. "Ethical Violence: Suicide as Authentic Act in the Films of Michael Haneke." In *The Cinema of Michael Haneke: Europe Utopia*, edited by Ben McCann and David Sorfa, 38–48. London: Wallflower.

Coulthard, Lisa. 2011b. "Interrogating the Obscene: Extremism and Michael Haneke." In *The New Extremism in Cinema: From France to Europe*, edited by Tanya C. Horeck and Tina Kendall, 180–191. Edinburgh: Edinburgh University Press Ltd.

Coulthard, Lisa. 2011c. "Negative Ethics: The Missed Event in the French Films of Michael Haneke." *Studies in French Cinema* 11(1): 71–82.

Cowan, Michael. 2008. "Between the Street and the Apartment: Disturbing the Space of Fortress Europe in Michael Haneke." *Studies in European Cinema* 5(2):117–129.

Crowley, Patrick. 2010. "When Forgetting Is Remembering: Haneke's *Caché* and the Events of October 17, 1961." In *On Michael Haneke*, edited by Brian Price and John David Rhodes, 267–279. Detroit, MI: Wayne State University Press.

Dalton, Mary M., and Kirsten James Fatzinger. 2003. "Choosing Silence: Defiance and Resistance without Voice in Jane Campion's *The Piano*." *Women and Language* 26(2): 34–39.

Davies, Luke. 2013. "Michael Haneke's 'Amour.'" *The Monthly: Australian Politics, Society & Culture*, March. Accessed November 1, 2016. https://www.themonthly.com.au/issue/2013/march/1361848248/luke-davies/love-time-ruin.

Debruge, Peter. 2012. "Review: *Amour.*" *Variety*, May 20. Accessed November 1, 2016. http://variety.com/2012/film/markets-festivals/amour-1117947583/.

Delahaye, Luc. 1999. *L'autre.* Introduction by Jean Baudrillard. London: Phaidon.

Dima, Vlad. 2015. "Sound, Death, and *Amour.*" *Studies in French Cinema* 15(2): 168–179.

Doane, Mary Ann. 1980. "The Voice in Cinema: The Articulation of Body and Space." *Yale French Studies* 60: 33–50.

Domizio, Ricardo. 2011. "Digital Cinema and the 'Schizophrenic' Image: The Case of Michael Haneke's Hidden." In *The Cinema of Michael Haneke: Europe Utopia*, edited by Ben McCann and David Sorfa, 237–246. London: Wallflower.

Dowd, Maureen. 2012. "Spellbound by Blondes, Hot and Icy." *The New York Times*. December 1. Accessed October 20, 2014. http://www.nytimes.com/2012/12/02/opinion/sunday/dowd-spellbound-by-blondes-hot-and-icy.html?pagewanted=all&_r=0.

Drukarczyk, Laura, Carten Klein, Christoph Ostgather, and Stephanie Stiel. 2014. "Life Threatening Illness in Popular Movies: A First Descriptive Analysis." *SpringerPlus* 3, August 5. Accessed November 14, 2016. https://www.ncbi.nlm.nih.gov/pmc/articles/PMC4143538/.

The Economist. 2009. "France's Ethnic Minorities: To Count or Not to Count." March 26. Accessed March 15, 2016. http://www.economist.com/node/13377324.

Edelstein, David. 2009. "Nasty Boys: Robert Downey Jr. Brightens a Grim Sherlock; Michael Haneke's *White Ribbon* Is Just a Grind." *New York Magazine*, December 28. Accessed April 29, 2016. http://nymag.com/movies/reviews/62895/.

Eisenstein, Sergei. (1942) 1947. *The Film Sense.* Edited and translated by Jay Leyda. New York: Harcourt, Brace & World, Inc.

Elsaesser, Thomas. 2010. "Performance Self-Contradictions: Michael Haneke's Mind Games." In *A Companion to Michael Haneke*, edited by Roy Grundmann, 53–74. Malden, MA: Wiley-Blackwell.

Everett, Wendy. 2005. "Fractal Films and the Architecture of Complexity." *Studies in European Cinema* 2(3): 159–171.

Ezra, Elizabeth, and Jane Sillers. 2007a. "The *Caché* Dossier: Introduction." *Screen* 48 (2): 211–213.

Ezra, Elizabeth, and Jane Sillers. 2007b. "Hidden in Plain Sight: Bringing Terror Home." *Screen* 48(2): 215–222.

Fenimore, Ross. 2010. "Voices That Lie Within: The Heard and Unheard in *Psycho.*" In *Music in the Horror Film: Listening to Fear*, edited by Neil Lerner, 80–97. New York: Routledge.

Fileva, Iskra. 2014. "Playing with Fire: Art and the Seductive Power of Pain." In *Suffering Art Gladly: The Paradox of Negative Emotion in Art*, edited by Jerrold Levinson, 171–185. Houndmills, Basingstoke, Hampshire: Palgrave Macmillan UK.

Fleming, Crystal. 2015. "France's Approach to Fighting Racism: Pretty Words and Magical Thinking." *The World Post*, May 7. Accessed October 1, 2016. http://www.huffingtonpost.com/crystal-fleming/frances-approach-to-fight_b_7231610.html.

Forrest, Tara. 2012. "A Negative Utopia: Michael Haneke's Fragmentary Cinema." In *A Companion to German Cinema*, edited by Terri Ginsberg and Andrew Mensch, 553–572. Malden, MA: Wiley-Blackwell.

France 24. 2013. "'No such thing as race,' Say French Lawmakers." May 17. Accessed March 1, 2016. http://www.france24.com/en/20130517-no-such-thing-as-race-french-lawmakers-france-racism-hollande.

Franklin, Ruth. 2013. "*Amour*, Directed by Michael Haneke: As Long as We Can Bear It." *Salmagundi* 211: 42–48.

Freedman, Carl. 2012. "Notes on Benjamin, Adorno, Mann, and the Cinema of Michael Haneke." *Film International* 57(3): 16–35.

French-American Foundation, United States. 2014. "September 2014: The New Black Elite." Accessed November 1, 2016. https://frenchamerican.org/events/new-black-elite.

Funny Games. 1997. Directed by Michael Haneke. Performed by Susanne Lothar, Ulriche Mühe, Arno Frisch, Frank Giering. Burbank, CA: Warner Home Video, 2008. DVD.

Garde, Ulrike. 2006. *Brecht & Co: German-Speaking Playwrights on the Australian Stage*. Oxford: Peter Lang & Co.

Geck, Martin. 2012. *Robert Schumann: The Life and Work of a Romantic Composer*. Translated by Stewart Spencer. Chicago: University of Chicago Press.

Gerbaz, Alex. 2011. "The Ethical Screen: *Funny Games* and the Spectacle of Pain." In *The Cinema of Michael Haneke: Europe Utopia*, edited by Ben McCann and David Sorfa, 163–171. London: Wallflower.

Gibbs, Christopher H. 2000. *The Life of Schubert*. Cambridge: Cambridge University Press.

Gilroy, Paul. 2007. "Shooting Crabs in a Barrel." *Screen* 48(2): 233–235.

Gleiberman, Owen. 2012. "Cannes: Can 'Amour' Really Be a Michael Haneke Film? It's a Tenderly Devastating Portrait of Old Age." *Entertainment Weekly*, May 20. Accessed November 14, 2016. http://www.ew.com/article/2012/05/20/cannes-michael-hanekes-love-is-a-tenderly-devastating-film?iid=sr-link2.

Gogröf, Andrea. 2015. "Endgame, Conflict, and Interest in Michael Haneke's *Amour*." *Excavatio* 26. Accessed November 14, 2016. https://sites.ualberta.ca/~aizen/excavatio/articles/v26/Gogrof.pdf.

Goldfield, Hannah. 2013. "Surviving *Amour*." *The New Yorker*, February 26. Accessed November 14, 2016. http://www.newyorker.com/culture/culture-desk/surviving-amour.

Goodrick, Steven. 2012. "Film: Chanson d'Amour." *The Lancet: Neurology* 11, 1027. Accessed November 14, 2016. http://www.thelancet.com/pdfs/journals/laneur/PIIS1474-4422(12)70282-X.pdf.

Gorbman, Claudia. 1987. *Unheard Melodies: Narrative Film Music*. Bloomington: Indiana University Press.

Gorbman, Claudia. 2000. "Music in *The Piano*." In *Jane Campion's "The Piano,"* edited by Harriet Margolis, 42–58. Cambridge: Cambridge University Press.

Grabner, Franz. 2010. "'We Live in a Permanent State of War': An Interview with Michael Haneke by Franz Grabner." In *Fascinatingly Disturbing: Interdisciplinary Perspectives on Michael Haneke's Cinema*, edited by Alexander D. Ornella and Stefanie Knauss, 13–33. Eugene, OR: Pickwick Publications.

Grønstad, Asbjørn. 2013. "Haneke's *Amour* and the Ethics of Dying." In *Death in Classic and Contemporary Film*, edited by Daniel Sullivan and Jeff Greenberg, 185–196. New York: Palgrave Macmillan.

Grundmann, Roy. 2007. "Auteur de Force: Michael Haneke's 'Cinema of Glaciation.'" *Cineaste* 32(2): 6–14.

Grundmann, Roy. 2010a. "Introduction: Haneke's Anachronism." In *A Companion to Michael Haneke*, edited by Roy Grundmann, 1–50. Malden, MA: Wiley-Blackwell.

Grundmann, Roy. 2010b. "Unsentimental Education: An Interview with Michael Haneke." In *A Companion to Michael Haneke*, edited by Roy Grundmann, 591–606. Malden, MA: Wiley-Blackwell.

Grundmann, Roy. 2012. "Love, Death, Truth—*Amour*." *Senses of Cinema* 65. Accessed November 14, 2016. http://sensesofcinema.com/2012/feature-articles/love-death-truth-amour/.

Gullette, Margaret Morganroth. 2014. "Euthanasia as a Caregiving Fantasy in the Era of New Longevity." *Age Culture Humanities*, 1. Accessed November 14, 2016. http://ageculturehumanities.org/WP/euthanasia-as-a-caregiving-fantasy-in-the-era-of-the-new-longevity/.

Gural-Migdal, Anna, and Romain Chareyron. 2009. "The Ghost Image of Horror and Pornography in Michael Haneke's *La Pianiste* (2001)." *Studies in French Cinema* 11(11): 57–70.

Haigh, Sam. 2011. "Integration or Interaction? Disability in France Today." In *Hexagonal Variations: Diversity, Plurality, and Reinvention in Contemporary France*, edited by Jo McCormack, Murray Pratt, and Alistair Rolls, 135–156. Amsterdam: Rodopi.

Haneke, Michael. 2000. "*71 Fragments of a Chronology of Chance*: Notes to the Film." In *After Postmodernism: Austrian Literature and Film in Transition*, edited by Willy Riemer, 171–175. Riverside, CA: Ariadne.

Haneke, Michael. 2010. *Das weisse Band (The White Ribbon or The Schoolteacher's tale)*. *The Screenplay Database*, January 25. Accessed November 1, 2016. http://www.screenplaydb.com/film/scripts/whiteribbonthe/.

Harriss, Joseph A. 2014. "Racist, Moi?: Marianne, Your Anti-Semitism Is Showing (Letter from Paris)." *The American Spectator*, November 19. Accessed February 12, 2016. http://spectator.org/61019_racist-moi/.

Hayward, Philip. 2009. "Introduction." In *Terror Tracks: Music, Sound, and Horror Cinema*, edited by Philip Hayward, 1–13. London: Equinox Publishing.

Hayward, Susan. 2006. *Cinema Studies: The Key Concepts*. 3rd ed. New York: Routledge.

Higgins, Lynn A. 2016. "Becoming a Song: Sound, History, and Cinema History in Michael Haneke's *Amour*." *South Central Review* 33(2): 80–95.

Hillman, Roger. 2015. "The Evening of Life, on Film: *Amour* and *Melancholia* in the *Abendland*." *Limbus: Australian Yearbook of German Literary and Cultural Studies* 8 ("Ageing"): 221–233.

Hornaday, Ann. 2013. "A Moving Story of Love and Loss." *The Washington Post*, January 11. Accessed November 14, 2016. http://www.washingtonpost.com/gog/movies/love-amour,1233121.html.

Horwath, A. 2009. "The Haneke Code: Talking Shop, Theory, and Practice with the Director of *The White Ribbon*." *Film Comment* 45(6): 26–31.

Hutchinson, Nina. 2003. "Between Action and Repression: *The Piano Teacher*." *Senses of Cinema* 26. Accessed November 11, 2016. http://sensesofcinema.com/2003/michael-haneke/piano_teacher/.

Ireland, D. I. 2012. "'It's a sin [. . .] using Ludwig van like that. He did no harm to anyone, Beethoven just wrote the music': The Role of the Incongruent Soundtrack in the Representation of the Cinematic Criminal." In *Constructing Crime: Discourse and*

Cultural Representations of Crime and "Deviance," edited by C. Gregoriou, 97–111. Basingstoke: Palgrave Macmillan.

Iveković, Rada. 2011. "The Global Nostalgia of a Non-Global Language." In *Hexagonal Variations: Diversity, Plurality and Reinvention in Contemporary France*, edited by Jo McCormack, Murray Pratt, and Alistair Rolls, 45–56. Amsterdam: Rodopi.

Jacks, Steven. 2013. "Petrushka Chord: Music Minute #22." *stevenjacks.com*, November 18. Accessed November 3, 2016. https://www.youtube.com/watch?v=oSZD6QSSq4c.

Jandey, Brigitte. 2011. "Frenchness in Perspectives(s)." In *Hexagonal Variations: Diversity, Plurality, and Reinvention in Contemporary France*, edited by Jo McCormack, Murray Pratt, and Alistair Rolls, 57–77. Amsterdam: Rodopi.

Jelinek, Elfriede. 1988. *The Piano Teacher: A Novel.* New York: Weidenfeld & Nicolson. Translated by Joachim Neugroschel. Originally published as *Die Klavierspielerin* (Reinbek: Rowohlt Verlag, 1983).

Jelloun, Tahar Ben. 1999. *French Hospitality: Racism and North African Immigrants.* Translated by Barbara Bray. New York: Columbia University Press.

Jennings, Murdoch. 2014. "Žižek's Dialectics, Critique of Ideology, and Emancipatory Politics in Michael Haneke's film *Caché* (2005)." *International Journal of Žižek Studies* 8(2): 1–30.

Johnson, Beth. 2009. "Masochism and the Mother, Pedagogy, and Perversion." *Angelaki* 14(3): 117–130.

Khanna, Ranjanna. 2007. "From Rue Morgue to Rue des Iris." *Screen* 48(2): 237–244.

Kiefer, Jonathan. 2010. "Dandified Sadism." *Newsreview.com*, January 28. Accessed November 1, 2016. https://www.newsreview.com/sacramento/dandified-sadism/content?oid=1361713.

Kline, T. Jefferson. 2010. "The Intertextual and Discursive Origins of Terror in Michael Haneke's *Caché.*" In *A Companion to Michael Haneke*, edited by Roy Grundmann, 551–561. Malden, MA: Wiley-Blackwell.

Konan, Aude. 2015. "Why Black People in France Are Still Invisible." *Media Diversified*, May 12. Accessed March 31, 2016. https://mediadiversified.org/2015/05/12/why-black-people-in-france-are-still-invisible/.

Kozloff, Sarah. 2000. *Overhearing Film Dialogue.* Berkeley, CA: University of California Press.

Kristeva, Julia. 2003. *Lettre au président de la République sur les citoyens en situation de handicap, à l'usage de ceux qui le sont et de ceux qui ne le sont pas.* Paris: Fayard.

Kroenert, Tim. 2013. "Love and Euthanasia." *Eureka Street* 23(3): 5.

Kulezic-Wilson, Danijela. 2015. *The Musicality of Narrative Film.* Houndmills, Basingstoke: Palgrave Macmillan.

Kumar, Niven, and Lucyna Swiatek. 2012. "Representations of New Terror: 'Auto-anomie' in the Films of Michael Haneke." *Journal of Postcolonial Writing* 48(3): 311–321.

Kunzru, Hari. 2009. "Nowhere to Hide." *The Guardian*, October 30. Accessed December 17, 2016. https://www.theguardian.com/film/2009/oct/31/michael-haneke-films-hari-kunzru.

Lacan, Jacques (1977) 1998. *The Seminar of Jacques Lacan, Book XI: The Four Fundamental Concepts of Psychoanalysis.* Edited by Jacques-Alain Miller, translated by Alan Sheridan. New York: W. W. Norton & Company, Inc.

Lacan, Jacques. 2002. *Écrits: A Selection.* Translated by Bruce Fink. New York: W. W. Norton & Company, Inc.

Laine, Tarja. 2010. "Haneke's 'Funny' Games with the Audience (Revisited)." In *On Michael Haneke*, edited by Brian Price and John David Rhodes, 267–279. Detroit, MI: Wayne State University Press.

Laing, Heather. 2007. *The Gendered Score: Music in 1940s Melodrama and the Woman's Film*. Hampshire, England: Ashgate Publishing Ltd.

Lawson, Mark. 2006. "Guilt, Lies and Videotape." *The Guardian*, January 20, 2006. Accessed January 20, 2013. http://film.guardian.co.uk/features/featurepages/0,4120,1690429,00. html.

Leitch, Thomas. 2007. *Film Adaptation and Its Discontents: From* Gone with the Wind *to* The Passion of the Christ. Baltimore, MD: The Johns Hopkins University Press.

Leitch, Thomas. 2008. "Adaptations without Sources: The Adventures of Robin Hood." *Literature/Film Quarterly* 36(1): 21–30.

Lerner, Neil. 2010. "Preface: Listening to Fear/Listening with Fear." In *Music in the Horror Film: Listening to Fear*, edited by Neil Lerner, vii–xi. New York: Routledge.

Levin, Thomas. 2010. "Five Tapes, Four Halls, Two Dreams: Vicissitudes of Surveillant Narration in Michael Haneke's *Caché*." In *A Companion to Michael Haneke*, edited by Roy Grundmann, 75–90. Malden, MA: Wiley-Blackwell.

Lloyd, Alexandra. 2016. "Songs of Innocence and Experience: Michael Haneke's Cinematic Visions of Childhood." *The Modern Language Review* 111(1): 183–207.

Loren, Scott, and Jörg Metelmann. 2013. *Irritation of Life: The Subversive Melodrama of Michael Haneke, David Lynch, and Lars von Trier*. Marburg, Germany: Schüren.

Lykidis, Alex. 2010. "Multicultural Encounters in Haneke's French-Language Cinema." In *A Companion to Michael Haneke*, edited by Roy Grundmann, 455–476. Malden, MA: Wiley-Blackwell.

Ma, Jean. 2010. "Discordant Desires, Violent Refrains: *La Pianiste* (*The Piano Teacher*)." In *A Companion to Michael Haneke*, edited by Roy Grundmann, 511–531. Malden, MA: Wiley-Blackwell.

Macallan, Helen, and Andrew Plain. 2007. "Haneke's Disinherited Children," *Senses of Cinema* 42. Accessed June 12, 2009. http://archive.sensesofcinema.com/contents/07/42/hidden.html.

MacCannell, Juliet Flower. 1994. "Between the Two Fears." In *Lacan and Contemporary Film*, edited by Todd McGowan and Sheila Kunkle, 47–82. New York: Other Press.

Maingueneau, Dominique. 2011. "Multiculturality in Discourse Analysis: The 'French' Example." *Journal of Multicultural Discourses* 6(2): 105–120.

Malomfălean, Laurenţiu. 2015. "The Nightmare-Body: Michael Haneke Reversing a Tarkovskian Dream Logic in *Amour*." *Caietele Echinox* 28: 299–307.

McFadden, Cybelle H. 2009. "Franco-Algerian Transcultural Tension and National Allegories." *South Atlantic Review* 74(2): 112–128.

McGowan, Todd. 2003. "Looking for the Gaze: Lacanian Film Theory and Its Vicissitudes." *Cinema Journal* 42(3): 27–47.

McKay, Elizabeth Norman. 1998. *Franz Schubert: A Biography*. Oxford: Clarendon Press.

Mecchia, Giuseppina. 2007. "The Children Are Still Watching Us: *Caché/Hidden* in the Folds of Time." *Studies in French Cinema* 7(2): 131–141.

Met, Philippe. 2012. "The Iceman Cometh (To a Theater Near You): Michael Haneke's Glaciation Trilogy." In *Film Trilogies: New Critical Approaches*, edited by Claire Perkins and Constantine Verevis, 164–180. London: Palgrave Macmillan.

Metelmann, Jörg. 2010. "Fighting the Melodramatic Condition: Haneke's Polemics." In *A Companion to Michael Haneke*, edited by Roy Grundmann, 168–186. Malden, MA: Wiley-Blackwell.

Michael H.—Profession: Director. 2013. Directed by Yves Montmayeur, Performed by Michael Haneke, Isabelle Huppert, Jean-Louis Trintignant, Emmanuelle Riva, Josef Bierbichler, Susanne Lothar. Artificial Eye. DVD.

Miller, Timothy D. 2009. "Doing Violence to 'Violence': Theodor W. Adorno and the Responsibilities of Music Criticism." MA Thesis. University of North Carolina at Chapel Hill Department of Music. Accessed November 15, 2015. https://cdr.lib.unc. edu/indexablecontent/uuid:8c31ed0c-a27e-4fab-bb0b-7243c2930e3d.

Mongrel Media. 2009. *The White Ribbon: A Film by Michael Haneke* (press kit). Accessed November 7, 2016. http://www.mongrelmedia.com/MongrelMedia/files/54/54d1314d-83b0-4013-882f-e4d489196dfe.pdf.

Monk, Leland. 2010. "Hollywood Endgames." In *A Companion to Michael Haneke*, edited by Roy Grundmann, 420–437. Malden, MA: Wiley-Blackwell.

Montmayeur, Yves. 2005. *Caché: A Documentary by Yves Montmayeur* (Les Films du Losange), *Caché*, DVD, directed by Michael Haneke (2005; Culver City, CA: Sony, 2006).

Montmayeur, Yves, dir. 2012. "Making of *Amour*" featurette. *Amour*. Directed by Michael Haneke. Culver City, CA: Sony Pictures. Blu-ray.

Mottram, James. 2006. "Michael Haneke: A Truly Shocking Director," *The Independent*, 20 January. Accessed May 22, 2009. http://www.independent.co.uk/arts-entertainment/ films/features/michael-haneke-a-truly-shocking-director-523700.html.

Müller, Wilhelm. *Winterreise*. Translated by Celia Sgroi. Accessed November 15, 2015. http://www.gopera.com/lieder/translations/schubert_911.pdf.

Murch, Walter. 1994. "Foreword." In *Audio-Vision: Sound on Screen*, by Michel Chion. Edited and translated by Claudia Gorbman, vii–xxiv. New York: Columbia University Press. Originally published as *L'Audio-Vision* (Paris, Editions Nathan, 1990).

Nair, Kartik. 2009. "*Caché* and the Secret Image." *Wide Screen* 1(1). Accessed May 22, 2009. http://widescreenjournal.org/index.php/journal/article/view/12/8.

Neher, Erick. 2013. "In Praise of Boring Films." *The Hudson Review*. Accessed November 14, 2016. http://hudsonreview.com/2013/08/in-praise-of-boring-films/#.V_UUnTKZNE4.

Nehme, Farran Smith. 2012. "Portrait of True 'Amour' till the End." *New York Post*. December 19. Accessed November 14, 2016. http://nypost.com/2012/12/19/portrait-of-true-amour-till-the-end/.

Noys, Benjamin. 2011. "Attenuating Austria: The Construction of Bourgeois Space in *The Seventh Continent*." In *The Cinema of Michael Haneke: Europe Utopia*, edited by Ben McCann and David Sorfa, 141–150. London: Wallflower.

O'Neill, Desmond. 2012. "*Amour*, ageing, and missed opportunities." *The BMJ*, November 23. http://blogs.bmj.com/bmj/2012/11/23/desmond-oneill-amour-ageing-and-missed-opportunities/.

Ornella, Alexander D. 2010. "Cat and Mouse: Haneke's Joy in the Spectator's Distress." In *Fascinatingly Disturbing: Interdisciplinary Perspectives on Michael Haneke's Cinema*, edited by Alexander D. Ornella and Stefanie Knauss, 145–168. Eugene, OR: Pickwick Publications.

Orr, John. 2011. "*The White Ribbon* in Michael Haneke's Cinema." In *The Cinema of Michael Haneke: Europe Utopia*, edited by Ben McCann and David Sorfa, 259–264. London: Wallflower Press.

Palmer, Landon. 2011. "Film Culture to Torture: Music and Violence in *Funny Games* and *The Piano Teacher*." In *The Cinema of Michael Haneke: Europe Utopia*, edited by Ben McCann and David Sorfa, 179–191. London: Wallflower Press.

Paul, L. A. 2014. *Transformative Experience*. Oxford: Oxford University Press.

Penney, James. 2010. "'You Never Look at Me from Where I See You': Postcolonial Guilt in *Caché*." *New Formations* 70: 77–93.

Peterson, Matt. 2006. "Shock Treatment: Michael Haneke's *The Seventh Continent* (1989, Kino) and Lars von Trier's *Manderlay* (2006, IFC Films)." *The Brooklyn Rail*, December 8. Accessed January 2, 2017. http://www.brooklynrail.org/2006/12/film/shock-treatment-michael-hanekes-i-the-se.

Peucker, Brigitte. 2000. "Fragmentation and the Real: Michael Haneke's Family Trilogy." In *After Postmodernism: Austrian Literature and Film in Transition*, edited by Willy Riemer, 176–188. Riverside, CA: Ariadne.

Peucker, Brigitte. 2010. "Games Haneke Plays: Reality and Performance." In *On Michael Haneke*, edited by Brian Price and John David Rhodes, 15–34. Detroit, MI: Wayne State University Press.

Phipps, Keith. 2009. "*The White Ribbon*." *A.V. Club*, December 30. Accessed October 15, 2016. http://www.avclub.com/review/the-white-ribbon-36647.

The Piano Teacher (*La pianiste*). 2001. Directed by Michael Haneke. Performed by Isabelle Huppert, Annie Girardot, Benoît Magimel. New York: Kino International. 2002. DVD.

Pine, Rachel Barton. "Program Notes: Berg Violin Concerto." Accessed October 28, 2014. http://industry.rachelbartonpine.com/rep_notes_view.php?id=2.

Plantinga, Harry. 2007. "Hymn Text: *Ein feste Burg ist unser Gott*." *Hymnary.org*. Accessed November 1, 2016. http://www.hymnary.org/text/ein_feste_burg_ist_unser_gott.

Porton, Richard. 2005. "Collective Guilt and Individual Responsibility: An Interview with Michael Haneke." *Cineaste* 31(1): 50–51.

Prentice, George. 2013. "This Thing Called Amour." *Boise Weekly*, February 13. Accessed November 14, 2016. http://www.boiseweekly.com/boise/this-thing-called-amour/Content?oid=2814828.

Price, Brian. 2010. "Pain and the Limits of Representation." In *On Michael Haneke*, edited by Brian Price and John David Rhodes, 35–50. Detroit, MI: Wayne State University Press.

Prose, Francine. 2013. "A Masterpiece You Might Not Want to See." *The New York Review of Books*, Jan. 7. Accessed November 14, 2016. http://www.nybooks.com/daily/2013/01/07/haneke-film-not-to-see/.

Quart, Leonard. 2016. "Aging in Films and Amour." *Logos* 15(2–3). Accessed November 14, 2016. http://logosjournal.com/2013/quart/.

Rea, Steven. 2010. "Pre-WW1 Aryan Progeny, Sowing Seeds of Fascism." *Philly.com*. January 21. Accessed April 29, 2016. http://www.philly.com/philly/entertainment/movies/20100122_Pre-WWI_Aryan_progeny__sowing_seeds_of_fascism.html.

Redman, Joshua. 2015. "Seeing and Hearing for the First Time, on YouTube." *The New Yorker*, 18 August. Accessed March 19, 2017. http://www.newyorker.com/culture/cultural-comment/seeing-and-hearing-for-the-first-time-on-youtube.

Rhodes, John David. 2010. "The Spectacle of Skepticism: Haneke's Long Takes." In *On Michael Haneke*, edited by Brian Price and John David Rhodes, 87–104. Detroit, MI: Wayne State University Press.

Riemer, Willy. 2000. "Beyond Mainstream Film: An Interview with Michael Haneke." In *After Postmodernism: Austrian Literature and Film in Transition*, edited by Willy Riemer, 159–170. Riverside, CA: Ariadne.

Riemer, Willy. 2004. "Michael Haneke: *Funny Games,* Violence, and the Media." In *Visions and Visionaries in Contemporary Austrian Literature and Film*, edited by Margarete Lamb-Faffelberger and Pamela S. Saur, 93–102. New York: Peter Lang.

Riemer, Willy. 2007. "Michael Haneke, *The Piano Teacher* [*Die Klavierspielerin*]: Repertoires of Power and Desire." In *Elfriede Jelinek: Writing Woman, Nation, and Identity: A Critical Anthology*, edited by Matthias Piccolruaz Konzett and Margarete Lamb-Faffelberger, 270–284. Madison, NJ: Fairleigh Dickinson University Press.

Ringstrom, Philip A. 2014. "Review of theMovie *Amour*." *International Journal of Psychoanalytic Self Psychology* 9: 157–161.

Roderick, Nemonie Craven. 2011. "Subject to Memory? Thinking after *Hidden*." In *The Cinema of Michael Haneke: Europe Utopia*, edited by Ben McCann and David Sorfa, 225–236. London: Wallflower.

Romney, Jonathan. 2009. "*The White Ribbon* (15)." *Independent*, November 14. Accessed November 1, 2016. http://www.independent.co.uk/arts-entertainment/films/reviews/the-white-ribbon-15-1820728.html.

Rose, Hilary, and Steven Rose. 2012. "Grow Old with Me." *The Lancet* 380, October 6. Accessed November 15, 2016. http://www.thelancet.com/pdfs/journals/lancet/PIIS0140-6736(12)61699-7.pdf.

Rosinski, Milosz Paul. 2015. "Touching Nancy's Ethics: Death in Michael Haneke's *Amour*." *Studies in French Cinema* 15(2): 180–196.

Royer, Michelle. 2015. "Star Embodiment and the Live Experience of Ageing in Cinema: The Case of *Amour*." In *Stars in World Cinema: Screen Icons and Star Systems Across Cultures*, edited by Andrea Bandhauer and Michelle Royer, 199–212. London: I. B. Tauris & Co. Ltd.

San Francisco Bach Choir (Magen Soloman, Artistic Director). 2013. "Illuminating an Ancient Art." Accessed August 1, 2016. http://www.sfbach.org/text-ein-feste-burg-ist-unser-gott-swv-143.

Saxton, Libby. 2008. "Close Encounters with Distant Suffering: Michael Haneke's Disturbing Visions." In *Five Directors: Auteurism from Assayas to Ozon*, edited by Kate Ince, 84–111. Manchester: Manchester University Press.

Scheurer, Timothy E. 2008. *Music and Mythmaking in Film: Genre and the Role of the Composer*. Jefferson, NC; London: McFarland & Company, Inc. http://www.seattle-symphony.org/symphony/buy/single/programnotes.aspx?id=12296.

Schrader, Paul. 1972. "Ozu." In *The Transcendental Style in Film: Ozu, Bresson, Dreyer* by Paul Schrader, 18–54. Berkeley: University of California Press, 1972.

Scott, A. O. 2009. "Wholesome Hamlet's Horror Sends a Jolt to the System." *The New York Times*, December 29. Accessed November 7, 2016. http://www.nytimes.com/2009/12/30/movies/30white.html?_r=0%27.

Seeßlen, Georg. 2010. "Structures of Glaciation: Gaze, Perspective, and Gestus in the Films of Michael Haneke." In *A Companion to Michael Haneke*, edited by Roy Grundmann, 323–336. Malden, MA: Wiley-Blackwell.

Service, Tom. 2010. "Schubert's Syphilitic Sonata." *The Guardian*, April 28. Accessed November 11, 2016. https://www.theguardian.com/music/tomserviceblog/2010/apr/28/schubert-syphilitic-sonata.

Seshadri, Kalpana Rahita. 2007. "Spectacle of the Hidden: Michael Haneke's *Caché.*" *Nottingham French Studies* 46(3): 32–48.

The Seventh Continent (Der siebente Kontinent). 1989. Directed by Michael Haneke. Performed by Birgit Doll, Dieter Berner, Leni Tanzer, Udo Samel. New York: Kino International Corp. 2006. DVD.

71 Fragments of Chronology of Chance. 1994. Directed by Michael Haneke. Performed by Gabriel Cosmin Urdes, Lukas Miko, Otto Grünmandl, Anne Bennet. New York: Kino International Corp. 2006. DVD.

Shambu, Girish. "*Code Unknown*: An Auto-Dialogue." February 13, 2006. Accessed November 1. http://girishshambu.blogspot.com/2006/02/code-unknown-auto-dialogue.html.

Sharkey, Betsy. 2013. "Amour Is a Horror Film for the Ages." *Los Angeles Times*, February 24. Accessed November 1, 2016. http://articles.latimes.com/2013/feb/24/entertainment/la-et-cm-betsy-amour-essay-20130224

Sharrett, Christopher. 2003. "The World That Is Known: An Interview with Michael Haneke." *Cineaste* 28(3): 28–31.

Sharrett, Christopher. 2004. "The World That Is Known: Michael Haneke Interviewed." *Kinoeye* 4(1). Accessed October 13, 2014. http://www.kinoeye.org/04/01/interview01.php.

Sharrett, Christopher. 2010. "Haneke and the Discontents of European Culture." In *On Michael Haneke*. Brian Price and John David Rhodes, 207–220. Detroit, MI: Wayne State University Press.

Silverman, Max. 2007. "The Empire Looks Back." *Screen* 48(2): 245–249.

Smith, Jeff. 2009. "Bridging the Gap: Reconsidering the Border between Diegetic and Nondiegetic Music." *Music and the Moving Image* 2(1): 1–25.

Smith, Kyle. 2009. "It Repels but Casts Its Spell." *New York Post*, December 30. Accessed November 1, 2016. http://nypost.com/2009/12/30/it-repels-but-casts-its-spell/.

Speck, Olivier C. 2010. *Funny Frames: The Filmic Concepts of Michael Haneke*. New York: Continuum.

Stam, Robert. 2000. "Permutations of Difference: Introduction." In *Film and Theory: An Anthology,* edited by Robert Stam and Toby Miller, 661–668. Malden, Massachusetts: Blackwell.

Stam, Robert, and Louise Spence. (1983) 2004. "Colonialism, Racism, and Representation." In *Film Theory and Criticism*, edited by Leo Braudy and Marshall Cohen, 9877–9891. New York: Oxford University Press. Originally published in *Screen* 24(2).

Sterritt, David. 2010. "A Shadow Poet: Michael Haneke." In *Cinema Inferno: Celluloid Explosions from the Cultural Margins*, edited by Robert G. Weiner and John Cline, 244–268. Lanham, MD: Scarecrow Press.

Stewart, Garrett. 2010. "Pre-War Trauma: Haneke's *The White Ribbon.*" *Film Quarterly* 63(4): 40–47.

Stoehr, Kevin L. 2010. "Haneke's Secession: Perspectivism and Anti-Nihilism in *Code Unknown* and *Caché.*" In *A Companion to Michael Haneke*, edited by Roy Grundmann, 477–494. Malden, MA: Wiley-Blackwell.

Szpilman, Wladyslaw. 1999. *The Pianist: The Extraordinary True Story of One Man's Survival in Warsaw, 1939–1945*. Translated by Anthea Bell. New York: Picador USA.

Tate, Adam Wyatt. 2011. "The Children Are Always Watching: Violence, Distressed Children, and Signs of Hope in the Cinema of Michael Haneke." MA Thesis.

University of Texas at Austin. Accessed March 28, 2016. https://repositories.lib.utexas. edu/bitstream/handle/2152/ETD-UT-2011-053304/TATE-THESIS.pdf?sequence=1.

Taubin, Amy. 2012. "Festivals: Cannes 2012: Death Foretold." *Film Comment* July/August. Accessed November 15, 2016. http://www.filmcomment.com/article/festivals-cannes-2012-amy-taubin/.

Thompson, Gary. 2010. "'Ribbon' Proves Dark Side of German Culture." *Philly.com*, January 21. Accessed November 1, 2016. http://www.philly.com/philly/entertainment/movies/20100121_white_ribbon.html.

Thuswaldner, Gregor. 2010. "'Mourning for the Gods Who Have Died': The Role of Religion in Michael Haneke's Glaciation Trilogy." In *A Companion to Michael Haneke*, edited by Roy Grundmann, 185–201. Malden, MA: Wiley-Blackwell.

Toubiana, Serge. 2005a. "Interview with Michael Haneke." *Benny's Video*, DVD, directed by Michael Haneke (1992; New York: Kino International, 2007).

Toubiana, Serge. 2005b. "Interview with Michael Haneke." *Caché*, DVD, directed by Michael Haneke (2005; Culver City, CA: Sony Pictures Home Entertainment, Inc., 2006).

Toubiana, Serge. 2005c. "Interview with Michael Haneke." *Funny Games*, DVD, directed by Michael Haneke (1997; New York: Kino International, 2007).

Trifonova, Temenuga. 2007. "*Code Unknown*: European Identity in Cinema." *Scope* 8. Accessed March 28, 2009. http://www.scope.nottingham.ac.uk/index.php.

Tweraser, Felix W. 2011. "Images of Confinement and Transcendence: Michael Haneke's Reception of Romanticism in *The Piano Teacher*." In *The Cinema of Michael Haneke: Europe Utopia*, edited by Ben McCann and David Sorfa, 195–205. London: Wallflower.

Vincendeau, Ginette. 2015. "Minority Report." *Sight and Sound* 22(6): 22–27.

Vinocur, Nicholas. 2015. "Why the National Front (Thinks It) Won in France." *Politico*, December 15. Accessed October 27, 2016. http://www.politico.eu/article/why-marine-le-pen-national-front-thinks-it-won-in-france-regional-elections/.

Vogel, Amos. 1996. "Of Nonexisting Continents: The Cinema of Michael Haneke." *Film Comment* 32(4): 73–75.

Von Maltzan, Carlotta. 2002. "Voyeurism and Film in Elfriede Jelinek's *The Piano Teacher*." In *Literature, Film, and the Culture Industry in Contemporary Austria*, edited by Margarete Lamb-Faffelberger, 98–108. New York: Peter Lang Publishing, Inc.

Waldron, Dara. 2013. *Cinema and Evil: Moral Complexities and the Dangerous Film*. Newcastle upon Tyne: Cambridge Scholars Publishing.

Walker, Elsie. 2015. *Understanding Sound Tracks through Film Theory*. New York: Oxford University Press.

Walker, Elsie. 2017. "Editorial: A New Moon for *LFQ*." *Literature Film Quarterly* 45(2). http://www.salisbury.edu/lfq.

Walsh, Timothy. 1992. "The Cognitive and Mimetic Function of Absence in Art, Music, and Literature." *Mosaic: A Journal for the Interdisciplinary Study of Literature* 25(2): 69–90.

Warren, Adrian. 2013. "Please, Love Me Do: Michael Haneke's *Amour*." *PopMatters*, March 28. Accessed November 5, 2016. http://www.popmatters.com/review/169739-amour/

Warren, Charles. 2010. "The Unknown Piano Teacher. In *A Companion to Michael Haneke*, edited by Roy Grundmann, 495–510. Malden, MA: Wiley-Blackwell.

Weigel, Moira. 2013. "Sadomodernism: Haneke in Furs." *Double Bind* 16. Accessed November 15, 2016. https://nplusonemag.com/issue-16/essays/sadomodernism/

Wheatley, Catherine. 2007 "Secrets, Lies, and Videotape." *Sight and Sound* 16(2): 32–36. Accessed May 22, 2009. http://www.bfi.org.uk/sightandsound/feature/49266.

Wheatley, Catherine. 2009. *Michael Haneke's Cinema: The Ethic of the Image*. Oxford: Berghahn.

Wheatley, Catherine, and Sheila Johnston. 2008. "Unkind Rewind." *Sight & Sound* 18(4): 18.

The White Ribbon (*Das weiße Bande: Eine deutsche Kindergeschichte*). 2009. Directed by Michael Haneke. Performed by Christian Friedel, Leonie Benesch, Ulrich Tukur, Ursina Lardi. London: Artificial Eye, 2010. Blu-ray.

Wierzbicki, James, ed. 2012. *Music, Sound, and Filmmakers: Sonic Style in Cinema*. New York: Routledge.

Wijdicks, Eelco F. M. 2013. "Film review: Palme d'Or-Awarded 'Amour'—The Neurologic Dying of a Loved One." *Neurology Today* 13(5): 25. Accessed November 15, 2016. http://mobile.journals.lww.com/neurotodayonline/_layouts/15/oaks.journals.mobile/articleviewer.aspx?year=2013&issue=03070&article=00011

Williams, James S. 2010. "Aberrations of Beauty: Violence and Cinematic Resistance in Haneke's *The White Ribbon*." *Film Quarterly* 63(4): 48–55.

Williams, Linda. 2012 (1991). "Film Bodies: Gender, Genre, and Excess." In *Film Genre Reader IV*, edited by Barry Keith Grant, 159–177. Austin: University of Texas Press. Originally published in *Film Quarterly* 44(4): 2–13.

Wood, Robin. 1979. "Der Erlkönig: the Ambiguities of Horror." In *American Nightmare: Essays on the Horror Film*, edited by Andrew Britton, Richard Lippe, Tony Williams, Robin Wood, 29–31. Toronto: Festival of Festivals.

Wood, Robin. 2007. "Michael Haneke: Beyond Compromise." *Cineaction* 73(4): 44–55.

Wortel, Elise. 2011. "From History to Haecceity: Spatial Reframings of the Past in Post-Heritage Cinema." *Alphaville: Journal of Film and Screen Media* 2: 1–16.

Wyatt, Jean. 2005. "Jouissance and Desire in Michael Haneke's *The Piano Teacher*." *American Imago: Psychoanalysis and the Human Sciences* 62(4): 453–482.

Yacowar, Maurice. 2006. "*Caché* and the Private/Public Secret." *Queen's Quarterly* 113(2): 225–233.

Žižek, Slavoj. 1991. *Looking Awry: An Introduction to Jacques Lacan through Popular Culture*. Cambridge, MA: The MIT Press.

Žižek, Slavoj. 2012. *Welcome to the Desert of the Real: Five Essays on September 11 and Related Dates*. London: Verso.

Zolkos, Magdalena. 2015. "The Origins of Fascism: Memory of Violence in Michael Haneke's *The White Ribbon*." *The European Legacy: Towards New Paradigms* 20(3): 205–223.

INDEX